Rick Doherty, MD
5528 Kuhn Street
Port Townsend, WA 98368
Phone 206.409.4918
rickarthdoherty@gmail.com

Praise for

DA[RK]
A[GE]
AME[RICA]

This is a great book for illuminating the clear flows and stark inevitabilities of the next Dark Age. It's a rich, provocative, thoughtful, reality based, if scary vision; highly informative and thorough, and brought forth with a positive internal spirit, and an occasional glimmer of hopeful possibility. If you think and worry about the near and distant future, you should definitely check this out.

— Jerry Mander, author, *Four Arguments for the Elimination of Television*, and *The Capitalism Papers; Fatal Flaws of an Obsolete System*, and Founder and Director, International Forum on Globalization

Greer's *Dark Age America* is the essential education and impetus for boomers who choose legacy focus over longevity fixation. We've lived through peak oil, peak debt, peak comfort, peak me-ness, peak pettiness. Now, let us become ancestors our grandchildren will be proud of.

— Connie Barlow, science writer, creator of Torreya Guardians and TheGreatStory.org

John Michael Greer is a modern-day prophet speaking on behalf of Reality. *Dark Age America* draws upon Greer's vast knowledge of the patterns and rhythms of history to yield insights grounded in our best evidential understandings of ecology, economics, systems science, and human nature. The result is a work of remarkable clarity and searing wisdom vital for these confusing times.

— Rev. Michael Dowd, author, *Thank God for Evolution* and host, "The Future Is Calling Us to Greatness"

If the future trajectory of our civilization follows the same general patterns laid down by previous ones, then John Michael Greer's new book gives us perhaps the best view of the future currently available. His thoughts on the great unraveling ahead are rooted in a broad and deep knowledge of history: even if you disagree with him about the future, you will learn a great deal from his survey of the relevant human past.

—Richard Heinberg, author, *The End of Growth*

Dark Age America argues cogently and compellingly the inevitable decline of industrial civilization and its ramifications within the next five centuries. Whereas the human psyche may hold out for a faux Great Turning or the fantasy that "this time it will be different," Greer demonstrates that ecologically, politically, economically, and technologically, the decline is not only inevitable but well underway. How the demise unfolds and whether any members of our species prevail may well be determined by the choices we make now. Business as usual is not an option.

—Carolyn Baker, Ph.D., author,
Love In The Age Of Ecological Apocalypse and *Collapsing Consciously*

Whether you only just figured it out or have known for a long time that globalized consumer culture is a sinking ship, it really helps when a polite steward comes to your cabin and offers to guide you to the lifeboat and then chats breezily, easing your fears, as he guides you down the metallic corridors with blinking fluorescent lights, describing all you may need to know to get your life back on track once the lifeboats reach safe harbor. *Dark Age America* is John Michael Greer's finest work. He does not cut any slack, even for his own predictions. Read it slowly, in a comfortable chair, with a cup of your favorite warm beverage.

— Albert Bates, author, *The Post-Petroleum Survival Guide and Cookbook*,
The Biochar Solution, and *The Paris Agreement*

Civilization isn't selling too well. The would-be masters of the universe want billions of consumers, productivity gains, growth and profits. In return they offer open borders, fancy widgets, gender equality for a rainbow of genders and space exploration pipe dreams. But there are no takers; what the people want is nine hours of sleep, summers in the country, family and friends around and somebody to buy their rutabagas. A dark age cometh, but don't worry. As Greer explains, this is perfectly normal—just takes some getting used to. A dark age is a great time to catch up on sleep.

—Dmitry Orlov, author, *Reinventing Collapse* and *The Five Stages of Collapse*

Dark Age America is a courageous, thoughtful, timely and well-researched prognosis for the next five centuries of life on Earth. John brings to bear a thorough knowledge of how past civilizations have unraveled, an appreciation of how complex systems work (and when they don't), and an understanding of how humans behave in crises that are not sudden and transitory, but gradual, uneven, profound and enduring. No matter where on the political spectrum your sensibilities lie, this intelligently reasoned, thought-provoking and important work will challenge your ways of thinking and prod you to take useful preparatory actions.

— Dave Pollard, author, *How to Save the World*

DARK
AGE
AMERICA

CLIMATE CHANGE, CULTURAL COLLAPSE,
and the HARD FUTURE AHEAD

JOHN MICHAEL GREER

new society
PUBLISHERS

Inquiries regarding requests to reprint all or part of *Dark Age America*
should be addressed to New Society Publishers at the address below.
To order directly from the publishers, please call toll-free (North America)
1-800-567-6772, or order online at www.newsociety.com

Any other inquiries can be directed by mail to:

New Society Publishers
P.O. Box 189, Gabriola Island, BC V0R 1X0, Canada
(250) 247-9737

LIBRARY AND ARCHIVES CANADA CATALOGUING IN PUBLICATION

Greer, John Michael, author
Dark age America : climate change, cultural collapse, and
the hard future ahead / John Michael Greer.

Includes bibliographical references and index.
Issued in print and electronic formats.
ISBN 978-0-86571-833-3 (paperback). — ISBN 978-1-55092-628-6 (ebook)

1. Climatic changes—Social aspects—United States.   2. Natural
resources—Social aspects—United States.   3. United States—
Civilization—21st century—Forecasting.   I. Title.

E169.12.G74 2016   306.0973   C2016-903935-8
                                            C2016-903936-6

Funded by the
Government
of Canada

Financé par le
gouvernement
du Canada

Canada

New Society Publishers' mission is to publish books that contribute in fundamental
ways to building an ecologically sustainable and just society, and to do so with the least
possible impact upon the environment, in a manner that models that vision.

MIX
Paper from
responsible sources
FSC® C016245

Certified
B
Corporation

new society
PUBLISHERS
www.newsociety.com

Contents

1. The Wake of Industrial Civilization 1

2. The Ecological Aftermath. 15

3. The Demographic Consequences 39

4. The Political Unraveling 59

5. The Economic Collapse 91

6. The Suicide of Science 123

7. The Twilight of Technology. 149

8. The Dissolution of Culture 177

9. The Road to a Renaissance 199

   Endnotes 227

   Bibliography. 231

   Index 239

   About the Author. 247

   A Note About the Publisher 248

1

THE WAKE OF INDUSTRIAL CIVILIZATION

IT HAS BEEN MORE THAN FOUR DECADES SINCE SCIENTISTS began warning of the inevitable consequences of trying to pursue limitless economic growth on a finite planet.[1] Since that time, as the limits to growth have become more and more clearly visible on the horizon of our future, a remarkable paradox has unfolded. The closer we get to those limits, the more they impact our daily lives, and the more clearly our current trajectory points toward the brick wall of a difficult future, the less most people in the industrial world seem to be able to imagine any alternative to driving the existing order of things ever onward until the wheels fall off.

This is as true in many corners of the activist community as it is in the most unregenerate of corporate boardrooms. For too many of today's environmentalists, renewable energy isn't something that they ought to produce for themselves, unless they happen to be wealthy enough to afford the rooftop PV systems that have become the latest status symbol in suburban neighborhoods on either coast. It's certainly not something that they ought to conserve. Rather, it's something that utilities and the government are supposed to produce as fast as possible, so that Americans can keep on using three times as much energy per capita as the average European and twenty times as much as the average Chinese.

Such enthusiasm for change that does appear in the activist community by and large focuses on world-changing events of one kind or another. As it happens, though, we have a serious shortage of world-changing events just now. There are good reasons for that, just as there are equally strong, if not equally good, reasons why so many people are pinning all their hopes on a world-changing event of one kind or another. Therapists like to point out that if you always do what you've always done, you'll always get what you've always gotten, and of late it's become a truism (though it's also a truth) that doing the same thing and expecting to get different results is a good working definition of insanity.

The attempt to find some way around that harsh but inescapable logic is the force that drove the prophetic hysteria about 2012 and drives end-of-the-world delusions more generally: if the prospect of changing the way you live terrifies you, but the thought of facing the consequences of the way you live terrifies you just as much, daydreaming that some outside force will come along and change everything for you can be a convenient way to avoid having to think about the future you're making for yourself.[2] Unfortunately, that sort of daydream has become far more common than the sort of constructive action that might actually make a difference.

That hard fact pretty much guarantees a future that is considerably worse than the present, by almost any imaginable definition. The difficulty here is that faith in the prospect of a better future has been so deeply ingrained in all of us that trying to argue against it is a bit like trying to tell a medieval peasant that heaven with all its saints and angels isn't there any more. The hope that tomorrow will be, or can be, or at the very least ought to be, better than today is hardwired into the collective imagination of the modern world. Behind that faith lies the immense inertia of three hundred years of industrial expansion, which cashed in the cheaply accessible fraction of the Earth's fossil fuel reserves for a brief interval of abundance so extreme that garbage collectors in today's America have access to things that emperors could not get before the Industrial Revolution dawned.

That age of extravagance has profoundly reshaped—in terms of the realities of human life before and after our age, a better word might be "distorted"—the way people nowadays think about nearly anything you care to name. In particular, it has blinded us to the ecological realities that provide the fundamental context to our lives. It's made nearly all of us think, for example, that unlimited exponential growth is possible, normal, and good, and so even as the disastrous consequences of unlimited exponential growth slam into our society one after another like waves hitting a sand castle, the vast majority of people nowadays still build their visions of the future on the fantasy that problems caused by growth can be solved by still more growth.

The distorted thinking we have inherited from three centuries of unsustainable growth crops up in full force even among many of those who think they're reacting against it. Activists at every point on the political spectrum have waxed rhetorical for generations about the horrors the future has in store, to be sure, but they always offer a way out—the adoption of whatever agenda they happen to be promoting—and it leads straight to a bright new tomorrow in which the hard limits of the present somehow no longer seem to apply. (Take away the shopworn trope of "the only way to rescue a better future from the jaws of imminent disaster" from today's activist rhetoric, for that matter, and in most cases there's very little left.)

Still, the bright new tomorrow we've all been promised is not going to arrive. This is the bad news brought to us by the unfolding collision between industrial society and the unyielding limits of the planetary biosphere. Peak oil, global warming, and all the other crises gathering around the world are all manifestations of a single root cause: the impossibility of infinite growth on a finite planet. They are warning signals telling us that we have gone into full-blown overshoot—the state, familiar to ecologists, in which a species outruns the resource base that supports it[3]—and they tell us also that growth is not merely going to stop; it's going to reverse, and that reversal will continue until our population, resource use, and waste production drop to levels that can be sustained over the long term by a damaged planetary ecosystem.

That bitter outcome might have been prevented if we had collectively taken decisive action before we went into overshoot. We didn't, and at this point the window of opportunity is firmly shut. Nearly all the proposals currently being floated to deal with the symptoms of our planetary overshoot assume, tacitly or otherwise, that this is not the case and that we still have as much time as we need. Such proposals are wasted breath, and if any of them are enacted—and some of them very likely will be enacted, once today's complacency gives way to tomorrow's stark panic—the resources poured into them will be wasted as well.

Thus I think it's time to pursue a different and more challenging project. We could have had a better future if we'd done the right things when there was still enough time to matter, but we didn't. That being the case, what kind of future can we expect to get?

There is a standard term in historical studies for that kind of future. That term is "dark age."

That label actually dates from before the period most often assigned it these days. Marcus Terentius Varro, who was considered the most erudite Roman scholar of his time, divided up the history known to him into three ages: an age of history, for which there were written records; before that, an age of fable, from which oral traditions survived; and before that, a dark age, about which no one knew anything at all.[4] It's a simple division but a surprisingly useful one. Even in those dark ages where literacy survived as a living tradition, records tend to be extremely sparse and unhelpful, and when records pick up again, they tend to be thickly frosted with fable and legend for a good long while thereafter. In a dark age, the thread of collective memory and cultural continuity snaps, the ends are lost, and a new thread must be spun from whatever raw materials happen to be on hand.

Dark ages of this kind are a recurrent phenomenon in human history, and the processes by which they come about have a remarkable degree of similarity even when the civilizations that precede them differ in every imaginable way. The historian Arnold Toynbee, whose massive twelve-volume work *A Study of History* remains the most comprehensive study of historical cycles ever penned, has explored this curious parallelism in detail.[5] On the way up, he noted, each civilization tends to diverge not merely from its neighbors but from all other civilizations throughout history. Its political and religious institutions, its arts and architecture, and all the other details of its daily life take on distinctive forms, so that as it nears maturity, even the briefest glance at one of its creations is often enough to identify its source.

Once the peak is past and the long road down begins, though, that pattern of divergence shifts into reverse, slowly at first, and then with increasing speed. A curious sort of homogenization takes place: distinctive features are lost, and common patterns emerge in their place. That doesn't happen all at once, and different cultural forms lose their distinctive outlines at different rates, but the further down the trajectory of decline and fall a civilization proceeds, the more it resembles every other civilization in decline. By the time that trajectory bottoms out, the resemblance is all but total; compare one post-collapse society to another—the societies of post-Roman Europe, let's say, with those of post-Mycenean Greece—and it can be hard to believe that dark age societies so similar could have emerged out of the wreckage of civilizations so different.

It's interesting to speculate about why this reversion to the mean should be so regular a theme in the twilight and aftermath of so many civilizations. Still, the recurring patterns of decline and fall have another implication—or, if you will, another application.

Modern industrial society, especially but not only here in North America, is showing all the usual symptoms of a civilization on its way toward history's compost bin. If, as the evidence suggests, we've started along the familiar track of decline and fall, it should be possible to map the standard features of the way down onto the details of our current situation, and come up with a fairly accurate sense of the shape of the future ahead of us.

Mind you, the part of history that can be guessed in advance is a matter of broad trends and overall patterns, not the sort of specific incidents that make up so much of history as it happens. Exactly how the pressures bearing down on late industrial America will work out in the day-by-day realities of politics, economics, and society will be determined by the usual interplay of individual choices and pure dumb luck. That said, the broad trends and overall patterns are worth tracking in their own right, and some things that look as though they ought to belong to the realm of the unpredictable—for example, the political and military dynamics of border regions, or the relations among the imperial society's political class, its increasingly disenfranchised lower classes, and the peoples outside its borders—follow predictable patterns in case after case in history, and show every sign of doing the same thing this time around too.

What I'm suggesting, in fact, is that in a very real sense, it's possible to map out the outlines of the history of North America over the next five centuries or so in advance. That's a sweeping claim, and I'm well aware that the immediate response of at least some of my readers will be to reject the possibility out of hand. I'd like to encourage those who have this reaction to try to keep an open mind.

This claim presupposes that the lessons of the past actually have some relevance to our future. That's a controversial proposal these days, but to my mind the controversy says more about the popular idiocies of our time than it does about the facts on the ground. People in today's America have taken to using thought-stoppers such as "But it's different this time!" to protect themselves from learning anything from history—a habit that no doubt does wonders for their peace of mind today, though it pretty much guarantees them a face-first collision with a brick wall of misery and failure not much further down time's road.

Among the resources I plan on using to trace out the history of the next five centuries is the current state of the art in the environmental sciences, and that includes the very substantial body of evidence and research on anthropogenic climate change. I'm aware that some people consider that controversial, and, of course, some very rich corporate interests have invested a lot of money into convincing people that it's controversial, but I've read extensively on all sides of the subject, and the arguments against taking anthropogenic climate change seriously strike me as specious. I don't propose to debate the matter here either—there are plenty of forums for that. While I propose to leaven current model-based estimates on climate change and sea-level rise with the evidence from paleoclimatology, those who insist that there's nothing at all the matter with treating the atmosphere as an aerial sewer for greenhouse gases are not going to be happy with everything I have to say.

I also propose to discuss industrial civilization's decline and fall without trying to sugarcoat the harsher dimensions of that process, and that's going to ruffle yet another set of feathers. Those who follow the news will doubtless already have noticed the desperate attempts to insist that it won't be that bad, really it won't, that are starting to show up these days whenever straight talk about the future slips through the fog of collective mythology that our society uses to blind itself to the consequences of its own actions. Those who dare to use words such as "decline" or "dark age" can count on being taken to task by critics who insist earnestly that such language is too negative, that of course we're facing a shift to a different kind of society but it shouldn't be described in such disempowering terms, and so on through the whole vocabulary of the obligatory optimism that's so fashionable among the privileged these days.

That sort of talk may be comforting, but it's not useful. The fall of a civilization is not a pleasant prospect—and that's what we're talking about, of course: the decline and fall of industrial civilization, the long passage through a dark age, and the first stirrings of the successor societies that will build on our ruins. That's how the life cycle of a civilization ends, and it's the way that ours is ending right now.

What that means in practice is that most of the familiar assumptions people in the industrial world like to make about the future will be stood on their heads in the decades and centuries ahead. Most of the rhetoric being splashed about these days in support of this or that or the other Great Turning that will save us from the consequences of our own actions assumes, as a matter of course, that a majority of people in the United States—or, heaven help us, in the whole industrial world—can and will come together around some broadly accepted set of values and some agreed-upon plan of action to rescue industrial civilization from the rising spiral of crises that surrounds it. My readers may have noticed that things seem to be moving in the opposite direction, and history suggests that they're quite correct.

Among the standard phenomena of decline and fall, in fact, is the shattering of the collective consensus that gives a growing society the capacity to act together to accomplish much of anything at all. The schism between the political class and the rest of the population—you can certainly call these "the one percent" and "the ninety-nine percent" if you wish—is simply the most visible of the fissures that spread through every declining civilization, breaking it into a crazy quilt of dissident fragments pursuing competing ideals and agendas. That process has a predictable endpoint, too: as the increasingly grotesque misbehavior of the political class loses whatever respect and loyalty it once received from the rest of society and the masses abandon their trust in the political institutions of their society, charismatic leaders from outside the political class fill the vacuum, violence becomes the normal arbiter of power, and the rule of law becomes a polite fiction when it isn't simply abandoned altogether.

The economic sphere of a society in decline undergoes a parallel fragmentation for different reasons. In ages of economic expansion, the labor of the working classes yields enough profit to cover the costs of a more or less complex superstructure, whether that superstructure consists of the pharaohs and priesthoods of ancient Egypt or the bureaucrats and investment bankers of late industrial America. As expansion gives way to contraction, the production of goods and services no longer yields the profit it once did, but the members of the political class, whose power and wealth depend on the superstructure, are predictably unwilling to lose their privileged status, and they have the power to keep themselves fed at everyone else's expense. The reliable result is a squeeze on productive economic activity that drives a declining civilization into one convulsive financial crisis after another and ends by shredding its capacity to produce even the most necessary goods and services.

In response, people begin dropping out of the economic mainstream altogether, because scrabbling for subsistence on the economic fringes is less futile than trying to get by in a system increasingly rigged against them. Rising taxes, declining government services, and systematic privatization of public goods by the rich compete to alienate more and more people from the established order, and the debasement of the money system in an attempt to make up for faltering tax revenues drives more and more economic activity into forms of exchange that don't involve money at all. As the monetary system fails, in turn, economies of scale become impossible to exploit; the economy fragments and simplifies until bare economic subsistence on local resources, occasionally supplemented by plunder, becomes the sole surviving form of economic activity.

Taken together, these patterns of political fragmentation and economic unraveling send the political class of a failing civilization on a feet-first journey through the exit doors of history. The only skills its members have, by and large, are those needed to manipulate the complex political and economic levers of their society, and their power depends entirely on the active loyalty of their subordinates, all the way down the chain of command, and the passive obedience of the rest of society. The collapse of political institutions strips the political class of any claim to legitimacy; the breakdown of the economic system limits its ability to buy the loyalty of those whom it can no longer inspire; the breakdown of the levers of control strips its members of the only actual power they've got; and that's when they find themselves having to compete for followers with the charismatic leaders rising just then from the lower echelons of society. The endgame, far more often than not, comes when the political class tries to hire the rising leaders of the disenfranchised as a source of muscle to control the rest of the populace and finds out the hard way that it's the people who carry the weapons, not the ones who think they're giving the orders, who actually exercise power.

The implosion of the political class has implications that go well beyond a simple change in personnel at the upper levels of society. The political and social fragmentation mentioned earlier applies just as forcefully to the less tangible dimensions of human life—its ideas and ideals, its beliefs and values and cultural practices. As a civilization tips over into decline, its educational and cultural institutions, its arts, literature, sciences, philosophies, and religions all become identified with its political class; this isn't an accident, as the political class generally goes out of its way to exploit all these things for the sake of its own faltering authority and influence. To those outside the political class, in turn, the high culture of the civilization becomes alien and hateful, and when the political class goes down, the cultural resources that it harnessed to its service go down with it.

Sometimes some of those resources get salvaged by subcultures for their own purposes, as Christian monks and nuns salvaged portions of classical Greek and Roman philosophy and science for the greater glory of God. That's not guaranteed, though, and even when it does happen, the salvage crew picks and chooses for its own reasons—the survival of classical Greek astronomy in the early medieval West, for example, happened simply because the Church needed to know how to calculate the date of Easter. Where no such motive exists, losses can be total: of the immense corpus of Roman music, the only thing that survives is a fragment of one tune that takes about twenty-five seconds to play, and there are historical examples in which even the simple trick of literacy got lost during the implosion of a civilization and had to be imported centuries later from somewhere else.

All these transformations impact the human ecology of a falling civilization—that is, the basic relationships with the natural world on which every human society depends for day-to-day survival. Most civilizations know perfectly well what has to be done to keep topsoil in place, irrigation water flowing, harvests coming in, and all the other details of human interaction with the environment on a stable footing. The problem is always how to meet the required costs as economic growth ends, contraction sets in, and the ability of central governments to enforce their edicts begins to unravel. The habit of feeding the superstructure at the expense of every-thing else impacts the environment just as forcefully as it does the working classes: just as wages drop to starvation levels and keep falling, funding for necessary investments in infrastructure, fallow periods needed for crop rotation, and the other inputs that keep an agricultural system going in a sustainable manner all get cut.

As a result, topsoil washes away, agricultural hinterlands de-grade into deserts or swamps, vital infrastructure collapses from malign neglect, and the ability of the land to support human life starts on the cascading descent that characterizes the end stage of decline—and so, in turn, does population, because human numbers in the last analysis are a dependent variable, not an independent one. Populations don't grow or shrink because people just up and decide one day to have more or fewer babies; they're constrained by ecolog-ical limits. In an expanding civilization, as its wealth and resource base increases, the population expands as well, since people can afford to have more children, and since more of the children born each year have access to the nutrition and basic health care that let them survive to breeding age themselves. When growth gives way to decline, population typically keeps rising for another generation or so due to sheer demographic momentum, and then begins to fall.

The consequences can be traced in the history of every collapsing civilization. As the rural economy implodes due to agricultural failure on top of the more general economic decline, a growing fraction of the population concentrates in urban slum districts, and as public health measures collapse, these turn into incubators for infectious disease. Epidemics are thus a common feature in the history of declining civilizations, and of course, war and famine are also significant factors; but an even larger toll is taken by the constant upward pressure exerted on death rates by poverty, malnutrition, crowding, and stress. As deaths outnumber births, population goes into a decline that can easily continue for centuries. It's far from uncommon for the population of an area in the wake of a civilization to equal less than ten percent of the figure it reached at the precollapse peak.

Factor these patterns together, follow them out over the usual one to three centuries of spiraling decline, and you have the standard picture of a dark age society: a mostly deserted countryside of small and scattered villages where subsistence farmers, illiterate and impoverished, struggle to coax fertility back into the depleted topsoil. Their governments consist of the personal rule of local warlords, who take a share of each year's harvest in exchange for protection from raiders and rough justice administered in the shade of any convenient tree. Their literature consists of poems, lovingly memorized and chanted to the sound of a simple stringed instrument, recalling the great deeds of the charismatic leaders of a vanished age, and these same poems also contain everything they know about their history. Their health care consists of herbs, a little rough surgery, and incantations cannily used to exploit the placebo effect. Their science—well, I'll let you imagine that for yourself.

And the legacy of the past? Here's some of what an anonymous poet in one dark age had to say about the previous civilization:

> *Bright were the halls then, many the bath-houses,*
> *High the gables, loud the joyful clamor,*
> *Many the meadhalls full of delights*
> *Until mighty Fate overthrew it all.*
> *Wide was the slaughter, the plague-time came,*
> *Death took away all those brave men.*
> *Broken their ramparts, fallen their halls,*
> *The city decayed; those who built it*
> *Fell to the earth. Thus these courts crumble,*
> *And roof-tiles fall from this arch of stone.*

Fans of Anglo-Saxon poetry will recognize that as a passage from "The Ruin."[6] If the processes of history follow their normal pattern, they will be chanting poems like this about the ruins of our cities four or five centuries from now. How we'll get there, and what is likely to happen en route, will be the subject of this book.

2

THE ECOLOGICAL
AFTERMATH

LIKE EVERY OTHER PROCESS IN THE REAL WORLD, HISTORY IS
shaped partly by the pressures of the environment and partly by
the way its own subsystems interact with one another and with the
subsystems of the other ecologies around it. That's not a common
view; most historical writing these days puts human beings at the
center of the picture, with the natural world as a supposedly static
background, while a minority view goes to the other extreme and
fixates on natural catastrophes as the sole cause of this or that
major historical change.

Neither of these approaches seems particularly useful. As our
civilization has been trying its level best not to learn for the past
couple of centuries, and thus will be learning the hard way in the
years immediately ahead, the natural world is not a static background to human history. It's an active and constantly changing
presence that responds in complex ways to human actions. I'd like
to propose, in fact, that history might best be understood as the
ecology of human communities, traced out along the dimension
of time.

Human societies are just as active and equally changeable as
their natural environments, and respond in complex ways to nature's actions. The strange loops generated by a dance of action and
interaction along these lines are difficult to track by the usual tools

of linear thinking, but they're the bread and butter of systems theory, and also of all those branches of ecology that treat the ecosystem rather than the individual organism as the basic unit.

The easiest way to show how this perspective works is to watch it in action, and it so happens that the systems approach makes unusually clear sense of one of the most important factors that will shape the history of North America over the next five centuries. The factor I have in mind is climate.

Now, of course, that's also a political hot potato just at the moment, due to the unwillingness of a great many people across the industrial world to deal with the hard fact that they can't continue to enjoy their current lifestyles if they want a climatically and ecologically stable planet to live on. It doesn't matter how often the planet sets new heat records, nor that the fabled Northwest Passage around the top of Canada and Alaska—which has been choked with ice since the beginning of recorded history—is open water every summer nowadays and is an increasingly important route for commercial shipping from Europe to the eastern shores of Asia.[1] Every time the planet's increasingly chaotic weather spits out unseasonably cold days in a few places, you can count on hearing well-paid corporate flacks and passionate amateurs alike insisting at the top of their lungs that this proves that anthropogenic climate change is nonsense.

To the extent that this reaction isn't just propaganda, it shows that too many people have forgotten that change in complex systems does not follow the sort of nice straight lines that our current habits of thought prefer. A simple experiment can help show how complex systems respond in the real world, and in the process make it easier to make sense of the sort of climate phenomena we can count on seeing in the decades ahead.

The next time you fill a bathtub, once you've turned off the tap, wait until the water is still. Slip your hand into the water, slowly and gently, so that you make as little disturbance in the water as possible. Then move your hand through the water about as fast as a snail moves, and watch and feel how the water adapts to the movement, flowing gently around your hand.

Once you've gotten a clear sense of that, gradually increase the speed with which your hand is moving. After you pass a certain threshold of speed, the movements of the water will take the form of visible waves—a bow wave in front of your hand, a wake behind it in which water rises and falls rhythmically, and wave patterns extending out to the edges of the tub. The faster you move your hand, the larger the waves become, and the more visible the interference patterns as they collide with one another.

Keep on increasing the speed of your hand. You'll pass a second threshold, and the rhythm of the waves will disintegrate into turbulence: the water will churn, splash, and spray around your hand, and chaotic surges of water will lurch up and down the sides of the tub. If you keep it up, you can get a fair fraction of the bathwater on your bathroom floor, but this isn't required for the experiment! Once you've got a good sense of the difference between the turbulence above the second threshold and the oscillations below it, take your hand out of the water, and watch what happens: the turbulence subsides into wave patterns, the waves shrink, and finally—after some minutes—you have still water again.

This same sequence of responses can be traced in every complex system, governing its response to every kind of disturbance in its surroundings. So long as the change stays below a certain threshold of intensity and rapidity—a threshold that differs for every system and every kind of change—the system will respond smoothly, with the least adjustment that will maintain its own internal balance. Once that threshold is surpassed, oscillations of various kinds spread through the system, growing steadily more extreme as the disturbance becomes stronger, until it passes the second threshold and the system's oscillations collapse into turbulence and chaos. When chaotic behavior begins to emerge in an oscillating system, in other words, that's a sign that real trouble may be sitting on the doorstep.

If global temperature were increasing in a nice smooth line, in other words, we wouldn't have as much to worry about, because it would be clear from that fact that the resilience of the planet's climate system was well able to handle the changes that were in process. Once things begin to oscillate, veering outside usual conditions in both directions, that's a sign that the limits to resilience are coming into sight, with the possibility of chaotic variability in the planetary climate as a whole waiting not far beyond that. We can fine-tune the warning signals a good deal by remembering that every system is made up of subsystems, and those of subsubsystems, and as a general rule of thumb, the smaller the system, the more readily it moves from local adjustment to oscillation to turbulence in response to rising levels of disturbance.

Local climate is sensitive enough, in fact, that ordinary seasonal changes can yield minor turbulence, which is why the weather is so hard to predict. Regional climates are more stable, and they normally cycle through an assortment of wavelike oscillations: the cycle of the seasons is one, but there are also multiyear and multidecade cycles of climate that can be tracked on a regional basis. The further up this geographical scale turbulence starts to show itself, the closer to massive trouble we are likely to be—which is why the drastic swings in regional and continental climate patterns in recent years deserve more attention than they generally get.

I'm not generally a fan of Thomas Friedman, but he scored a direct hit when he warned that what we have to worry about from anthropogenic climate change is not global warming but "global weirding."[2] A linear change in global temperatures would be harsh, but it would be possible to some extent to shift crop belts smoothly north in the Northern Hemisphere and south in the Southern. If the crop belts disintegrate—if you don't know whether the next season is going to be warm or cold, wet or dry, short or long—famines become hard to avoid, and cascading impacts on an already strained global economy add to the fun and games. At this point, for the reasons just shown, that's the most likely shape of the century or two ahead of us.

In theory, some of that could be avoided if the world's nations were to stop treating the skies as an aerial sewer in which to dump greenhouse gases. In practice—well, I've met far too many people who claim to be deeply concerned about climate change but who still insist that they have to have SUVs to take their kids to soccer practice, and I recall the embarrassed silence that spread across the media a while back when British climate scientist Kevin Anderson pointed out that maybe jetting all over the place to climate conferences was communicating the wrong message at a time when climate scientists and everyone else needed to decrease their carbon footprint.[3] Until the people who claim to be passionate about climate change start showing a willingness to burn much less carbon, it's unlikely that anyone else will do so, and so I think it's a pretty safe bet that fossil fuels will continue to be extracted and burned as long as geological and economic realities permit.

The one bleak consolation here is that those realities are a good deal less flexible than worst-case scenarios generally assume. There are two factors in particular to track here, and both unfold from net energy—the difference between the energy content of fossil fuels as they reach the end consumer and the energy input needed to get them all the way there. The first factor is simply that if it takes more energy to extract, process, and transport a deposit of fossil carbon than the end user can get out of it by burning it, the fossil carbon will stay in the ground. The poster child here is kerogen shale, which has been the bane of four decades of enthusiastic energy projects in the American West and elsewhere. There's an immense amount of energy locked up in the Green River shale and its equivalents, but every attempt to break into that cookie jar has come to grief on the hard fact that, if everything is included in the analysis, it takes more energy to extract kerogen from shale than you get from burning the kerogen.

The second factor is subtler and considerably more damaging. As fossil fuel deposits with abundant net energy are exhausted, and have to be replaced by deposits with lower net energy, a larger and larger fraction of the total energy supply available to an industrial society has to be diverted from all other economic uses to the process of keeping the energy flowing. Thus it's not enough to point to high total energy production and insist that all's well. The logic of net energy has to be applied here as well; the total energy input that gets used up in energy resource extraction, processing, and distribution has to be subtracted from total energy production, to get a realistic sense of how much energy is available to power the rest of the economy—and the rest of the economy, remember, is what produces the wealth that makes it possible for individuals, communities, and nations to afford fossil fuels in the first place.

Long before the last physically extractable deposit of fossil fuel is exhausted, in other words, fossil fuel extraction will stop because it's become an energy sink rather than an energy source. Well before that latter point is reached, furthermore, global and national economies will no longer be able to produce enough wealth to meet the rising energy costs of fossil fuel extraction. Demand destruction, which is what economists call the process by which people who can't afford to buy a product stop using it, is as important here as raw physical depletion; as economies reel under the twin burdens of depleting reserves and rising energy costs for energy production, carbon footprints will shrink willy-nilly as rapid downward mobility becomes the order of the day for most people. Combine these factors with the economic impacts of "global weirding" itself, and you've got a good first approximation of the forces that are already massing around us and will terminate the fossil fuel economy with extreme prejudice in the decades ahead.

What that means for the future climate of North America is difficult to predict in detail but not so hard to trace in outline. From now until the end of the twenty-first century, perhaps longer, we can expect climate chaos, accelerating in its geographical spread and collective impact until a couple of decades after CO_2 emissions begin to decline, due to the lag time between when greenhouse gases hit the atmosphere and when their effects finally peak. As the rate of emissions slows thereafter, the turbulence will gradually abate, and some time after that—exactly when is anybody's guess, but 2300 is as good a guess as any—the global climate will have settled down into a "new normal" that won't be normal by our standards at all. Barring further curveballs from humanity or nature, that "new normal" will remain until enough excess CO_2 has been absorbed by natural cycles—a process that will take millennia to complete.

An educated guess at the shape of the "new normal" is possible because, for the past few million years, the paleoclimatology of North America has shown a fairly reliable pattern.[4] The colder North America has been, by and large, the heavier the rainfall in the western half of the continent. During the most recent Ice Age, for example, rainfall in what's now the desert Southwest was so heavy that it produced a chain of huge pluvial (rain-fed) lakes and supported relatively abundant grassland and forest ecosystems across much of what's now sagebrush and cactus country. Some measure of the difference can be caught from the fact that 18,000 years ago, when the last Ice Age was at its height, Death Valley was a sparkling lake surrounded by pine forests. By contrast, the warmer North America becomes, the dryer the western half of the continent gets, and the drying effect spreads east a very long way.

After the end of the latest Ice Age, for example, the world entered what nowadays gets called the Holocene Climatic Optimum. That term's a misnomer, at least for this continent, because conditions over a good bit of North America then were optimum only for sand fleas and Gila monsters. There's been a running debate for several decades about whether the Hypsithermal, to use the so-called Optimum's other name, was warmer than today all over the planet or just in some regions. Current opinion tends to favor the latter, but the difference doesn't actually have that much impact on the issue we're considering: the evidence from a broad range of sources shows that North America was significantly warmer in the Hypsithermal than it is today, and so that period makes a fairly good first approximation of the conditions this continent is likely to face in a warmer world.

To make sense of the long-term change to North American climates, it's important to remember that rainfall is far more important than temperature as a determining factor for local ecosystems. On average, if a given region gets more than about 40 inches of rain a year, no matter what the temperature, it'll normally support some kind of forest; if it gets between 40 and 10 inches a year, the usual ecosystem is grassland or, in polar regions, mosses and lichens; with less than 10 inches a year, you've got desert, whether it's as hot as the Sahara or as bitterly cold as the Takla Makan.[5] In the Hypsithermal, as the West dried out, tallgrass prairie extended straight across the Midwest to western Pennsylvania, and much of the Great Plains were desert, complete with sand dunes.

In a world with ample fossil fuel supplies, it's been possible to ignore such concerns by such expedients as pumping billions of gallons of water a year from aquifers or distant catchment basins to grow crops in deserts and the driest of grasslands. As fossil fuel supplies sunset out, though, the shape of human settlement will once again be a function of annual rainfall, as it was everywhere on the planet before 1900. If the Hypsithermal's a valid model, as seems most likely, most of North America from the Sierra Nevada and Cascade ranges east across the Great Basin and Rocky Mountains to the Great Plains and south through most of inland Mexico will be sun-scorched desert, as harsh as any on today's Earth. Human settlement will be accordingly sparse: scattered towns in those few places where geology allows a permanent water supply, separated by vast desolate regions inhabited by few hardy nomads or by no one at all.

Around the Great Desert, grassland will extend for a thousand miles or more, east to the Allegheny foothills, north to a thinner and dryer boreal forest belt shifted several hundred miles closer to the Arctic Ocean, and south to the tropical jungles of the Gulf Coast. Further south, in what's now Mexico, the Gulf Coast east of the Sierra Madre Oriental will shift to tropical ecosystems all the way north to, and beyond, the current international border.

Between the greatly expanded tropical zone along the coasts and the hyperarid deserts of the north, Mexico will be a land of sharp ecological contrasts.

Climate isn't the only factor governing human settlement, though. Two other crucial factors will also shape the future environments of North America—rising sea levels and the deadly legacies of today's frankly brainless handling of nuclear and chemical wastes. We'll examine them one at a time.

෯ৡৡ

History, as noted earlier, can be seen as human ecology in its transformations over time, and every ecosystem depends in the final analysis on the available habitat. For human beings, the habitat that matters is dry land with adequate rainfall and moderate temperatures; we've talked about the way that anthropogenic climate change is interfering with the latter two, but it promises to have significant impacts on the first of those requirements as well.

It's helpful to put all this in the context of deep time. For most of the last billion years or so, the Earth has been a swampy jungle planet where ice and snow were theoretical possibilities only. Four times in that vast span, though, something—scientists are still arguing about exactly what it was—turned the planet's thermostat down sharply, resulting in ice ages millions of years in length. The most recent of these downturns began cooling the planet maybe ten million years ago, in the Miocene epoch. A little less than two million years ago, at the beginning of the Pleistocene epoch, the first of the great continental ice sheets began to spread across the Northern Hemisphere, and the Ice Age was on.

We're still in it. During an ice age, a complex interplay of the Earth's rotational and orbital wobbles drives the Milankovich cycle, a cyclical warming and cooling of the planet that takes hundreds of thousands of years to complete, with long glaciations broken by much shorter interglacials. We're approaching the end of the current interglacial, and it's estimated that the current Ice Age has maybe another ten million years to go; one consequence is that at some point a few millennia in the future, we can pretty much count on glaciers pushing south across the face of North America once again. In the meantime, we've still got continental ice sheets covering Antarctica and Greenland, and a significant amount of year-round ice in mountains in various corners of the world. That's normal for an interglacial, though not at all normal for most of the planet's history.

The back-and-forth flip-flop between glaciations and inter-glacials has a galaxy of impacts on the climate and ecology of the planet, but one of the most obvious comes from the simple fact that all the frozen water needed to form a continental ice sheet has to come from somewhere, and the only available "somewhere" on this planet is the oceans. As glaciers build up and spread across the land, sea level drops accordingly; 18,000 years ago, when the most recent glaciation hit its final peak, sea level was more than 400 feet lower than today, and roaming tribal hunters could walk all the way from Holland to Ireland on dry land and keep going, following reindeer herds a good distance into what's now the northeast Atlantic.[6]

What followed has plenty of lessons on offer for our future. It used to be part of the received wisdom that ice ages began and ended with, ahem, glacial slowness, and there still seems to be good reason to think that the beginnings are fairly gradual, but the ending of the most recent Ice Age involved periods of very sudden change.[7] As already mentioned, 18,000 years ago, the ice sheets were at their peak; about 16,000 years ago, the planetary climate began to warm, pushing the ice into a slow retreat. Around 14,700 years ago, the warm Bölling phase arrived, and the ice sheets retreated hundreds of miles; according to several studies, the West Antarctic ice sheet collapsed completely at this time.

The Bölling gave way after around 600 years to the Older Dryas cold period, putting the retreat of the ice on hold. After another six centuries or so, the Older Dryas gave way to a new warm period, the Alleröd, which sent the ice sheets reeling back and raised sea levels hundreds of feet worldwide. Then came a new cold phase, the frigid Younger Dryas, which brought temperatures back to their Ice Age lows, cold enough to allow the West Antarctic ice sheet to re-establish itself and to restore tundra conditions over large sections of the Northern Hemisphere. Ice core measurements suggest that the temperature drop hit fast, in a few decades or less.

Just over a millennium later, right around 9600 BC, the Boreal phase arrived, and brought even more spectacular change. According to oxygen isotope measurements from Greenland ice cores, global temperatures spiked 7°C in less than a decade, pushing the remaining ice sheets into rapid collapse and sending sea levels soaring.[8] Over the next few thousand years, the planet's ice cover shrank toward its current level, and sea level rose a bit above what it is today; a gradual cooling trend beginning around 6000 BCE brought both to the status they had at the beginning of the industrial era.

Scientists still aren't sure what caused the stunning temperature spike at the beginning of the Boreal phase, but one widely held theory is that it was driven by large-scale methane releases from the warming oceans and thawing permafrost. The ocean floor contains huge amounts of methane trapped in unstable methane hydrates; permafrost contains equally huge amounts of dead vegetation that's kept from rotting by subfreezing temperatures, and when the permafrost thaws, that vegetation rots and releases more methane. Methane is a far more powerful greenhouse gas than carbon dioxide, but it's also much more transient—once released into the atmosphere, methane breaks down into carbon dioxide and water relatively quickly, with an estimated average lifespan of ten years or so—and so it's quite a plausible driver for the sort of sudden shock that can be traced in the Greenland ice cores.

If that's what did it, of course, we're arguably well on our way there, since methane is already being released from the Arctic Ocean and Siberian permafrost in spectacular amounts. On top of the carbon dioxide being pumped into the atmosphere by human industry, a methane spike would do a fine job of producing "global weirding" on the grand scale. Meanwhile, two of the world's three remaining ice sheets—the West Antarctic and Greenland sheets— have already been destabilized by rising temperatures.[9] Between them, these two ice sheets contain enough water to raise sea level around 50 feet globally, and the likely anthropogenic carbon dioxide emissions over the next century provide enough warming to cause the collapse and total melting of both of them. All that water isn't going to hit the world's oceans overnight, of course, and a great deal depends on just how fast the melting happens.

The predictions for sea-level rise included in recent IPCC reports assume a slow, linear process of glacial melting. That's appropriate as a baseline, but evidence from paleoclimatology shows that ice sheets collapse in relatively sudden bursts of melting, producing what are termed "global meltwater pulses" that can be tracked worldwide by a variety of proxy measurements.[10] Mind you, "relatively sudden" in geological terms is slow by the standards of a human lifetime; the complete collapse of a midsized ice sheet like Greenland's or West Antarctica's can take five or six centuries, and that in turn involves periods of relatively fast melting and sea-level rise, interspersed with slack periods when sea level creeps up much more slowly.

So far, at least, the vast East Antarctic ice sheet has shown only very modest changes, and most current estimates suggest that it would take something far more drastic than the carbon output of our remaining economically accessible fossil fuel reserves to tip it over into instability. This is a good thing, as East Antarctica's ice fields contain enough water to drive sea level up 250 feet or so. Thus a reasonable estimate for sea-level change over the next five hundred years involves the collapse of the Greenland and West Antarctic sheets and some melting on the edges of the East Antarctic sheet, raising sea level by something over 50 feet, delivered in a series of unpredictable bursts divided by long periods of relative stability or slow change.

The result will be what paleogeographers call "marine transgression"—the invasion of dry land and fresh water by the sea. Fifty feet of sea-level change adds up to quite a bit of marine transgression in some areas, much less in others, depending always on local topography. Where the ground is low and flat, the rising seas can penetrate a very long way; in California, for example, the state capital at Sacramento is many miles from the ocean, but since it's only 30 feet above sea level and connected to the sea by a river, its skyscrapers will be rising out of a brackish estuary long before Greenland and West Antarctica are bare of ice. The port cities of the Gulf Coast are also on the front lines. New Orleans is actually below sea level— only extensive levees keep it above water now, and it will likely be an early casualty, but every other Gulf port from Brownsville, Texas, (elevation 43 feet) to Tampa, Florida, (elevation 15 feet) faces the same fate, and most East and West Coast ports face substantial flooding of economically important districts.

The flooding of Sacramento isn't the end of the world, and there may even be some among my readers who would consider it to be a good thing. What I'd like to point out, though, is the economic impact of the rising waters. Faced with an unpredictable but continuing rise in sea level, communities and societies face one of two extremely expensive choices. They can abandon many billions of dollars of infrastructure to the sea and rebuild further inland, or they can invest roughly the same amount in sea walls and flood-control measures. Because the rate of sea-level change can't be anticipated, furthermore, there's no way to know in advance how far to relocate or how high to build the barriers at any given time, and there are often hard limits to how much change can be done in advance: port cities, for example, can't just move away from the sea and still maintain a functioning economy.

This is a pattern we'll be seeing over and over again in this survey. Societies descending into dark ages reliably get caught on the horns of a brutal dilemma. For any of a galaxy of reasons, crucial elements of infrastructure no longer do the job they once did, but reworking or replacing them runs up against two critical difficulties that are hardwired into the process of decline itself. The first is that, as time passes, the resources needed to do the necessary work become increasingly scarce. The second is that, as time passes, the uncertainties about what needs to be done become increasingly large.

The result can be tracked in the decline of every civilization. At first, failing systems are replaced with some success, but the economic impact of the replacement process becomes an ever-increasing burden, and the new systems never do quite manage to work as well as the older ones did in their heyday. As the process continues, the costs keep mounting and the benefits become less reliable; more and more often, scarce resources end up being wasted because the situation is too uncertain to allow them to be allocated where they're most needed. With each passing year, decision makers have to figure out how much of the dwindling stock of resources can be put to productive uses and how much has to be set aside for crisis management, and the raw uncertainty of the times guarantees that these decisions will very often turn out wrong. Eventually, the declining curve in available resources and the rising curve of uncertainty intersect to produce a crisis that spins out of control, and what's left of a community, an economic sector, or a whole civilization goes to pieces under the impact.

It's not too hard to anticipate how that will play out in the century or so immediately ahead of us. If, as I've suggested, we can expect the onset of a global meltwater pulse from the breakup of the Greenland and West Antarctic ice sheets at some point in the years ahead, the first upward jolt in sea level will doubtless be met with grand plans for flood-control measures in some areas and relocation of housing and economic activities in others. Some of those plans may even be carried out, though the raw economic impact of worldwide coastal flooding on a global economy already under severe strain from a chaotic climate and a variety of other factors won't make that easy. Some coastal cities will hunker down behind hurriedly built or enlarged levees; others will abandon low-lying districts and try to rebuild further upslope; still others will simply founder and be partly or wholly abandoned—and all these choices impose costs on society as a whole.

Thereafter, when sea level rises only slowly, the costs of maintaining flood-control measures and replacing vulnerable infrastructure with new facilities on higher ground will become an unpopular burden, and the same shortsighted appeal that drives climate change denialism today will doubtless find plenty of hearers then as well. When sea level surges upwards, the flood-control measures and relocation projects will face increasingly severe tests, which some of them will inevitably fail. The twin spirals of rising costs and rising uncertainty will have their usual effect, shredding the ability of a failing society to cope with the challenges that beset it.

If human beings behave as they usually do, what will most likely happen is that the port cities of North America will keep on trying to maintain business as usual until well after that stops making any kind of economic sense. The faster the seas rise, the sooner that response will tip over into its opposite, and people will begin to flee in large numbers from the coasts in search of safety for themselves and their families. My working guess is that the Eastern and Western seaboards of dark age America will be much more sparsely populated than they are today, with communities concentrated in those areas where land well above sea level lies close to the sea. The Gulf Coast, where very little rises much above sea level and marine transgression will therefore swallow large areas very quickly, may be all but abandoned until the seas stop rising.

These factors make for a shift in the economic and political geography of the continent that will be of quite some importance. In times of rapid sea-level change, maintaining the infrastructure for maritime trade in seacoast ports is a losing struggle; maritime trade is still possible without port infrastructure, but it's rarely economically viable; and that means that inland waterways with good navigable connections to the sea will take on an even greater importance than they have today. In North America, the most crucial of those are the St. Lawrence Seaway, the Hudson River-Erie Canal linkage to the Great Lakes, and whatever port further inland replaces New Orleans—Baton Rouge is a likely candidate, due to its location and elevation above sea level—once the current Mississippi delta drowns beneath the rising seas. Even in dark ages, maritime trade is a normal part of life, and that means that the waterways just listed will become the economic, political, and strategic keys to most of the North American continent.

❧❧❧

The rising seas set in motion by anthropogenic climate change are one part of a broader pattern, which is the impact of today's actions on tomorrow's environment. Civilizations normally leave a damaged environment behind them when they fall, and ours shows every sign of following that wearily familiar pattern. The nature and severity of the ecological damage a civilization leaves behind, though, depend on two factors, one obvious, the other less so. The obvious factor derives from the nature of the technologies the civilization deployed in its heyday; the less obvious one depends on how many times those technologies had been through the same cycle of rise and fall before the civilization under discussion got to them.

There's an important lesson in this latter factor. Human technologies almost always start off their trajectory through time as environmental disasters looking for a spot marked X, which they inevitably find, and then have the rough edges knocked off them by centuries or millennia of bitter experience. When our species first developed the technologies that enabled hunting bands to take down big game animals, the result was mass slaughter and the extinction of entire species of megafauna, followed by famine and misery; repeat the same cycle dozens of times, and you end up with the exquisite ecological balance that most hunter-gatherer societies maintained in historic times. In much the same way, early field agriculture yielded bumper crops of topsoil loss and subsistence failure to go along with its less reliable yields of edible grain, and the hard lessons from that experience have driven the rise of more sustainable agricultural systems—a process completed in our time with the emergence of organic agricultural methods that build soil rather than depleting it.

Any brand-new mode of human subsistence is thus normally cruising for a bruising, and will get it in due time at the hands of the biosphere. That's not precisely good news for modern industrial civilization, because ours is a brand-new mode of human subsistence; it's the first human society ever to depend almost entirely on extrasomatic energy—energy, that is, that doesn't come from human or animal muscles fueled by food crops. In my book *The Ecotechnic Future*, I've suggested that industrial civilization is simply the first and most wasteful of a new mode of human society, the technic society. Eventually, I proposed, technic societies will achieve the same precise accommodation to ecological reality that hunter-gatherer societies worked out long ago and that agricultural societies have spent the last eight thousand years or so pursuing. Unfortunately, that doesn't help us much just now.

Modern industrial civilization, in point of fact, has been stunningly clueless in its relationship with the planetary cycles that keep us all alive. Like those early bands of roving hunters who slaughtered every mammoth they could find and then looked around blankly for something to eat, we've drawn down the finite stocks of fossil fuels on this planet without the least concern about what the future would bring—well, other than the occasional pious utterance of thought-stopping mantras of the "I'm sure they'll think of something" variety. That's not the only thing we've drawn down recklessly, of course, and the impact of our idiotically short-term thinking on our long-term prospects will be among the most important forces shaping the next five centuries of North America's future.

Let's start with one of the most obvious: topsoil, the biologically active layer of soil that can support food crops. On average, as a result of today's standard agricultural methods, North America's arable land loses almost three tons of topsoil from each cultivated acre every single year. Most of the topsoil that made North America the breadbasket of the twentieth-century world is already gone, and at the current rate of loss, all of it will be gone by 2150.[11] That would be bad enough if we could rely on artificial fertilizer to make up for the losses, but by 2150 that won't be an option: the entire range of chemical fertilizers are made from nonrenewable resources—natural gas is the main feedstock for nitrate fertilizers, rock phosphate for phosphate fertilizers, and so on—and all of these are depleting fast.

Topsoil loss driven by bad agricultural practices is actually quite a common factor in the collapse of civilizations. Sea-floor cores in the waters around Greece, for example, show a spike in sediment deposition from rapidly eroding topsoil right around the end of the Mycenean civilization, and another from the latter years of the Roman Empire.[12] If archeologists thousands of years from now try the same test, they'll find yet another eroded topsoil layer at the bottom of the Gulf of Mexico, the legacy of an agricultural system that put quarterly profits ahead of the relatively modest changes that might have preserved the soil for future generations.

The methods of organic agriculture mentioned earlier could help very significantly with this problem, since those include techniques for preserving existing topsoil and rebuilding depleted soil at a rate considerably faster than nature's pace. To make any kind of difference, though, those methods would have to be deployed on a very broad scale and then passed down through the difficult years ahead. Lacking that, even where desertification driven by climate change doesn't make farming impossible, a very large part of today's North American farm belt will likely be unable to support crops for centuries or millennia to come. Eventually, the same slow processes that replenished the soil on land scraped bare by the Ice Age glaciers will do the same thing to land stripped of topsoil by industrial farming, but "eventually" will not come quickly enough to spare our descendants many hungry days.

The same tune in a different key is currently being played across the world's oceans, and as a result my readers can look forward, in the not too distant future, to tasting the last piece of seafood they will ever eat.[13] Conservatively managed, the world's fish stocks could have produced large yields indefinitely, but they were not conservatively managed. Where regulation was attempted, political and economic pressure consistently drove catch limits above sustainable levels, and of course, cheating was pervasive and the penalties for being caught were merely another cost of doing business. Fishery after fishery has accordingly collapsed, and the increasingly frantic struggle to feed seven billion hungry mouths is unlikely to leave any of those that remain intact for long.

Worse, all of this is happening in oceans that are being hammered by other aspects of our collective ecological stupidity. Global climate change, by boosting the carbon dioxide content of the atmosphere, is acidifying the oceans and causing sweeping shifts in oceanic food chains. Those shifts involve winners as well as losers; where calcium-shelled diatoms and corals are suffering population declines, seaweeds and other forms of algae, which are not so sensitive to changes in the acid-alkaline balance, are thriving on the increased CO_2 in the water[14]—but the fish that feed on seaweeds and algae are not the same as those that feed on diatoms and corals, and the resulting changes are whipsawing ocean ecologies.

Close to shore, toxic effluents from human industry and agriculture are also adding to the trouble. The deep oceans, all things considered, offer sparse pickings for most saltwater creatures. The vast majority of ocean life thrives within a few hundred miles of land, where rivers, upwelling zones, and the like provide nutrients in relative abundance. We're already seeing serious problems with toxic substances concentrating up through oceanic food chains, and unless communities close to the water's edge respond to rising sea levels with consummate care, hauling every source of toxic chemicals out of reach of the waters, that problem is only going to grow worse. Different species react differently to this or that toxin; some kind of aquatic ecosystem will emerge and thrive even in the most toxic estuaries of deindustrial North America, but it's unlikely that those ecosystems will produce anything fit for human beings to eat, and making the attempt may not be particularly good for one's health.

Over the long run, that, too, will right itself. Bioaccumulated toxins will end up entombed in the muck on the ocean's floor, providing yet another interesting data point for the archeologists of the far future; food chains and ecosystems will reorganize, quite possibly in very different forms from the ones they have now. Changes in water temperature, and potentially in the patterns of ocean currents, will bring unfamiliar species into contact with one another, and living things that survive the deindustrial years in isolated refugia will expand into their former range. These are normal stages in the adaptation of ecosystems to large-scale shocks. Still, those processes of renewal take time, and the deindustrial dark ages ahead of us will be long gone before the seas are restored to biological abundance.

Barren lands and empty seas aren't the only bitter legacies we're leaving our descendants, of course. One of the others has received quite a bit of attention of late—since March 11, 2011, to be precise, when the Fukushima Daiichi nuclear disaster got under way. Nuclear power exerts a curious magnetism on the modern mind, drawing it toward extremes in one direction or the other; the wildly unrealistic claims about its limitless potential to power the future that have been made by its supporters are neatly balanced by the wildly unrealistic claims about its limitless potential as a source of human extinction on the other. Negotiating a path between those extremes is not always an easy matter.

In both cases, though, it's easy enough to clear away at least some of the confusion by turning to documented facts. It so happens, for instance, that no nation on Earth has ever been able to launch or maintain a nuclear power program without huge and continuing subsidies. Nuclear power, in other words, never pays for itself; absent a steady stream of government handouts, it doesn't make enough economic sense to attract enough private investment to cover its costs, much less meet the huge and so far unmet expenses of nuclear waste storage, and in the great majority of cases, the motive behind the program, and the subsidies, is pretty clearly the desire of the local government to arm itself with nuclear weapons at any cost. Thus the tired fantasy of cheap, abundant nuclear power needs to be buried alongside the Eisenhower-era propagandists who dreamed it up in the first place.

It also happens, of course, that there have been quite a few catastrophic nuclear accidents since the dawn of the atomic age just over seventy years ago, especially but not only in the former Soviet Union.[15] Thus it's no secret what the consequences are when a reactor melts down, or when mismanaged nuclear waste storage facilities catch fire and spew radioactive smoke across the countryside. What results is an unusually dangerous industrial accident, on a par with the sudden collapse of a hydroelectric dam or a chemical plant explosion that sends toxic gases drifting into a populated area; it differs from these mostly in that the contamination left behind by certain nuclear accidents remains dangerous for many years after it comes drifting down from the sky.

There are currently 69 operational nuclear power plants scattered unevenly across the face of North America, with 127 reactors among them; there are also 48 research reactors, most of them much smaller and less vulnerable to meltdown than the power plant reactors. Most North American nuclear power plants store spent fuel rods in pools of cooling water onsite, since the spent rods continue to give off heat and radiation and the project of building long-term storage facilities for high-level nuclear waste has been at a standstill for decades. Neither a reactor nor a fuel rod storage pool can be left untended for long without serious trouble, and a great many things—including natural disasters and human stupidity—can push them over into meltdown, in the case of reactors, or conflagration, in the case of spent fuel rods. In either case, or both, you'll get a plume of toxic, highly radioactive smoke drifting in the wind, and a great many people immediately downwind will die quickly or slowly, depending on the details and the dose.

It's entirely reasonable to predict that this is going to happen to some of those 175 reactors. In a world racked by climate change, resource depletion, economic disintegration, political and social chaos, mass movements of populations, and the other normal features of the decline and fall of a civilization and the coming of a dark age, the short straw is going to be drawn sooner or later, and serious nuclear disasters are going to happen. That doesn't justify the claim made by some people that every one of those reactors is going to melt down catastrophically, every one of the spent-fuel storage facilities is going to catch fire, and so on—though, of course, that claim does make for more colorful rhetoric.

In the real world, we don't face the kind of sudden collapse that could make all the lights go out at once. Some nations, regions, and local areas within regions will slide faster than others, or be deliberately sacrificed so that resources of one kind or another can be used somewhere else. As long as governments retain any kind of power at all, keeping nuclear facilities from adding to the ongoing list of disasters will be high on their agendas; shutting down reactors that are no longer safe to operate is one step they can certainly do, and so is hauling spent fuel rods out of the pools and putting them somewhere less immediately vulnerable.

It's probably a safe bet that the further we go along the arc of decline and fall, the further these decommissioning exercises will stray from the optimum. I can all too easily imagine fuel rods being hauled out of their pools by condemned criminals or political prisoners, loaded on flatbed rail cars, taken to some desolate corner of the expanding western deserts, and tipped one at a time into trenches dug in the desert soil, then covered over with a few meters of dirt and left to the elements. Sooner or later the radionuclides will leak out, and that desolate place will become even more desolate, a place of rumors and legends where those who go don't come back.

Meanwhile, the reactors and spent-fuel pools that don't get shut down even in so cavalier a fashion will become the focal points of dead zones of a slightly different kind. The facilities themselves will be off-limits for some thousands of years, and the invisible footprints left behind by the plumes of smoke and dust will be dangerous for centuries. The vagaries of deposition and erosion are impossible to predict; in areas downwind from Chernobyl or some of the less famous Soviet nuclear accidents, one piece of overgrown former farmland may be relatively safe while another a quarter-hour's walk away may still set a Geiger counter clicking at way-beyond-safe rates. Here I imagine cow skulls on poles, or some such traditional marker, warning the unwary that they stand on the edge of accursed ground.

It's important to keep in mind that not all the accursed ground in deindustrial North America will be the result of nuclear accidents. There are already areas on the continent so heavily contaminated with toxic pollutants of less glow-in-the-dark varieties that anyone who attempts to grow food or drink the water there can count on a short life and a wretched death. As the industrial system spirals toward its end, and those environmental protections that haven't been gutted already get flung aside in the frantic quest to keep the system going just a little bit longer, spills and other industrial accidents are very likely to become a good deal more common than they are already.

There are methods of soil and ecosystem bioremediation that can be done with very simple technologies—for example, plants that concentrate toxic metals in their tissues so they can be hauled away to a less dangerous site and fungi that break down organic toxins—but if they're to do any good at all, these will have to be preserved and deployed in the teeth of massive social changes and equally massive hardships. Lacking that, and it's a considerable gamble at this point, the North America of the future will be spotted with areas where birth defects are a common cause of infant mortality and it will be rare to see anyone over the age of forty or so without the telltale signs of cancer.

There's a bitter irony in the fact that cancer, a relatively uncommon disease a century and a half ago—childhood cancers were so rare that individual cases were written up in medical journals —has become the signature disease of industrial society, expanding its occurrence and death toll in lockstep with our mindless dumping of chemical toxins and radioactive waste into the environment. What, after all, is cancer? A disease of uncontrolled growth.

I sometimes wonder if our descendants in the deindustrial world will appreciate that irony. One way or another, I have no doubt that they'll have their own opinions about the bitter legacy we're leaving them. As they think back on the people of the twentieth and early twenty-first centuries who gave them the barren soil and ravaged fisheries, the chaotic weather and rising oceans, the poisoned land and water, the birth defects and cancers that embitter their lives, how will they remember us? I think I know. I think we will be the orcs and Nazgûl of their legends, the collective Satan of their mythology, the ancient race who ravaged the Earth and everything on it so they could enjoy lives of wretched excess at the future's expense. They will remember us as evil incarnate—and from their perspective, it's by no means easy to dispute that judgment.

3

THE DEMOGRAPHIC CONSEQUENCES

THE THREE ENVIRONMENTAL SHIFTS DISCUSSED IN THE PRE-
vious chapter—the ecological impacts of a sharply warmer and
dryer climate, the flooding of coastal regions due to rising sea
levels, and the long-term consequences of industrial America's
frankly brainless dumping of persistent radiological and chemical
poisons—all involve changes to the North American continent
that will endure straight through the deindustrial dark age ahead
and will help shape the history of the successor cultures that will
rise amid our ruins. For millennia to come, the peoples of North
America will have to contend with drastically expanded deserts,
coastlines many miles further inland than they are today, and the
presence of dead zones where nuclear or chemical wastes in the soil
and water make human settlement impossible.

Agriculture can adapt to a wide range of climate shifts, and some
highly promising moves toward adapting agricultural methods
to the changed climate of the deindustrial era are already under
way.[1] That said, there is a fairly limited set of regions in which field
agriculture of something like the familiar sort will be viable in a
post-fossil fuel age. Those regions cluster in the Eastern Seaboard
from the new coast west to the Alleghenies and the Great Lakes
and in river valleys in the eastern half of the Mississippi basin.

The Midwestern grasslands will support pastoral grazing, and the jungle belts around the new Gulf Coast will be suitable for tropical horticulture once the soil has a chance to recover. The vast inland deserts will support a few people, much the way the inland regions of the Sahara Desert do today, and a narrow strip of land along the Pacific coast will be habitable to roughly the same degree that the northern shores of Africa are at present. Meanwhile, all through these regions, the fertile and the barren alike, there will be dead zones contaminated by nuclear or chemical poisons, where no one can live.

As a result, deindustrial North America will support many fewer people than it did in 1880 or so, before new agricultural technologies dependent on fossil fuels launched the population boom that is peaking in our time. This also implies, of course, that deindustrial North America will support many, many fewer people than it does today. For obvious reasons, it's worth talking about the processes by which today's seriously overpopulated North America will become the sparsely populated continent of the coming dark age—but that discussion is going to require a confrontation with a certain kind of petrified irrelevancy all too common in our time.

There are two officially sanctioned scripts into which discussions of overpopulation are inevitably shoehorned in today's industrial world. Like most cultural phenomena in today's industrial world, the scripts just mentioned hew closely to the faux-liberal and faux-conservative narratives that dominate so much of contemporary thought.[2] The scripts differ along the usual lines: that is to say, the faux-liberal script is well-meaning and ineffectual, while the faux-conservative script is practicable and evil.

Thus the faux-liberal script insists that overpopulation is a terrible problem, we ought to do something about it, and the things we should do about it are all things that don't work, won't work, and have been being tried over and over again for decades without having the slightest effect on the situation. The faux-conservative script insists that overpopulation is a terrible problem but only because it's people of, ahem, the wrong skin color who are overpopulating, ahem, *our* country: that is, overpopulation means immigration, and immigration means let's throw buckets of gasoline onto the flames of ethnic conflict, so it can play its standard role in ripping apart a dying civilization with even more verve than it otherwise would.

Overpopulation and immigration policy are not the same thing. Neither are depopulation and the mass migrations of whole peoples for which German historians of the post-Roman dark ages coined the neat term *völkerwanderung*, "the wandering of nations," which are the corresponding phenomena in eras of decline and fall. For that reason, the faux-conservative side of the debate, along with the usually unmentioned realities of immigration policy in today's America and the far greater and more troubling realities of mass migration and ethnogenesis that will follow in due time, will be covered a little later in this chapter. For now I want to talk about overpopulation as such, and therefore about the faux-liberal side of the debate and the stark realities of depopulation that are waiting in the future.

All this needs to be put in its proper context. In 1962, the year I was born, there were about three and a half billion human beings on this planet. Today, there are more than seven billion of us. That staggering increase in human numbers has played an immense and disastrous role in backing today's industrial world into the corner where it now finds itself. Among all the forces driving us toward an ugly future, the raw pressure of human overpopulation, with the huge and rising resource requirements it entails, is among the most important.

That much is clear. What to do about it is something else again. You'll still hear people insisting that campaigns to convince people to limit their reproduction voluntarily ought to do the trick, but such campaigns have been ongoing since many decades before I was born, and human numbers more than doubled anyway. If a strategy has failed every time it's been tried, insisting that we ought to do it again isn't a useful suggestion. That applies not only to the campaigns just noted, but to all the other proposals to slow or stop population growth that have been tried repeatedly and failed just as repeatedly over the decades just past.

These days, a great deal of the hopeful talk around the subject of limits to overpopulation has refocused on what's called the demographic transition: the process, visible in the population history of most of today's industrial nations, whereby people start voluntarily reducing their reproduction when their income and access to resources rise above a certain level. It's a real effect, though its causes are far from clear. The problem here is simply that the resource base that would make it possible for enough of the world's population to have the income and access to resources necessary to trigger a worldwide demographic transition simply don't exist.

As fossil fuels and a galaxy of other nonrenewable resources slide down the slope of depletion at varying rates, for that matter, it's becoming increasingly hard for people in the industrial nations to maintain their familiar standards of living. It may be worth noting that this hasn't caused a sudden upward spike in population growth in those countries where downward mobility has become most visible. The demographic transition, in other words, doesn't work in reverse, and this points to a crucial fact that hasn't necessarily been given the weight it deserves in conversations about overpopulation.

The vast surge in human numbers that dominates the demographic history of modern times is wholly a phenomenon of the industrial age. Other historical periods have seen modest population increases but nothing on the same scale, and those have reversed themselves promptly when ecological limits came into play. Whatever the specific factors and forces that drove the population boom, then, it's a pretty safe bet that the underlying cause was the one factor present in industrial civilization that hasn't played a significant role in any other human society: the exploitation of vast quantities of extrasomatic energy—that is, energy that doesn't come from human or animal muscle. Place the curve of increasing energy per capita worldwide next to the curve of human population worldwide, and the two move very nearly in lockstep: thus it's fair to say that human beings, like yeast, respond to increased access to energy with increased reproduction.

Does that mean that we're going to have to deal with soaring population worldwide for the foreseeable future? No, and hard planetary limits to resource extraction are the reasons why. Without the huge energy subsidy to agriculture contributed by fossil fuels, producing enough food to support seven billion people won't be possible. We saw a preview of the consequences in 2008 and 2009, when the spike in petroleum prices caused a corresponding spike in food prices and a great many people around the world found themselves scrambling to get enough to eat on any terms at all. The riots and revolutions that followed grabbed the headlines, but another shift that happened around the same time deserves more attention: birth rates in many Third World countries decreased noticeably and have continued to trend downward since then.[3]

The same phenomenon can be seen elsewhere. Since the collapse of the Soviet Union, most of the former Soviet republics have seen steep declines in rates of live birth, life expectancy, and most other measures of public health, while death rates have climbed well above birth rates and stayed there.[4] For that matter, since the financial crisis of 2008, birth rates in the United States have dropped sharply; these days, immigration is the only reason the population of the United States doesn't register significant declines year after year.

This is the wave of the future. As fossil fuel and other resources dwindle, and economies dependent on those resources become less and less able to provide people with the necessities of life, the population boom will turn into a population bust. The base scenario in 1972's *The Limits to Growth*, still the most accurate (and thus inevitably the most vilified) model of the future into which we're stumbling blindly just now, put the peak of global population somewhere around 2030: that is, fourteen years from now. Recent declines in birth rates in areas that were once hotbeds of population growth, such as Latin America and the Middle East, can be seen as the leveling off that always occurs in a population curve before decline sets in.

That decline is likely to go very far indeed. That's partly a matter of straightforward logic: because global population has been artificially inflated by pouring extrasomatic energy into boosting the food supply and providing other necessary resources to human beings, the exhaustion of economically extractable reserves of the fossil fuels that made that process possible will knock the props out from under global population figures. Still, historical parallels also have quite a bit to offer here: extreme depopulation is a common feature of the decline and fall of civilizations, with up to ninety-five percent population loss over the one to three centuries that the fall of a civilization usually takes.

Suggest that to people nowadays and, once you get past the usual reactions of denial and disbelief, the standard assumption is that population declines so severe could happen only if there were catastrophes on a truly gargantuan scale. That's an easy assumption to make, but it doesn't happen to be true. Just as it didn't take vast public orgies of copulation and childbirth to double the planet's population over the last half-century, it wouldn't take equivalent exercises in mass death to halve the planet's population over the same time frame. The ordinary processes of demographic change can do the trick all by themselves.

Let's explore that by way of a thought experiment. Between family, friends, coworkers, and the others that you meet in the course of your daily activities, you probably know something close to a hundred people. Every so often, in the ordinary course of events, one of them dies—depending on the age and social status of the people you know, that might happen once a year, once every two years, or what have you. Take a moment to recall the most recent death in your social circle, and the one before that, to help put the rest of the thought experiment in context.

Now imagine that from this day onward, among the hundred people you know, one additional person—one person more than you would otherwise expect to die—dies every year, while the rate of birth remains the same as it is now. Imagine that modest increase in the death rate affecting the people you know. One year, an elderly relative of yours doesn't wake up one morning; the next, a barista at the place where you get coffee on the way to work dies of cancer; the year after that, a coworker's child comes down with an infection the doctors can't treat, and so on. A noticeable shift? Granted, but it's not Armageddon; you attend a few more funerals than you're used to, make friends with the new barista, and go about your life until one of those additional deaths is yours.

Now take that process and extrapolate it out. (Those of my readers who have the necessary math skills should take the time to crunch the numbers themselves.) Over the course of three centuries, an increase in the crude death rate of one percent per annum, given an unchanged birth rate, is sufficient to reduce a population to five percent of its original level. Vast catastrophes need not apply; of the traditional four horsemen, War, Famine, and Pestilence can sit around drinking beer and playing poker. The fourth horseman, in the shape of a modest change in crude death rates, can do the job all by himself.

Now imagine the same scenario, except that there are three additional deaths each year in your social circle, rather than one. That would be considerably more noticeable, but it still doesn't look like the end of the world—at least until you do the math. An increase in the crude death rate of three percent per annum, given an unchanged birth rate, is enough to reduce a population to five percent of its original level within a single century. In global terms, if world population peaks around eight billion in 2030, a decline on that scale would leave four hundred million people on the planet by 2130.

In the real world, of course, things are not as simple or smooth as they are in the thought experiment just offered. Birth rates are subject to complex pressures and vary up and down depending on the specific pressures a population faces, and even small increases in infant and child mortality have a disproportionate effect by removing potential breeding pairs from the population before they can reproduce. Meanwhile, population declines are rarely anything like so even as the thought experiment suggests. Those other three horsemen, in particular, tend to get bored of their poker game at intervals and go riding out to give the guy with the scythe some help with the harvest. War, famine, and pestilence are common events in the decline and fall of a civilization, and the twilight of the industrial world is likely to get its fair share of them.

Thus it probably won't be a matter of one or two or three more deaths a year, every year. Instead, one year, war breaks out, most of the young men in town get drafted, and half of them come back in body bags. Another year, after a string of bad harvests and food shortages, the flu comes through, and a lot of people who would have shaken it off under better conditions are just that little bit too malnourished to survive. Yet another year, a virus shaken out of its tropical home by climate change and ecosystem disruption goes through town, and fifteen percent of the population dies in eight ghastly months. That's the way population declines happen in history.

In the twilight years of the Roman world, to cite an example we'll be using repeatedly in the chapters ahead, a steady demographic contraction was overlaid by civil wars, barbarian invasions, economic crises, famines, and epidemics.[5] The total population decline varied significantly from one region to another, but even the relatively stable parts of the Eastern Empire seem to have had around a fifty percent loss of population, while some areas of the Western Empire suffered far more drastic losses—Britain in particular was transformed from a rich, populous, and largely urbanized province to a land of silent urban ruins and small, scattered villages of subsistence farmers where even so simple a technology as wheel-thrown pottery became a lost art.

The classic lowland Maya are another good example along the same lines. Hammered by climate change and topsoil loss, the Maya heartland went through a rolling collapse a century and a half in length that ended with population levels maybe five percent of what they'd been at the start of the Terminal Classic period, and most of the great Maya cities became empty ruins rapidly covered by the encroaching jungle.[6] Those of my readers who have seen pictures of tropical foliage burying the pyramids of Tikal and Copan may find it helpful to imagine scenes of the same kind in the ruins of Atlanta and Austin a few centuries from now. That's the kind of thing that happens when an urbanized society suffers severe population loss during the decline and fall of a civilization.

That, in turn, is what has to be factored into any realistic forecast of dark age America: there will be many, many fewer people inhabiting North America a few centuries from now than there are today. Between the depletion of the fossil fuel resources necessary to maintain today's hugely inflated numbers and the degradation of North America's human carrying capacity by climate change, sea level rise, and persistent radiological and chemical pollution, the continent simply won't be able to support all that many people. The current total is about 470 million—35 million in Canada, 314 million in the US, and 121 million in Mexico, according to the latest figures I was able to find—and something close to five percent of that—say, 20 to 25 million—might be a reasonable midrange estimate for the human population of the North American continent when the population implosion finally bottoms out a few centuries from now.

Now, of course, those 20 to 25 million people won't be scattered evenly across the continent. There will be very large regions—for example, the nearly lifeless, sun-blasted wastelands that climate change will make of the southern Great Plains, the Great Basin, and the Sonoran Desert—where human settlement will be as sparse as it is today in the bleakest parts of the Sahara Desert. There will be other areas—for example, the Great Lakes region and the Gulf Coast from Mexico around to the shallow seas where Florida used to be—where population will be relatively dense by Dark Age standards, and towns of modest size may even thrive if they happen to be in defensible locations.

The nomadic herding folk of the Midwestern prairies, and the other human ecologies that will spring up in the varying ecosystems of deindustrial North America, will all gradually settle into a more or less stable population level, at which births and deaths balance each other and the consumption of resources stays at or below sustainable levels of production. That's what happens in human societies that don't have the dubious advantage of a torrent of non-renewable energy reserves to distract them temporarily from the hard necessities of survival.

It's getting to that level that's going to be a bear. The mechanisms of population contraction are simple enough, and as suggested above, they can have a dramatic impact on historical time scales without cataclysmic impact on the scale of individual lives. The same principle applies to the second half of the demography of dark age America: the role of mass migration and ethnogenesis in the birth of the cultures that will emerge on this continent when industrial civilization is a fading memory.

⁂

It's one thing to suggest that North America a few centuries from now might have something like five percent of its current population. It's quite another thing to talk about exactly whose descendants will comprise that five percent—and yes, I know that raising that issue is normally a very good way to spark a shouting match in which who-did-what-to-whom rhetoric plays its usual role in drowning out everything else.

Now, of course, there's a point to talking about, and learning from, the abuses inflicted by groups of people on other groups of people over the last five centuries or so of North American history. Such discussions, though, have very little to offer the theme of this book, because history may be a source of moral lessons, but it's not a moral phenomenon. A glance back over our past shows clearly enough that who won, who lost, who ended up ruling a society, and who ended up enslaved or exterminated by that same society, was not determined by moral virtue or by the justice of one or another cause but by the crassly pragmatic factors of military, political, and economic power. No doubt most of us would rather live in a world that didn't work that way, but here we are, and morality remains a matter of individual choices—yours and mine—in the face of a cosmos that's sublimely unconcerned with our moral beliefs.

Thus we can take it for granted that just as the borders that currently divide North America were put there by force or the threat of force, the dissolution of those borders and their replacement with new lines of division will happen the same way. For that matter, it's a safe bet that the social divisions, ethnic and otherwise, of the successor cultures that emerge in the aftermath of our downfall will be established and enforced by means no more just or fair than the ones that distribute wealth and privilege to the different social and ethnic strata in today's North American nations. Again, it would be pleasant to live in a world where that isn't true, but we don't.

I apologize to any of my readers who are offended or upset by these points. In order to make any kind of sense of the way that civilizations fall—and more to the point, the way that ours is falling—it's essential to get past the belief that history is under any obligation to hand out rewards for good behavior and punishments for the opposite, or for that matter, the other way around. Over the years and decades and centuries ahead of us, as industrial civilization crumbles, a great many people who believe with all their hearts that their cause is right and just are going to die anyway, and there will be no shortage of brutal, hateful, vile individuals who claw their way to the top—for a while, at least. One of the reliable features of dark ages is that while they last, the top of the heap is a very unsafe place to be.

North America being what it is today, a great many people considering the sort of future I've just sketched out start thinking about the potential for ethnic conflict, especially but not only in the United States. It's an issue worth discussing, and not only for the obvious reasons. Conflict between ethnic groups is quite often a major issue in the twilight years of a civilization, for reasons we'll discuss shortly, but it's also self-terminating, for an interesting reason: traditional ethnic divisions don't survive dark ages. In an age of political dissolution, economic implosion, social chaos, demographic collapse, and mass migration, the factors that maintain ethnic divisions in place don't last long. In their place, new ethnicities emerge. It's a commonplace of history that dark ages are the cauldron from which nations are born.

So we have three stages, which overlap to a greater or lesser degree: a stage of ethnic conflict, a stage of ethnic dissolution, and a stage of ethnogenesis. Let's take them one at a time.

The stage of ethnic conflict is one effect of the economic contraction that's inseparable from the decline of a civilization. If a rising tide lifts all boats, as economists of the trickle-down school used to insist, a falling tide has a much more differentiated effect, since each group in a declining society does its best to see to it that as much as possible of the costs of decline land on someone else.[7] Since each group's access to wealth and privilege determines fairly exactly how much influence it has on the process, it's one of the constants of decline and fall that the costs and burdens of decline trickle down, landing with most force on those at the bottom of the pyramid.

That heats up animosities across the board: between ethnic groups, between regions, between political and religious divisions, you name it. Since everyone below the uppermost levels of wealth and power loses some of what they've come to expect, and since it's human nature to pay more attention to what you've lost than to the difference between what you've retained and what someone worse off than you has to make do with, everyone's aggrieved, and everyone sees any attempt by someone else to better their condition as a threat. That's by no means entirely inaccurate—if the pie's shrinking, any attempt to get a wider slice has to come at somebody else's expense—but it fans the flames of conflict even further, helping to drive the situation toward the inevitable explosions.

One very common and very interesting feature of this process is that the increase in ethnic tensions tends to parallel a process of ethnic consolidation. In the United States a century ago, for example, the division of society by ethnicity wasn't anything so like as simple as it is today. The uppermost caste in most of the country wasn't simply white, it was white male Episcopalians whose ancestors got here from northwestern Europe before the Revolutionary War. Irish ranked below Germans but above Italians, who looked down on Jews, and so on down the ladder to the very bottom, which was occupied by either African Americans or Native Americans depending on locality. Within any given ethnicity, furthermore, steep social divisions existed, microcosms of a hierarchically ordered macrocosm. Gender distinctions and a great many other lines of fracture combined with the ethnic divisions just noted to make American society in 1916 as intricately caste-ridden as any culture on the planet.

The partial dissolution of many of these divisions has resulted inevitably in the hardening of those that remain. That's a common pattern, too: consider the way that the rights of Roman citizenship expanded step by step from the inhabitants of the city of Rome itself to larger and larger fractions of the people it dominated, until finally every free adult male in the Empire was a Roman citizen by definition. Parallel to that process came a hardening of the major divisions, between free persons and slaves on the one hand, between citizens of the Empire and the barbarians outside its borders, and between adherents of the major religious blocs into which the tolerant paganism of Rome's heyday was divided. The result was the same in that case as it is in ours: traditional, parochial jealousies and prejudices focused on people one step higher or lower on the ladder of caste give way to new loyalties and hatreds, uniting ever-greater fractions of the population into increasingly large and explosive masses.

The way that this interlocks with the standard mechanisms of decline and fall will be a central theme throughout this book. The crucial detail, though, is that a society riven by increasingly bitter divisions of the sort just sketched out is very poorly positioned to deal with external pressure or serious crisis. "Divide and conquer," the Romans liked to say during the centuries of their power: splitting up their enemies and crushing them one at a time was the fundamental strategy they used to build their empire. On the way down, though, it was the body of Roman society that did the dividing, tearing itself apart along every available line of schism, and Rome was accordingly conquered in its turn. That's usual for falling civilizations, and we're well along the same route in the United States today.

Ethnic divisions thus routinely play a significant role in the crash of civilizations. Still, as noted above, the resulting chaos quickly shreds the institutional arrangements that make ethnic divisions endure in a settled society. Charismatic leaders emerge out of the chaos, and those who are capable of envisioning and forming alliances across ethnic lines succeed where their rivals fail; the reliable result is a chaotic melting pot of armed bands and temporary communities drawn from all available sources. When the Huns first came west from the Eurasian steppes around 370 CE, for example, they were apparently a federation of related Central Asian tribes; by the time of Attila, rather less than a century later, his vast armies included warriors from most of the ethnic groups of Eastern Europe.[8] We don't even know what their leader's actual name was. "Attila" was a nickname—"Daddy"—in Visigothic, the lingua franca among the eastern barbarians at that time.

The same chaotic reshuffling was just as common on the other side of the collapsing Roman frontiers. The province of Britannia, for instance, had long been divided into ethnic groups with their own distinct religious and cultural traditions. In the wake of the Roman collapse and the Saxon invasions, the survivors who took refuge in the mountains of the West forgot the old divisions, and took to calling themselves by a new name: *Combrogi*, "fellow-countrymen" in old Brythonic.[9] Nowadays that's *Cymry*, the name the Welsh use for themselves. Not everyone who ended up as *Com-brogi* was British by ancestry—one of the famous Welsh chieftains in the wars against the Saxons was a Visigoth named Theodoric.[10] Nor were all the people on the other side Saxons—one of the leaders of the invaders was a Briton named Caradoc ap Cunorix, the "Cerdic son of Cynric" of the Anglo-Saxon Chronicle.[11]

It's almost impossible to overstate the efficiency of the blender into which every political, economic, social, and ethnic manifestation got tossed in the last years of Rome. My favorite example of the raw confusion of that time is the remarkable career of another Saxon leader named Odoacer. He was the son of one of Attila the Hun's generals, but he got involved in Saxon raids on Britain after Attila's death. Sometime in the 460s, when the struggle between the Britons and the Saxons was more or less stuck in deadlock, Odoacer decided to look for better pickings elsewhere and led a Saxon fleet that landed at the mouth of the Loire in western France.[12] For the next decade or so, more or less in alliance with Childeric, king of the Franks, he fought the Romans, the Goths, and the Bretons there.

When the Saxon hold on the Loire was finally broken, Odoacer took the remains of his force and joined Childeric in an assault on Italy. No records survive of the fate of that expedition, but it apparently didn't go well. Odoacer next turned up, without an army, in what's now Austria and was then the province of Noricum. It took him only a short time to scrape together a following from the random mix of barbarian warriors to be found there, and in 476 he marched on Italy again and overthrew the equally random mix of barbarians who had recently seized control of the peninsula.

The Emperor of the West just then, the heir of the Caesars and titular lord of half the world, was a boy named Romulus Augustulus. In a fine bit of irony, he also happened to be the son of Attila the Hun's Greek secretary, a sometime ally of Odoacer's father. This may be why, instead of doing the usual thing and having the boy killed, Odoacer basically told the last Emperor of Rome to run along and play. That sort of clemency was unusual, and it wasn't repeated by the next barbarian warlord in line; fourteen years later Odoacer was murdered by order of Theodoric, king of the Ostrogoths, who proceeded to take his place as temporary master of the corpse of imperial Rome.

Soldiers of fortune, or of misfortune, weren't the only people engaged in this sort of heavily armed tour of the post-Roman world during those same years. Entire nations were doing the same thing. Those of my readers who have been watching North America's climate come unhinged may be interested to know that severe droughts in Central Asia may have been the trigger that kickstarted the process, pushing nomadic tribes out of their traditional steppe territories in a desperate quest for survival. Whether or not that's what pushed the Huns into motion, the westward migration of the Huns forced other barbarian peoples further west to flee for their lives, and the chain of dominoes thus set in motion played a massive role in creating the chaos in which figures like Odoacer rose and fell. It's a measure of the sheer scale of these migrations that, before Rome started to topple, many of the ancestors of today's Spaniards lived in what's now the Ukraine.

And afterward? The migrations slowed and finally stopped; the warlords became kings; and the people who found themselves in some more or less stable kingdom began the slow process by which a random assortment of refugees, barbarian invaders, and military veterans from the far corners of the Roman world became the first draft of a nation. The former province of Britannia, for example, became seven Saxon kingdoms and a varying number of Celtic ones; and then began the slow process of war and coalescence out of which England, Scotland, Wales, and Cornwall gradually emerged. Elsewhere, the same process moved at varying rates; new nations, languages, ethnic groups came into being. The cauldron of nations had come off the boil, and the history of Europe settled down to a somewhat less frenetic rhythm.

I've used post-Roman Europe as a convenient and solidly documented example, but transformations of the same kind are commonplace whenever a civilization goes down. The smaller and more isolated the geographical area of the civilization that falls, the less likely mass migrations are—ancient China, Mesopotamia, and central Mexico had plenty of them, while the collapse of the classic Maya and Heian Japan featured a shortage of wandering hordes— but the rest of the story is among the standard features you get with societal collapse. North America is neither small nor isolated, and so it's a safe bet that we'll get a tolerably complete version of the usual process right here in the centuries ahead.

What does that mean in practice? It means, to begin with, that a rising spiral of conflict along ethnic, cultural, religious, political, regional, and social lines will play an ever-larger role in North American life for decades to come. Those of my readers who have been paying attention to events, especially but not only in the United States, will have already seen that spiral getting under way. As the first few rounds of economic contraction have begun to bite, the standard response of every group you care to name has been to try to get the bite taken out of someone else. Listen to the insults being flung around in the political controversies of the present day—the thieving rich, the shiftless poor, and the rest of it—and notice how many of them amount to claims that wealth that ought to belong to one group of people is being unfairly held by another. In those claims, you can hear the first whispers of the battle cries that will be shouted as the usual internecine wars begin to tear our civilization apart.

As those get under way, for reasons we'll discuss at length later on, governments and the other institutions of civil society will come apart at the seams, and the charismatic leaders already mentioned will rise to fill their place. In response, existing loyalties will begin to dissolve as the normal process of warband formation kicks into overdrive. In such times a strong and gifted leader like Attila the Hun can unite any number of contending factions into a single overwhelming force, but at this stage such things have no permanence; once the warlord dies, ages, or runs out of luck, the forces so briefly united will turn on each other and plunge the continent back into chaos.

There will also be mass migrations, and far more likely than not, these will be on a scale that would have impressed Attila himself. That's one of the ways that the climate change our civilization has unleashed on the planet is a gift that just keeps on giving; until the climate settles back down to some semblance of stability and sea levels have risen as far as they're going to rise, people in vulnerable areas are going to be forced out of their homes by one form of unnatural catastrophe or another, and the same desperate quest for survival that may have sent the Huns crashing into Eastern Europe will send new hordes of refugees streaming across the landscape. Some of those hordes will have starting points within the United States—I expect mass migrations from Florida as the seas rise, and from the Southwest as drought finishes tightening its fingers around the Sun Belt's throat—while others will come from further afield.

Five centuries from now, as a result, it's entirely possible that most people in the upper Mississippi valley will be of Brazilian ancestry, and that the inhabitants of the Hudson's Bay region sing songs about their long-lost homes in drowned Florida, while languages descended from English may be spoken only in a region extending from New England to the isles of deglaciated Greenland. Nor will these people necessarily think of themselves in any of the national and ethnic terms that come so readily to our minds today. It's by no means impossible that somebody may claim to be the President of the United States (though it may be pronounced Presden of Meriga by that time), or what have you, just as Charlemagne and his successors claimed to be the emperors of Rome. Just as the Holy Roman Empire was proverbially neither holy, nor Roman, nor an empire, neither the office nor the nation at that future time is likely to have much of anything to do with its nominal equivalent today—and there will certainly be nations and ethnic groups in that time that have no parallel today.

One implication of these points may be worth noting here, as we move deeper into the stage of ethnic conflict. No matter what your ethnic group, dear reader, no matter how privileged or under-privileged it may happen to be in today's world, it will almost certainly no longer exist as such when industrial civilization on this continent descends into the deindustrial dark age ahead. Such of your genes as make it through centuries of die-off and ruthless Darwinian selection will be mixed with genes from many other nationalities and corners of the world, and it's probably a safe bet that the people who carry those genes won't call themselves by whatever label you call yourself. When a civilization falls the way ours is falling, that's how things generally go.

4

THE POLITICAL
UNRAVELING

THE FATE OF THE POLITICAL INSTITUTIONS OF A FALLING CIV-
ilization is governed by an unexpected dynamic. Outside the elites,
which generally have a different and considerably more gruesome
destiny than the other inhabitants of a falling civilization, it's surprisingly rare for people to have to be forced to trade civilization
for barbarism, either by human action or by the pressure of events.
By and large, by the time that choice arrives, the great majority are
more than ready to make the exchange. What's more, they generally
have very good reasons to do so.

Let's start by reviewing some basics. The collapse of civilizations has a surprisingly simple basis: the mismatch between the
maintenance costs of capital and the resources that are available
to meet those costs. Capital here is meant in the broadest sense of
the word and includes everything in which a civilization invests its
wealth: buildings, roads, imperial expansion, urban infrastructure,
information resources, trained personnel, or what have you. Capital
of every kind has to be maintained, and as a civilization adds to its
stock of capital, the costs of maintenance rise steadily, until the resource base available to the civilization won't meet the maintenance
costs any more.

The only way to resolve the resulting crisis is to stop maintaining
some of the capital, so that its maintenance costs drop to zero and

any useful resources locked up in the capital can be put to other uses. Human beings being what they are, the conversion of capital to waste generally isn't carried out in a calm, rational manner. Instead, kingdoms fall, cities get sacked, ruling elites are torn to pieces by howling mobs, and the like. If a civilization depends on renewable resources, each round of capital destruction is followed by a return to relative stability, and the process begins all over again. The history of imperial China is a good example of how the resulting cycle works out in practice.

If a civilization depends on nonrenewable resources for essential functions, though, abandoning some of its capital yields only a brief reprieve from the crisis of maintenance costs. Once the nonrenewable resource base tips over into depletion, there's less and less available each year thereafter to meet the remaining maintenance costs, and the result is the stairstep pattern of decline and fall so familiar from history: each crisis leads to a round of capital destruction, which leads to renewed stability, which gives way to crisis as the resource base drops further. Here again, human beings being what they are, this process isn't carried out in a calm, rational manner. The difference here is simply that kingdoms keep falling, cities keep getting sacked, ruling elites are slaughtered one after another in ever more inventive and colorful ways, until finally contraction has proceeded far enough that the remaining capital can be supported on the available stock of renewable resources.

That's a thumbnail sketch of the theory of catabolic collapse. I'd encourage those who have questions about the details of the theory to read the original paper, which was published as an appendix to my book *The Long Descent*.[1] What I want to do here is to go a little more deeply into the social implications of the theory.

It's common these days to hear people insist that our society is divided into two and only two classes, an elite class that receives all the benefits of the system, and everyone else, who bears all the burdens. The reality, in ours and every other human society, is a great deal more nuanced. It's true, of course, that the benefits move up the ladder of wealth and privilege and the burdens get shoved toward the bottom, but in most cases—ours very much included— you have to go a good long way down the ladder before you find people who receive no benefits at all.

There have admittedly been a few human societies in which most people receive only such benefits from the system as will enable them to keep working until they drop. The early days of plantation slavery in the United States and the Caribbean islands, when the average lifespan of a slave from purchase to death was under ten years, fell into that category, and so do a few others—for example, Cambodia under the Khmer Rouge. These are exceptional cases; they emerge when the cost of unskilled labor drops close to zero and either abundant profits or ideological considerations make the fate of the laborers a matter of complete indifference to their masters.

Under any other set of conditions, such arrangements are un-economical. It's more profitable to the elites, by and large, to allow the laboring classes to get enough from the system that they can survive and raise families, and use those rewards to motivate them to do more than the bare minimum that will evade the overseer's lash. That's what generates the standard peasant economy, for ex-ample, in which the rural poor pay the landowners in labor and a share of agricultural production for access to arable land.

There are any number of arrangements of this kind, in which the laboring classes do the work, the ruling classes allow them ac-cess to productive capital, and the results are divided between the two classes in a proportion that allows the ruling classes to get rich and the laboring classes to get by. If that sounds familiar, it should. In terms of the distribution of labor, capital, and production, the latest offerings of today's job market are indistinguishable from the arrangements between an ancient Egyptian landowner and the peasants who planted and harvested his fields.

The more complex a society becomes, the more intricate the caste system that divides it, and the more diverse the changes that are played on this basic scheme. A relatively simple medieval society might get by with four castes—the feudal Japanese model, which divided society into warriors, farmers, craftspeople, and merchants, is as good an example as any.[2] A stable society near the end of a long age of expansion, by contrast, might have hundreds or even thousands of distinct castes, each with its own niche in the social and economic ecology of that society. In every case, each caste represents a particular balance between benefits received and burdens exacted, and given a stable economy entirely dependent on renewable resources, such a system can continue intact for a very long time.

Factor in the process of catabolic collapse, though, and an otherwise stable system turns into a fount of cascading instabilities. The point that needs to be grasped here is that social hierarchies are a form of capital, in the broad sense mentioned above. Like the other forms of capital included in the catabolic collapse model, social hierarchies facilitate the production and distribution of goods and services, and they have maintenance costs that have to be met. If the maintenance costs aren't met, as with any other form of capital, social hierarchies are converted to waste; they stop fulfilling their economic function, and they become available for salvage.

That sounds very straightforward. Here as so often, though, it's the human factor that transforms it from a simple equation to the raw material of history. As the maintenance costs of a civilization's capital begin to mount up toward the point of crisis, corners get cut and malign neglect becomes the order of the day. Among the various forms of capital, though, some benefit people at one point on the ladder of social hierarchy more than people at other levels. As the maintenance budget runs short, people normally try to shield the forms of capital that benefit them directly, and push the cutbacks off onto forms of capital that benefit others instead. Since the ability of any given person to influence where resources go corresponds very precisely to that person's position in the social hierarchy, this means that the forms of capital that benefit the people at the bottom of the ladder get cut first.

Now, of course, this isn't what you hear from Americans today, and it's not what you hear from people in any society approaching catabolic collapse. When contraction sets in, as already noted, people tend to pay much more attention to whatever they're losing than to the even greater losses suffered by others. The middle-class Americans who denounce welfare for the poor at the top of their lungs while demanding that funding for Medicare and Social Security remain intact are a classic example of the type; so, for that matter, are the other middle-class Americans who denounce the admittedly absurd excesses of the so-called one percent while carefully neglecting to note the immense differentials of wealth and privilege that separate them from those still further down the ladder.

This sort of thing is inevitable in a fight over slices of a shrinking pie.[3] Set aside the inevitable partisan rhetoric, though, and a society moving into the penumbra of catabolic collapse is a society in which more and more people are receiving less and less benefit from the existing order of society, while being expected to shoulder an ever-increasing share of the costs of a faltering system. To those who receive little or no benefits in return, the maintenance costs of social capital rapidly become an intolerable burden, and as the supply of benefits still available from a faltering system becomes more and more a perquisite of the upper reaches of the social hierarchy, that burden becomes an explosive political fact.

Every society depends for its survival on the passive acquiescence of the majority of the population and the active support of a large minority. That minority—call them the overseer class—are the people who operate the mechanisms of social hierarchy: the bureaucrats, media personnel, police, soldiers, and other functionaries who are responsible for maintaining social order. They are not drawn from the ruling elite; by and large, they come from the same classes they are expected to control, and if their share of the benefits of the existing order falters, if their share of the burdens increases too noticeably, or if they find other reasons to make common cause with those outside the overseer class against the ruling elite, then the ruling elite can expect to face the brutal choice between flight into exile and a messy death. The mismatch between maintenance costs and available resources, in turn, makes some such turn of events extremely difficult to avoid.

A ruling elite facing a crisis of this kind has at least three available options. The first, and by far the easiest, is to ignore the situation. In the short term, this is actually the most economical option, since it requires the least investment of scarce resources and doesn't require potentially dangerous tinkering with fragile social and political systems. The only drawback is that once the short term runs out, it pretty much guarantees a horrific fate for the members of the ruling elite, and in many cases, this is a less convincing argument than one might think. It's always easy to find an ideology that insists that things will turn out otherwise, and since members of a ruling elite are generally well insulated from the unpleasant realities of life in the society over which they preside, it's usually just as easy for them to convince themselves of the validity of whatever ideology they happen to choose. The behavior of the French aristocracy in the years leading up to the French Revolution is worth consulting in this context.

The second option is to try to remedy the situation by increased repression. This is the most expensive option, and it's generally even less effective than the first, but ruling elites with a taste for jackboots tend to fall into the repression trap fairly often. What makes repression a bad choice is that it does nothing to address the sources of the problems it attempts to suppress. Furthermore, it increases the maintenance costs of social hierarchy drastically—secret police, surveillance gear, prison camps, and the like don't come cheap—and it enforces the lowest common denominator of passive obedience while doing much to discourage active engagement of people outside the elite in the project of saving the society. A survey of the fate of the Communist dictatorships of Eastern Europe is a good antidote to the delusion that an elite with enough spies and soldiers can stay in power indefinitely.

That leaves the third option, which requires the ruling elite to sacrifice some of its privileges and perquisites so that those further down the social ladder still have good reason to support the existing order of society. That isn't common, but it does happen. It happened in the United States as recently as the 1930s, when Franklin Roosevelt spearheaded changes that spared the United States the sort of fascist takeover or civil war that occurred in so many other failed democracies in the same era. Roosevelt and his allies among the very rich realized that fairly modest reforms would be enough to convince most Americans that they had more to gain from supporting the system than they would gain by overthrowing it. A few job-creation projects and debt-relief measures, a few welfare programs, and a few perp walks by the most blatant of the con artists of the preceding era of high finance were enough to stop the unraveling of the social hierarchy, and restore a sense of collective unity strong enough to see the United States through a global war in the following decade.

Of course, Roosevelt and his allies had huge advantages that any comparable project would not be able to duplicate today. In 1933, though it was hamstrung by a collapsed financial system and a steep decline in international trade, the economy of the United States still had the world's largest and most productive industrial plant and some of the world's richest deposits of petroleum, coal, and many other natural resources. Fifty years later, in the Reagan era, the industrial plant was abandoned in an orgy of offshoring motivated by short-term profit-seeking, and today nearly every resource the American land once offered in abundance has been mined and pumped right down to the dregs. That means that any attempt to imitate Roosevelt's feat under current conditions will face much steeper obstacles, and it would also require the ruling elite to relinquish a much greater share of its current perquisites and privileges than they did in Roosevelt's day.

I could be mistaken, but I don't think it will even be tried this time around. Just at the moment, the squabbling coterie of competing power centers that constitutes the ruling elite of the United States seems committed to an approach halfway between the first two options I've outlined. The militarization of US domestic police forces and the rising spiral of civil rights violations carried out with equal enthusiasm by both mainstream political parties fall on the repressive side of the scale. At the same time, for all these gestures in the direction of repression, the overall attitude of American politicians and financiers seems to be that nothing really that bad can actually happen to them or to the system that provides them with their power and their wealth.

They're wrong, and at this point it's probably a safe bet that a great many of them will die because of that mistake. Already, a large fraction of Americans—probably a majority—accept the continuation of the existing order of society in the United States only because a viable alternative has yet to emerge. As the United States moves deeper into the penumbra of crisis, and the burden of propping up an increasingly dysfunctional status quo bears down ever more intolerably on ever more people outside the narrowing circle of wealth and privilege, the bar that any alternative has to leap will be set lower and lower. Sooner or later, something will make that leap and convince enough people that there's a workable alternative to the status quo, and the passive acquiescence on which the system depends for its survival will no longer be something that can be taken for granted.

It's not necessary for such an alternative to be more democratic or more humane than the order that it attempts to replace. It can be considerably less so, so long as it imposes fewer costs on the majority of people and distributes benefits more widely than the existing order does. That's why, in the last years of Rome, so many people of the collapsing empire readily accepted the rule of barbarian warlords in place of the imperial government. That government had become hopelessly dysfunctional by the time of the barbarian invasions, centralizing authority in distant bureaucratic centers out of touch with current realities, and imposing tax burdens on the poor so crushing that many people were forced to sell themselves into slavery or flee to depopulated regions of the countryside to take up the uncertain life of *Bacaudae*, half guerrilla and half bandit, hunted by imperial troops whenever those latter had time to spare from the defense of the frontiers.

By contrast, the local barbarian warlord might be brutal and capricious, but he was there on the scene, and thus unlikely to exhibit the serene detachment from reality so common in centralized bureaucratic states at the end of their lives. What's more, the warlord had good pragmatic reasons to protect the peasants who put bread and meat on his table, and the cost of supporting him and his retinue in the relatively modest style of barbarian kingship was considerably less expensive than the immense economic burden of helping to prop up the baroque complexities of the late Roman imperial bureaucracy. That's why the peasants and agricultural slaves of the late Roman world acquiesced so calmly in the implosion of Rome and its replacement by a patchwork of petty kingdoms. It wasn't just that it was merely a change of masters—it was that in a great many cases, the new masters were considerably less burdensome than the old ones had been.

We can expect much the same process to unfold in North America as the United States passes through its own trajectory of decline and fall. Before tracing the ways that process might work out, though, it's going to be necessary to sort through some common misconceptions, and that requires us to examine the ways that ruling elites destroy themselves.

ॐ

One of the persistent tropes in current speculations on the future of our civilization revolves around the notion that the current holders of wealth and influence will entrench themselves even more firmly in their positions as things fall apart. Thus it's worth discussing what tends to happen to elite classes in the decline and fall of a civilization, and seeing what that has to say about the fate of the industrial world's elite class as our civilization follows the familiar path.

It's probably necessary to say up-front that we're not talking about the evil space lizards that haunt David Icke's paranoid delusions,[4] or for that matter the faux-Nietzschean supermen who play a parallel role in Ayn Rand's dreary novels and pseudophilosophical rants. What we're talking about, rather, is something far simpler, which all of my readers will have experienced in their own lives. Every group of social primates has an inner core of members who have more access to the resources controlled by the group, and more influence over the decisions made by the group, than other members. How individuals enter that core and maintain themselves there against their rivals varies from one set of social primates to another—baboons settle such matters with threat displays backed up with violence, church ladies do the same thing with social maneuvering and gossip, and so on—but the effect is the same: a few enter the inner core, the rest are excluded from it. That process, many times amplified, gives rise to the ruling elite of a civilization.

I don't happen to know much about the changing patterns of leadership in baboon troops, but among human beings, there's a predictable shift over time in the way that individuals gain access to the elite. When institutions are new and relatively fragile, it's fairly easy for a gifted and ambitious outsider to bluff and bully his way into the elite. As any given institution becomes older and more firmly settled in its role, that possibility fades. What happens instead in a mature institution is that the existing members of the elite group select, from the pool of available candidates, those individuals who will be allowed to advance into the elite. The church ladies just mentioned are a good example of this process in action. If any of my readers are doctoral candidates in sociology looking for a dissertation topic, I encourage them to consider joining a local church and tracking the way the elderly women who run most of its social functions groom their own replacements and exclude those they consider unfit for that role.

That process is a miniature version of the way the ruling elite of the world's industrial nations select new additions to their number.

There, as among church ladies, there are basically two routes in. You can be born into the family of a member of the inner circle, and if you don't run off the rails too drastically, you can count on a place in the inner circle yourself in due time. Alternatively, you can work your way in from outside by being suitably deferential and supportive to the inner circle, meeting all of its expectations and conforming to its opinions and decisions, until the senior members of the elite start treating you as a junior member and the junior members have to deal with you as an equal. You can watch that at work, as already mentioned, in your local church—and you can also watch it at work in the innermost circles of power and privilege in American life.

Here in America, the top universities are the places where the latter version of the process stands out in all its dubious splendor. To these universities, every autumn, come the children of rich and influential families to begin the traditional four-year rite of passage. It would require something close to a superhuman effort on their part to fail. If they don't fancy attending lectures, they can hire impecunious classmates as "note takers" to do that for them. If they don't wish to write papers, the same principle applies, and those same impecunious classmates are more than ready to help out, since that can be the first step to a career as an executive assistant, speechwriter, or the like. The other requirements of college life can be met in the same manner as needed, and the university inevitably looks the other way, knowing that they can count on a generous donation from the parents as a reward for putting up with Junior's antics.

Those of my readers who've read the novels of Thomas Mann, and recall the satiric portrait of central European minor royalty in *Royal Highness*, already know their way around the sort of life I'm discussing here. Those who don't may want to recall everything they learned about the education and business career of George W. Bush. All the formal requirements are met, every gracious gesture is in place—the diploma, the prestigious positions in business or politics or the stateside military, maybe a book written by one of those impecunious classmates turned ghostwriter and published to bland and favorable reviews in the newspapers of record—it's all there, and the only detail that nobody sees fit to mention is that the whole thing could be done just as well by a well-trained cockatiel, and much of it is well within the capacities of a department store mannequin—provided, of course, that one of those impecunious classmates stands close by, pulling the strings that make the hand wave and the head nod.

The impecunious classmates, for their part, are aspirants to the second category mentioned above, those who work their way into the elite from outside. They also come to the same top universities every autumn, but they don't get there because of who their parents happen to be. They get there by devoting every spare second to that goal from elementary school on. They take the right classes, get the right grades, play the right sports, pursue the right extracurricular activities, and rehearse for their entrance interviews by the hour. They are bright, earnest, amusing, pleasant, because they know that that's what they need to be in order to get where they want to go. Scratch that glossy surface, and you'll find an anxious conformist terrified of failing to measure up to expectations, and it's a reasonable terror—most of them will in fact fail to do that, and never know how or why.

Once in an Ivy League university or the equivalent, they're pretty much guaranteed passing grades and a diploma unless they go out of their way to avoid them. Most of them, though, will be shunted off to midlevel posts in business, government, or one of the professions. Only the lucky few will catch the eye of someone with elite connections and be gently nudged out of their usual orbit into a place from which further advancement is possible. Whether the rich kid whose exam papers you ghostwrote takes a liking to you and arranges to have you hired as his executive assistant when he gets his first job out of school, or the father of a friend of a friend meets you on some social occasion, chats with you, and later on has the friend of a friend mention in passing that you might consider a job with this senator or that congressman, or what have you, it's not what you know, it's who you know, not to mention how precisely you conform to the social and intellectual expectations of the people you know who have the power to give or withhold the prize you crave so desperately.

That's how the elite of today's America recruits new members. *Mutatis mutandis*, it's how the governing elite of every stable, long-established society recruits new members. That procedure has significant advantages, and not just for the elites. Above all else, it provides stability. Over time, any elite self-selected in this fashion converges asymptotically on the standard model of a mature aristocracy, with an inner core of genial duffers surrounded by an outer circle of rigid conformists—the last people on the planet who are likely to disturb the settled calm of the social order. Like the lead-weighted keel of a deepwater sailboat, their inertia becomes a stabilizing force that only the harshest of tempests can overturn.

Inevitably, though, this advantage comes with certain disadvantages, two of which are of particular importance for our subject. The first is that stability and inertia are not necessarily a good thing in a time of crisis. In particular, if the society governed by an elite of the sort just described happens to depend for its survival on some unsustainable relationship with surrounding societies, the world of nature, or both, the leaden weight of a mature elite can make necessary change impossible until it's too late for any change at all to matter. One of the most consistent results of the sort of selection process I've sketched out is the elimination of any tendency toward original thinking on the part of those selected. Creativity may be lauded in theory, but what counts as creativity in such a system consists solely of taking some piece of accepted conventional wisdom one very carefully measured step further than anyone else has quite gotten around to going yet.

In a time of drastic change, that sort of limitation is lethal. More deadly still is the other disadvantage I have in mind, which is the curious and consistent habit such elites have of blind faith in their own invincibility. The longer a given elite has been in power, and the more august and formal and well-aged the institutions of its power and wealth become, the easier it seems to be for members of the elite to forget that their forefathers established themselves in that position by some form of more or less blatant piracy, and that they themselves could be deprived of it by that same means. Thus elites, shall we say, "misunderestimate" exactly those crises and sources of conflict that pose an existential threat to the survival of their class and its institutions, precisely because they can't imagine that an existential threat to these things could be posed by anything at all.

The irony, and it's a rich one, is that the same conviction tends to become just as widespread outside elite circles as within it. The illusion of invincibility, the conviction that the existing order of things is impervious to any but the most cosmetic changes, tends to be pervasive in any mature society and remains fixed in place right up to the moment that everything changes and the existing order of things is swept away forever. The intensity of the illusion very often has nothing to do with the real condition of the social order to which it applies. France in 1789 and Russia in 1917, to cite two of the obvious examples, were both brittle, crumbling, jerry-rigged hulks waiting for the push that would send them tumbling into oblivion, which they each received shortly thereafter, but next to no one saw the gaping vulnerabilities at the time. In both cases, even the urban rioters that applied the push were left standing there slack-jawed when they saw how readily the whole thing came crashing down.

The illusion of invincibility is far and away the most important asset a mature ruling elite has, because it discourages deliberate attempts at regime change from within. Everyone in the society, in the elite or outside it, assumes that the existing order is so firmly bolted into place that only the most apocalyptic events would be able to shake its grip. In such a context, most activists either beg for scraps from the tables of the rich or content themselves with futile gestures of hostility at a system they don't seriously expect to be able to harm, while the members of the elite go their genial way, stumbling from one preventable disaster to another, convinced of the inevitability of their positions, and blissfully unconcerned with the possibility—which normally becomes a reality sooner or later—that their own actions might be sawing away at the old and brittle branch on which they're seated.

If this doesn't sound familiar to you, dear reader, you definitely need to get out more. The behavior of the holders of wealth and power in contemporary America, as already suggested, is a textbook example of the way that a mature elite turns senile. Each round of freewheeling financial fraud, each preventable economic slump, increases the odds that an already brittle, crumbling, and jerry-rigged system will crack under the strain, opening a window of opportunity that hostile foreign powers and domestic demagogues alike will not be slow to exploit.

Do such considerations move the supposed defenders of the status quo to rein in the manufacture of worthless financial paper? Surely you jest. Secure in their sense of their own invulnerability, they amble down the familiar road that led so many of their equivalents in past societies to dispossession or annihilation.

৽৪৽

The senility that afflicts ruling elites in their last years is far from the only factor leading the rich and influential members of a failing civilization to their eventual destiny as lamppost decorations or some-close equivalent. Another factor, at least as important, is a lethal mismatch between the realities of power in an age of decline and the institutional frameworks inherited from a previous age of ascent.

That sounds very abstract, and appropriately so. Power in a mature civilization *is* very abstract, and the further you ascend the social ladder, the more abstract it becomes. Conspiracy theorists of a certain stripe have invested vast amounts of time and effort in quarrels over which specific group of people it is that runs everything in today's America. All of it was wasted, because the nature of power in a mature civilization precludes the emergence of any one center of power that dominates all others.

Look at the world through the eyes of an elite class and it's easy to see how this works. Members of an elite class compete against one another to increase their own wealth and influence and form alliances to pool resources and counter the depredations of their rivals. The result, in every human society complex enough to have an elite class in the first place, is an elite composed of squabbling factions that jealously resist any attempt at further centralization of power. In times of crisis, at least before senility sets in, that resistance can be overcome, but in less troubled times, any attempt by an individual or faction to seize control of the whole system faces the united opposition of the rest of the elite class.

One result of the constant defensive stance of elite factions against each other is that as a society matures, power tends to pass from individuals to institutions.[5] Bureaucratic systems take over more and more of the management of political, economic, and cultural affairs, and the policies that guide the bureaucrats in their work slowly harden until they are no more subject to change than the law of gravity. Among its other benefits to the existing order of society, this habit—we may as well call it policy mummification—limits the likelihood that an ambitious individual can parlay control over a single bureaucracy into a weapon against his rivals.

Our civilization is no exception to any of this. In the modern industrial world, some bureaucracies are overtly part of the political sphere. Others—we call them corporations—are supposedly apart from government, and still others like to call themselves "non-governmental organizations" as a form of protective camouflage. They are all part of the institutional structure of power, and thus function in practice as arms of government. They have more in common than this. Most of them have the same hierarchical structure and organizational culture, and those that are large enough to matter have executives who went to the same schools, share the same values, and crave the same handouts from higher up the ladder. No matter how revolutionary their rhetoric, for that matter, upsetting the system that provides them with their status and its substantial benefits is the last thing any of them want to do.

All these arrangements make for a great deal of stability, which the elite classes of mature civilizations generally crave. The downside is that it's not easy for a society that's proceeded more than a short distance along this path to change its ways to respond to new circumstances. Getting an entrenched bureaucracy to set aside its mummified policies in the face of changing conditions is generally so difficult that it's often easier to leave the old system in place while redirecting all its important functions to another, newly founded bureaucracy oriented toward the new policies. If conditions change again, the same procedure repeats, producing a layer cake of bureaucratic organizations that all supposedly exist to do the same thing.

Consider, as one example out of many, the shifting of responsibility for US foreign policy over the years. Officially, the State Department has charge of foreign affairs. In practice, direct power over foreign policy passed many decades ago to the staff of the National Security Council, and more recently has shifted again to coteries of advisers assigned to the office of the President. In each case, what drove the shift was the attachment of the older institution to a set of policies and procedures that stopped being relevant to the world of foreign policy—in the case of the State Department, the customary notions of old-fashioned diplomacy, and in the case of the National Security Council, the bipolar power politics of the Cold War era—but could not be dislodged from the bureaucracy in question due to the immense inertia of policy mummification in institutional frameworks.

The layered systems that result are not without their practical advantages to the existing order. Having many bureaucracies provides even more stability than a single bureaucracy, since it's often necessary for the people who actually have day-to-day responsibility for this or that government function to get formal approval from the top officials of the agency or agencies that used to have that responsibility. Even when those officials no longer have any formal way to block a policy they don't like, the personal and contextual nature of elite politics means that informal options usually exist. Furthermore, since the titular headship of some formerly important body such as the US State Department confers prestige but not power, it makes a good consolation prize to be handed out to also-rans in major political contests, a place to park well-connected incompetents, or what have you.

One problem with this layering process comes from points already made in this chapter: the maintenance bill for so baroque a form of capital is not small. In a mature civilization, a large fraction of available resources and economic production ends up being consumed by institutions that no longer have any real function beyond perpetuating their own existence and the salaries and prestige of their upper-level functionaries. It's not unusual for the maintenance costs of unproductive capital of this kind to become so great a burden on society that the burden in itself forces a crisis—that was one of the major forces that brought about the French Revolution, for instance. Still, I'd like to focus for a moment on a different issue, which is the effect that the institutionalization of power and the multiplication of bureaucracy has on the elites who allegedly run the system from which they so richly benefit.

France in the years leading up to the Revolution makes a superb example, one that John Kenneth Galbraith discussed with his trademark sardonic humor in his useful book *The Culture of Contentment*. The role of ruling elite in pre-1789 France was occupied by close equivalents of the people who fill that same position in America today: the "nobility of the sword," the old feudal aristocracy who had roughly the same role as the holders of inherited wealth in today's America, and the "nobility of the robe," who owed their position to education, political office, and a talent for social climbing, and thus had roughly the same role as successful Ivy League graduates do here and now. These two elite classes sparred constantly against each other, and just as constantly competed against their own peers for wealth, influence, and position.

One of the most notable features of both sides of the French elite in those days was just how little either group actually had to do with the management of public affairs, or for that matter the management of their own considerable wealth. The great aristocratic estates of the time were bureaucratic societies in miniature, ruled by hierarchies of feudal servitors and middle-class managers, while the hot new financial innovation of the time, the stock market, allowed those who wanted their wealth in a less tradition-infested form to neglect every part of business ownership but the profits. Those members of the upper classes who held offices in government, the Church, and the other venues of power thus presided decorously over institutions that were perfectly capable of functioning without them.

The elite classes of mature civilizations almost always seek to establish arrangements of this sort, and understandably so. It's easy to recognize the attractiveness of a state of affairs in which the holders of wealth and influence get all the advantages of their positions and have to put up with as few as possible of the inconveniences thereof. That said, this attraction is also a death wish, because it rarely takes the people who actually do the work long to figure out that a ruling class in this situation has become entirely parasitic and that society would continue to function perfectly well were something suitably terminal to happen to the titular holders of power.

This is why most of the revolutions in modern history have taken place in nations in which the ruling elite has followed its predilections and handed over all its duties to subordinates. In the case of the American Revolution, the English nobility had been directly involved in colonial affairs in the first century or so after Jamestown. Once it left the colonists to manage their own affairs, the latter needed very little time to realize that the only thing they had to lose by seeking independence was the steady hemorrhage of wealth from the colonies to England. In the case of the French and Russian Revolutions, much the same thing happened without the benefit of an ocean in the way: the middle classes who actually ran both societies recognized that the monarchy and aristocracy had become disposable, and promptly disposed of them once a crisis made it possible to do so.

The crisis just mentioned is a significant factor in the process. Under normal conditions, a society with a purely decorative ruling elite can keep on stumbling along indefinitely on sheer momentum. It usually takes a crisis—Britain's military response to colonial protests in 1775, the effective bankruptcy of the French government in 1789, the total military failure of the Russian government in 1917, or what have you—to convince the people who actually handle the levers of power that their best interests no longer lie with their erstwhile masters. Once the crisis hits, the unraveling of the institutional structures of authority can happen with blinding speed, and the former ruling elite is rarely in a position to do anything about it. All they have ever had to do, and all they know how to do, is issue orders to deferential subordinates. When there are none of these latter to be found, or (as more often happens) when the people to whom the deferential subordinates are supposed to pass the orders are no longer interested in listening, the elite has no options left.

The key point to be grasped here is that power is always contextual. A powerful person is a person able to exert particular kinds of power, using particular means, on some particular group of other people, and someone thus can be immensely powerful in one setting and completely powerless in another. What renders the elite classes of a mature society vulnerable to a total collapse of power is that they almost always lose track of this unwelcome fact. Hereditary elites are particularly prone to falling into the trap of thinking of their position in society as an accurate measure of their own personal qualifications to rule, but it's also quite common for those who are brought into the elite from the classes immediately below to think of their elevation as proof of their innate superiority. That kind of thinking is natural for elites, but once they embrace it, they're doomed.

It's dangerous enough for elites to lose track of the contextual and contingent nature of their power when the mechanisms through which power is enforced can be expected to remain in place—as it was in the American colonies in 1776, France in 1789, and Russia in 1917. It's far more dangerous if the mechanisms of power themselves are in flux. That can happen for any number of reasons, but the one that's of central importance to the theme of this book is the catabolic collapse of a declining civilization, in which the existing mechanisms of power come apart because their maintenance costs can no longer be met.

That poses at least two challenges to the ruling elite, one obvious and the other less so. The obvious one is that any deterioration in the mechanisms of power limits the ability of the elite to keep the remaining mechanisms of power funded, since a great deal of power is always expended in paying the maintenance costs of power. Thus in the declining years of Rome, for example, the crucial problem the empire faced was precisely that the sprawling system of imperial political and military administration cost more than the imperial revenues could support, but the weakening of that system made it even harder to collect the revenues on which the rest of the system depended, and forced more of what money there was to go for crisis management.[6] Year after year, as a result, roads, fortresses, and the rest of the infrastructure of Roman power sank under a burden of deferred maintenance and malign neglect, and the consequences of each collapse became more and more severe because there was less and less in the treasury to pay for rebuilding when the crisis was over.

That's the obvious issue. More subtle is the change in the nature of power that accompanies the decay in the mechanisms by which it's traditionally been used. Power in a mature civilization, as already noted, is very abstract, and the people who are responsible for administering it at the top of the social ladder rise to those positions precisely because of their ability to manage abstract power through the complex machinery that a mature civilization provides them. As the mechanisms collapse, though, power suddenly stops being abstract, and the skills that allow the manipulation of abstract power have almost nothing in common with the skills that allow concrete power to be wielded.

Late imperial Rome, again, is a fine example. There, as in other mature civilizations, the ruling elite had a firm grip on the intricate mechanisms of social control at their uppermost and least tangible end. The inner circle of each imperial administration—which sometimes included the emperor himself and sometimes treated him as a sock puppet—could rely on sprawling, many-layered civil and military bureaucracies to put their orders into effect. They were by and large subtle, ruthless, well-educated men, schooled in the intricacies of imperial administration, oriented toward the big picture, and completely dependent for their power, and indeed their survival, on the obedience of their underlings and the permanence of the Roman system itself.

The people who replaced them, as the empire came apart, shared none of these characteristics except the ruthlessness. The barbarian warlords who carved up the corpse of Roman power had a completely different set of skills and characteristics: raw physical courage, a high degree of competence in the warrior's trade, and the kind of charisma that attracts cooperation and obedience from those who have many other options. Their power was concrete, personal, and astonishingly independent of institutional forms. That's why Odoacer, whose remarkable career was mentioned earlier, could turn up alone in a border province, patch together an army out of a random mix of barbarian warriors, and promptly lead them to the conquest of Italy.

There were a very few members of the late Roman elite who could exercise power in the same way as Odoacer and his equivalents, and they're the exceptions that prove the rule. The greatest of them, Flavius Aetius, spent many years in youth as a hostage in the royal courts of the Visigoths and the Huns and got his practical education there, rather than in Roman schools. He was, for all practical purposes, a barbarian warlord who happened to be Roman by birth, and played the game as well as any of the other warlords of his age. His vulnerabilities were all on the Roman side of the frontier, where the institutions of Roman society still retained a fingernail grip on power, and so—having defeated the Visigoths, the Franks, the Burgundians, and the massed armies of Attila the Hun, all for the sake of Rome's survival—he was assassinated by the emperor he served.

Fast forward close to two thousand years and it's easy to see how the same pattern of elite extinction through the collapse of political complexity will likely work out here in North America. The ruling elites of our society, like those of the late Roman Empire, are superbly skilled at manipulating and parasitizing a fantastically elaborate bureaucratic machine that includes governments, business firms, universities, and many other institutions among its components. That's what they do; that's what they know how to do; and that's what all their training and experience has prepared them to do. Thus their position is exactly equivalent to that of French aristocrats before 1789, but they're facing the added difficulty that the vast mechanism on which their power depends has maintenance costs that their civilization can no longer meet. As the machine fails, so does their power.

Nor are they particularly well prepared to make the transition to a radically different way of exercising power. Imagine for a moment that one of the current US elite—an executive from a too-big-to-fail investment bank, a top bureaucrat from inside the DC beltway, a trust-fund multimillionaire with a pro forma job at the family corporation, or what have you—were to turn up in some chaotic failed state on the fringes of the industrial world, with no money, no resources, no help from abroad, and no ticket home. What's the likelihood that, without anything other than whatever courage, charisma, and bare-knuckle fighting skills he might happen to have, some such person could equal Odoacer's feat, win the loyalty and obedience of thousands of gang members and unemployed mercenaries, and lead them in a successful invasion of a neighboring country?

There are people in North America who could probably carry off a feat of that kind, but you won't find them in the current ruling elite. That in itself defines part of the path to dark age America: the replacement of a ruling class that specializes in managing abstract power through institutions with a ruling class that specializes in expressing power up close and in person, using the business end of the nearest available weapon. The process by which the new elite emerges and elbows its predecessors out of the way, in turn, is among the most reliable dimensions of decline and fall.

⸙

To make sense of that process, it's going to be necessary to take a step back and revisit some of the points made earlier, when I discussed the way that the complex social hierarchies common to mature civilizations break down into larger and less stable masses in which new loyalties and hatreds more easily build to explosive intensity. America is as good an example of that as any. A century ago, as already noted, racists in this country were at great pains to distinguish various classes of whiteness, with people of Anglo-Saxon ancestry at the pinnacle of whiteness and everybody else fitting into an intricate scheme of less-white categories below. Over the course of the twentieth century, those categories collapsed into a handful of abstract ethnicities—white, black, Hispanic, Asian—and can be counted on to collapse further as we proceed, until there are just two categories left, which are not determined by ethnicity but purely by access to the machinery of power.

Arnold Toynbee called those two the dominant minority and the internal proletariat.[7] The dominant minority is the governing elite of a civilization in its last phases, a group of people united not by ethnic, cultural, religious, or ideological ties, but purely by their success in either clawing their way up the social ladder to a position of power, or hanging on to a position inherited from their forebears. Toynbee draws a sharp division between a dominant minority and the governing elite of a civilization that hasn't yet begun to decline, which he calls a creative minority. The difference is that a creative minority hasn't yet gone through the descent into senility that afflicts elites, and it still recalls its dependence on the loyalty of those further down the social ladder. A dominant minority or, in my terms, a senile elite has lost track of that dependence, and has to demand and enforce obedience because it can no longer inspire respect.

Everyone else in a declining civilization belongs to the second category, the internal proletariat. Like the dominant minority, the internal proletariat has nothing to unite it but its relationship to political power: it consists of all those people who have none. In the face of that fact, other social divisions gradually evaporate. Social hierarchies are a form of capital, and like any form of capital, they have maintenance costs, which are paid out in the form of influence and wealth. The higher someone stands in the social hierarchy, the more access to influence and wealth they have; that's their payoff for cooperating with the system and enforcing its norms on those further down.

As resources run short and a civilization in decline has to start cutting its maintenance costs, though, the payoffs get cut. For obvious reasons, the higher someone is on the ladder to begin with, the more influence they have over whose payoffs get cut, and that reliably works out to "not mine." The further down you go, by contrast, the more likely people are to get the short end of the stick. That said, until the civilization actually comes apart, there's normally a floor to the process, somewhere around the minimum necessary to actually sustain life. An unlucky few get pushed below this, but normally it's easier to maintain social order when the very poor get just enough to survive. Thus social hierarchies disintegrate from the bottom up, as more and more people on the lower rungs of the latter are pushed down to the bottom, erasing the social distinctions that once differentiated them from the lowest rung.

That happens in society as a whole, and it also happens in each of the broad divisions of the caste system—in the United States, those would be the major ethnic divisions. The many shades of relative whiteness that used to divide white Americans into an intricate array of castes, for instance, have almost entirely gone by the board. You have to go pretty far up the ladder to find white Americans who differentiate themselves from other white Americans on the basis of whose descendants they are. Further down the ladder, Americans of Italian, Irish, and Polish descent—once strictly defined castes with their own churches, neighborhoods, and institutions—now as often as not think of themselves as white without further qualification.

The same process has gotten under way to one extent or another in the other major ethnic divisions of American society, and it's also started to dissolve even those divisions among the growing masses of the very poor. I have something of a front-row seat on that last process, as I live on the edge of the low-rent district in an old mill town in the north central Appalachians, and shopping and other errands take me through the neighborhood on foot quite often. I walk past couples pushing baby carriages, kids playing in backyards or vacant lots, neighbors hanging out together on porches, and more often as not these days, the people in these groups don't all have the same skin color. Head into the expensive part of town, and you won't see that; the dissolution of the caste system hasn't extended that far up the ladder—yet.

This is business as usual in a collapsing civilization. Sooner or later, no matter how intricate the caste system you start with, you end up with a society divided along the lines sketched out by Toynbee, with a dominant minority defined solely by its access to power and wealth, and an internal proletariat defined solely by its exclusion from these things. We're not there yet in today's North

America. There is still an assortment of intermediate castes between the two final divisions of society, but as Bob Dylan sang a long time ago, you don't have to be a weatherman to know which way the wind is blowing.

The political implications of this shift are worth watching. Ruling elites in mature civilizations don't actually exercise power themselves; rather, they issue general directives to their immediate subordinates, who hand them further down the pyramid. Along the way the general directives are turned into specific orders, which finally go to the ordinary working Joes and Janes who actually do the work of maintaining the status quo against potential rivals, rebels, and dissidents. A governing elite that hasn't yet gone senile knows that it has to keep the members of its overseer class happy, and it provides them with appropriate perks and privileges toward this end. As the caste system starts to disintegrate due to a shortage of resources to meet maintenance costs, though, the salaries and benefits at the bottom of the overseer class get cut, and more and more of the work of maintaining the system is assigned to poorly paid, poorly trained, and poorly motivated temp workers whose loyalties don't necessarily lie with their putative masters.

You might think that even an elite gone senile would have enough basic common sense left to notice that losing the loyalty of the people who keep the elite in power is a fatal error. In practice, though, the disconnection between the world of the dominant elite and the world of the internal proletariat quickly becomes total, and the former can be completely convinced that everything is fine when the latter know otherwise. So the gap that opens up between the dominant minority and the internal proletariat is much easier to see from below than from above. Left to itself, that gap would probably keep widening until the dominant minority toppled into it. It's an interesting regularity of history, though, that this process is almost never left to run its full length. Instead, another series of events generally overtakes it, with the same harsh consequences for the dominant minority.

To understand this, it's necessary to include another aspect of Toynbee's analysis and look at what's going on just outside the borders of a civilization in decline. Civilizations prosper by preying on their neighbors.[8] The mechanism may be invasion and outright pillage, demands for tribute backed up by the threat of armed force, unbalanced systems of exchange that concentrate wealth in an imperial center at the expense of the periphery, or what have you, but the process is the same in every case, and so are the results. One way or another, the heartland of every civilization ends up surrounded by an impoverished borderland, scaled according to the transport technologies of the era. In the case of the ancient Maya, the borderland extended only a modest distance in any direction; in the case of ancient Rome, it extended north to the Baltic Sea and east up to the borders of Parthia; in the case of modern industrial society, the borderland includes the entire Third World.

However large the borderland may be, its inhabitants fill a distinctive role in the decline and fall of a civilization. Toynbee calls them the external proletariat.[9] As a civilization matures, their labor provides a steadily increasing share of the wealth that keeps the civilization and its dominant elite afloat, but they receive essentially nothing in return, and they're keenly aware of this. Civilizations in their prime keep their external proletariats under control by finding and funding compliant despots to rule over the borderlands and, not incidentally, distract the rage of the external proletariat to some target more expendable than the civilization's dominant minority. Here again, though, maintenance costs are the critical issue. When a dominant minority can no longer afford the subsidies and regular military expeditions needed to keep their puppet despots on their thrones, and try to maintain peace along the borders on the cheap, they invariably catalyze the birth of the social form that brings them down.

Historians call it the warband: a group of young men whose sole trade is violence, gathered around a charismatic leader. Warbands spring up in the borderlands of a civilization as the dominant minority or its pet despots lose their grip, and they go through a brutally Darwinian process of evolution thereafter in constant struggle with each other and with every other present or potential rival in range. Once they start forming, there seems to be little that a declining civilization can do to derail that evolutionary process.[10]

Warbands are born of chaos; their activities add to the chaos; and every attempt to pacify the borderlands by force simply adds to the chaos that feeds them. In their early days, warbands cover their expenses by whatever form of violent activity will pay the bills, from armed robbery to smuggling to mercenary service. As they grow, raids across the border are the next step, and as the civilization falls apart and the age of migrations begins, warbands are the cutting edge of the process that shreds nations and scatters their people across the map.

The process of warband formation itself can quite readily bring a civilization down. Very often, though, the dominant minority of the declining civilization gives the process a good hard shove in the same direction. As the chasm between the dominant minority and the internal proletariat becomes wider, remember, the overseer class that used to take care of crowd control and the like for the dominant minority becomes less and less reliable, as their morale and effectiveness are hammered by ongoing budget cuts, and the social barriers that once divided them from the people they are supposed to control will have begun to dissolve if they haven't entirely given way yet. What's the obvious option for a dominant minority that is worried about its ability to control the internal proletariat, can no longer rely on its own overseer class, and also has a desperate need to find something to distract the warbands on its borders?

They hire the warbands, of course.

That's what inspired the Roman-British despot Vortigern to hire the Saxon warlord Hengist and three shiploads of his heavily armed friends to help keep the peace in Britannia after the legions departed.[11] That's what led the Fujiwara family, the uncrowned rulers of Japan, to hire uncouth samurai from the distant, half-barbarous

Kanto plain to maintain peace in the twilight years of the Heian period.[12] That's why scores of other ruling elites have made the obvious, logical, and lethal choice to hire their own replacements and hand over the actual administration of power to them.

That latter is the moment toward which all the political trends examined in this chapter converge. The disintegration of social hierarchies, the senility of ruling elites, and the fossilization of institutions all lead to the hour of the knife, the point at which those who think they still rule a civilization discover the hard way— sometimes the *very* hard way—that effective power has transferred to new and more muscular hands. Those of the elites who attempt to resist this transfer rarely survive the experience. Those who promptly accommodate themselves to the new state of affairs may be able to prosper for a time, but only so long as their ability to manipulate what's left of the old system makes them useful to its new overlords. As what was once a complex society governed by bureaucratic institutions dissolves into a much simpler society governed by the personal rule of warlords, that skill set does not necessarily wear well.

In some cases—Hengist is an example—the warlords allow the old institutions to fall to pieces all at once, and the transition from an urban civilization to a protofeudal rural society takes place in a few generations at most. In others—the samurai of the Minamoto clan, who came out on top in the furious struggles that surrounded the end of the Heian period, are an example here—the warlords try to maintain the existing order of society as best they can, and they get dragged down by the same catabolic trap that overwhelmed their predecessors. In an unusually complex case—for example, post-Roman Italy—one warlord after another can seize what's left of the institutional structure of a dead empire, try to run it for a while, and then get replaced by someone else with the same agenda, each change driving one more step down the long stair that turned the Forum into a sheep pasture.

One way or another, though, that process will eventually come to an end. Just as the survivors of the era of mass migration finally settle down in the places they've ended up, those warlords who survive the brutal Darwinian environment of dark age politics and warfare sooner or later become political as well as military figures, and some of the territories they control develop enough political and economic cohesion to endure as units after the death of the warlords who seized them. This is the way that new nations begin to form.

By the time the political unraveling of industrial North America ends, as a result of these processes, the parts of the continent capable of supporting agriculture will be divided into hundreds of statelets, some of which will owe a nominal allegiance to some wider polity, and some of which will be entirely independent. Outside the agricultural regions, where human habitation is possible at all, patterns much more tribal in nature will emerge, as they have done over and over again in the past. Thereafter, the long process of consolidation will begin, as the deindustrial dark age passes and successor societies begin to build on the ruins of the industrial age.

5

THE ECONOMIC COLLAPSE

THE POLITICAL TRANSFORMATIONS EXPLORED IN THE PREVI-
ous chapter can also be traced in detail in the economic sphere. A
strong case could be made, in fact, that the economic dimension is
the more important of the two and that the political struggles that
pit the elites of a failing civilization against the rising warbands of
the nascent dark age reflect deeper shifts in the economic sphere.
Whether or not that's the case—and in some sense, it's simply a
difference in emphasis—the economics of decline and fall need to
be understood in order to make sense of the trajectory ahead of us.

One of the more useful ways of understanding that trajectory
was traced out some years ago by Joseph Tainter in his book *The
Collapse of Complex Societies*. While I've taken issue with some of
the details of Tainter's analysis in various other writings, the general
model of collapse he offers is sound and deserves to be summarized
here.

Tainter begins with the law of diminishing returns: the rule,
applicable to an astonishingly broad range of human affairs, that
the more you invest—in any sense—in any one project, the smaller
the additional return is on each unit of additional investment. The
point at which this starts to take effect is called the point of diminishing returns. Off past that point is a far more threatening
landmark, the point of zero marginal return: the point, that is,
when additional investment costs as much as the benefit it yields.

Beyond that lies the territory of negative returns, where further investment yields less than it costs, and the gap grows wider with each additional increment.

The attempt to achieve infinite economic growth on a finite planet makes a fine example of the law of diminishing returns in action. Given the necessary preconditions—a point we'll discuss in more detail a bit later—economic growth in its early stages produces benefits well in excess of its costs. Once the point of diminishing returns is past, though, further growth brings less and less benefit in any but a purely abstract, financial sense. Broader measures of well-being fail to keep up with the expansion of the economy, and eventually the point of zero marginal return arrives and further rounds of growth actively make things worse.

Mainstream economists these days shove these increments of what John Ruskin used to call "illth"[1]—yes, that's the opposite of wealth—into the category of "externalities," where they are generally ignored by everyone who doesn't have to deal with them in person. If growth continues far enough, though, the production of illth overwhelms the production of wealth, and we end up more or less where we are today, where the benefits from continued growth are outweighed by the increasingly ghastly impact of the social, economic, and environmental "externalities" driven by growth itself. That's the nature of our predicament: the costs of growth rise faster than the benefits and eventually force the industrial economy to its knees.

The role of externalities in concealing the true cost of today's industrial society is almost impossible to exaggerate. It's been pointed out, for example, that none of the twenty biggest industries in today's world could break even, much less make a profit, if they had to pay for the damage they do to the environment.[2]

The conventional wisdom these days interprets that statement to mean that it's unfair to make those industries pay for the costs they impose on the rest of us—after all, they have a God-given right to profit at everyone else's expense, right? That's certainly the attitude of fracking firms in North Dakota, who have proposed that they ought to be exempted from the state's rules on dumping radioactive waste, because following the rules would cost them too much money.[3] That the costs externalized by the fracking industry will sooner or later be paid by others, as radionuclides in fracking waste work their way up the food chain and start producing cancer clusters, is, of course, not something anyone in the industry or the media is interested in discussing.

Watch this sort of thing, and you can see the chasm opening up under the foundations of industrial society. Externalized costs don't just go away; one way or another, they're going to be paid, and costs that don't appear on a company's balance sheet still affect the economy. That's the argument of *The Limits to Growth*, still the most accurate of the studies from the 1970s that tried unavailingly to turn industrial society away from its suicidal path.[4]

On a finite planet, once an inflection point is passed, the costs of economic growth rise faster than growth does, and sooner or later force the global economy to its knees. The tricks of accounting that let corporations pretend that their externalized costs vanish into thin air don't change that bleak prognosis. Quite the contrary, the pretense that externalities don't matter just makes it harder for a society in crisis to recognize the actual source of its troubles. I've come to think that that's the unmentioned context behind a dispute currently roiling those unhallowed regions where economists lurk in the shrubbery: the debate over secular stagnation.[5]

Secular stagnation? That's the concept, unmentionable until recently, that the global economy could stumble into a rut of slow, no, or negative growth and stay there for years. There are still plenty of economists who insist that this can't happen, which is rather funny, really, when you consider that this has basically been the state of the global economy since 2009. (My back-of-the-envelope calculations suggest, in fact, that if you subtract the hallucinatory paper wealth manufactured by derivatives and similar forms of financial gamesmanship from the world's GDP, the production of nonfinancial goods and services worldwide has actually been declining since before the 2008 housing crash.)

Even among those who admit that what's happening can indeed happen, there's no consensus as to how or why such a thing could occur. On the off chance that any mainstream economists are listening, I have a hypothesis to propose: the most important cause of secular stagnation is the increasing impact of externalities on the economy. The dishonest macroeconomic bookkeeping that leads economists to think that externalized costs go away because they're not entered into anyone's ledger books doesn't actually make them disappear. Instead, they become an unrecognized burden on the economy as a whole, an unfelt headwind blowing with hurricane force in the face of economic growth.

Thus there's a profound irony in the insistence by North Dakota fracking firms that they ought to be allowed to externalize even more of their costs in order to maintain their profit margin. If I'm right, the buildup of externalized costs is what's causing the ongoing slowdown in economic activity worldwide that's driving down commodity prices, forcing interest rates in many countries to zero or below, and resurrecting the specter of deflationary depression. The fracking firms in question thus want to respond to the collapse in oil prices—a result of secular stagnation—by doing even more of what's causing secular stagnation. To say that this isn't likely to end well is to understate the case considerably.

๛

This awareness of diminishing returns and unmentioned externalities formed the launching point for Joseph Tainter's exploration of the nature of collapse. His core insight was that the same rules can be applied to social complexity. When a society begins to add layers of social complexity—for example, expanding the reach of the division of labor, setting up hierarchies to centralize decision-making, and so on—the initial rounds pay off substantially in terms of additional wealth and the capacity to deal with challenges from other societies and the natural world. Here again, though, there's a point of diminishing returns, after which additional investments in social complexity yield less and less in the way of benefits, and there's a point of zero marginal return, after which each additional increment of complexity subtracts from the wealth and resilience of the society.

There's a mordant irony to what happens next. Societies in crisis reliably respond by doing what they know how to do. In the case of complex societies, what they know how to amounts to adding on new layers of complexity; after all, that's what's worked in the past. I mentioned in the previous chapter the way this plays out in political terms. The same thing happens in every other sphere of collective life—economic, cultural, intellectual, and so on down the list. If too much complexity is at the root of the problems besetting a society, though, what happens when its leaders keep adding even more complexity to solve those problems, and then treat the additional problems as externalities that aren't supposed to be taken into account?

Any of my readers who have trouble coming up with the answer might find it useful to take a look out the nearest window. Whether or not Tainter's theory provides a useful description of every complex society in trouble—for what it's worth, it's a significant part of the puzzle in every historical example known to me—it certainly applies to contemporary industrial society. Here in America, certainly, we've long since passed the point at which additional investments in complexity yield any benefit at all, but the manufacture of further complexity goes on apace, unhindered by the mere fact that it's making a galaxy of bad problems worse. Do I need to cite the US health care system, which is currently collapsing under the sheer weight of the baroque superstructure of corporate and government bureaucracies heaped on top of what was once the simple process of paying a visit to the doctor?

We can describe this process as intermediation: the insertion of an assortment of persons, professions, and institutions between the producer and the consumer of any given good or service. It's a standard feature of social complexity, and it tends to blossom in the latter years of every civilization, as part of the piling up of complexity on complexity that Tainter discussed. There's an interesting parallel between intermediation and ecological succession—the process by which barren ground is colonized by one wave after another of organisms, each of which forms a more complex and more stable ecosystem than the one before it.[6] Just as an ecosystem, as it moves from one stage in succession to the next, tends to produce ever more elaborate food webs linking the plants whose photosynthesis starts the process with the consumers of detritus at its end, the rise of social complexity in a civilization tends to produce ever more elaborate patterns of intermediation between producers and consumers.

Contemporary industrial civilization has taken intermediation to an extreme not reached by any previous civilization, and there's a reason for that. White's law, one of the fundamental rules of human ecology, states that economic development is a function of energy per capita. The jackpot of cheap, concentrated energy that industrial civilization obtained from fossil fuels threw that equation into overdrive, and economic development is simply another name for complexity. The US health care system, again, is one example out of many; as the American economy expanded metastatically over the course of the twentieth century, an immense army of medical administrators, laboratory staff, specialists, insurance agents, government officials, and other functionaries inserted themselves into the notional space between physician and patient, turning what was once an ordinary face-to-face business transaction into a bureaucratic nightmare reminiscent of Franz Kafka's *The Castle*.

In one way or another, that's been the fate of every kind of economic activity in modern industrial society. Pick an economic sector, any economic sector, and the producers and consumers of the goods and services involved in any given transaction are hugely outnumbered by the people who earn a living from that transaction in some other way—by administering, financing, scheduling, regulating, taxing, approving, overseeing, facilitating, supplying, or in some other manner getting in there and grabbing a piece of the action. Take the natural tendency for social complexity to increase over time and put it to work in a society that's surfing a gargantuan tsunami of cheap energy, in which most work is done by machines powered by fossil fuels and not by human hands and minds, and that's pretty much what you can expect to get.

That's also a textbook example of the sort of excess complexity Joseph Tainter discussed in *The Collapse of Complex Societies,* but industrial civilization's dependence on nonrenewable energy resources puts the entire situation in a different and even more troubling light. On the one hand, continuing increases in complexity in a society already burdened to the breaking point with too much complexity pretty much guarantee a rapid decrease in complexity not too far down the road—and no, that's not likely to unfold in a nice neat orderly way, either. On the other, the ongoing depletion of energy resources and the decline in net energy that unfolds from that inescapable natural process means that energy per capita will be decreasing in the years ahead. That, according to White's law, means that the ability of industrial society to sustain current levels of complexity, or anything like them, will be going away in the tolerably near future.

In order to sort out the implications of this fact, it's worth starting from the big picture. In any human society, whether it's a tribe of hunter-gatherers, an industrial nation-state, or anything else, people apply energy to raw materials to produce goods and services. This is what we mean by the word "economy." The goods and services that any economy can produce are strictly limited by the energy sources and raw materials that it can access.

A principle that ecologists call Liebig's law of the minimum is relevant here: the amount of anything that a given species or ecosystem can produce in a given place and time is limited by whichever resource is in shortest supply. Most people get that when thinking about the nonhuman world, since it's obvious that plants can't use extra sunlight to make up for a shortage of water and that soil deficient in phosphates can't be treated by adding extra nitrates. It's when you apply this same logic to human societies that the mental gears jam up, because we've been told so often that one resource can always be substituted for another that most people believe it without a second thought.

What's going on here, though, is considerably more subtle than current jargon reflects. Examine the cases of resource substitution that find their way into economics textbooks, and you'll find that what's happened is that a process of resource extraction that uses less energy on a scarcer material has been replaced by another process that takes more energy but uses more abundant materials. The shift from high-quality iron ores to low-grade taconite that reshaped the iron industry in the twentieth century, for example, was possible because ever-increasing amounts of highly concentrated energy could be put into the smelting process without making the resulting iron too expensive for the market.

The point made by this and comparable examples is applicable across the board to industrial societies. Far more often than not, in such societies, *concentrated energy is the limiting resource*. Given an abundant enough supply of concentrated energy at a low enough price, it would be possible to supply a technic society with raw materials by extracting dissolved minerals from seawater or chewing up ordinary rock to get a part per million or so of this or that useful element. Lacking that kind of absurdly vast energy supply, access to concentrated energy is where Liebig's law bites down hard.

Another way to make this same point is to think of how much of any given product a single worker can make in a day using a set of good hand tools, and comparing that to the quantity of the same thing that the same worker could make using the successive generations of factory equipment, from the steam-driven and belt-fed power tools of the late nineteenth century straight through to the computerized milling machines and assembly-line robots of today. The difference can be expressed most clearly as a matter of the amount of energy being applied directly and indirectly to the manufacturing process—not merely the energy driving the tools through the manufacturing process, but the energy that goes into manufacturing and maintaining the tools, supporting the infrastructure needed for manufacture and maintenance, and so on through the whole system involved in the manufacturing process.

Maverick economist E. F. Schumacher pointed out that the cost per worker of equipping a workplace is one of the many crucial factors that mainstream economic thought invariably neglects.[7] That cost is usually expressed in financial terms, but underlying the abstract tokens we call money is a real cost in energy, expressed in terms of the goods and services that have to be consumed in the process of equipping and maintaining the workplace. If you have energy to spare, that's not a problem; if you don't, on the other hand, you're actually better off using a less complex technology: what Schumacher called "intermediate technology" and the movement in which I studied green wizardry thirty years ago called "appropriate technology."

The cost per worker of equipping a workplace, in turn, also has a political dimension—a point that Schumacher did not neglect, though nearly all other economists pretend that it doesn't exist. The more costly it is to equip a workplace, the more certain it is that workers won't be able to set themselves up in business and the more control the very rich will then have over economic production and the supply of jobs. As Tainter pointed out, social complexity correlates precisely with social hierarchy; one of the functions of complexity, in the workplace as elsewhere, is thus to maintain existing social pecking orders.

Schumacher's arguments, though, focused on the Third World nations of his own time, which had very little manufacturing capacity at all. Most of them had been colonies of European empires, assigned the role of producing raw materials and buying finished products from the imperial center as part of the wealth pump that drove them into grinding poverty while keeping their imperial overlords rich. He focused on advising client nations on how to build their own economies and extract themselves from the political grip of their former overlords, who were usually all too eager to import high-tech factories, which their upper classes inevitably controlled. The situation is considerably more challenging when your economy is geared to immense surpluses of concentrated energy and the supply of energy begins to run short. That's the situation we're in today.

Even if it were just a matter of replacing factory equipment, that would be a huge challenge, because all those expensive machines—not to mention the infrastructure that manufactures them, maintains them, supplies them, and integrates their products into the wider economy—count as sunk costs, subject to what social psychologists call the "Concorde fallacy," the conviction that it's less wasteful to keep on throwing money into a failing project than to cut your losses and do something else.[8] The real problem is that it's not just factory equipment; the entire economy has been structured from the ground up to use colossal amounts of highly concentrated energy, and everything that's been invested in that economy since the beginning of the modern era thus counts as a sunk cost to one degree or another.

Add these trends together, and you have a recipe for the radical simplification of the economy, a politer way of saying "decline and fall." The state of affairs in which most people in the workforce have only an indirect connection to the production of concrete goods and services to meet human needs is, in James Howard Kunstler's useful phrase, an arrangement without a future.[9] The unraveling of that arrangement, and the return to a state of affairs in which most people produce goods and services with their own labor for their own, their families', and their neighbors' use, will be the great economic trend of the next several centuries.

That's not to say that this unraveling will be a simple process. All those millions of people whose jobs depend on intermediation, and thus on the maintenance of current levels of economic complexity, have an understandable interest in staying employed. That interest in practice works out to an increasingly frantic quest to keep people from sidestepping the baroque corporate and bureaucratic economic machine and getting goods and services directly from producers.

That's a great deal of what drives the ongoing crusade against alternative health care—every dollar spent on herbs from a medical herbalist or treatments from an acupuncturist is a dollar that doesn't go into feeding the gargantuan corporations and bureaucracies that are supposed to provide health care for Americans, and sometimes even do so. The same thing is driving corporate and government attacks on local food production, since every dollar a consumer spends buying zucchini from a backyard farmer doesn't prop up the equally huge and tottering mass of institutions that attempt to control the production and sale of food in America.

It's not uncommon for those who object to these maneuvers to portray them as the acts of a triumphant corporate despotism on the brink of seizing total power over the planet. I'd like to suggest that they're something quite different. While the American and global economies are both still growing in a notional sense, the measures of growth that yield that result factor in such things as the manufacture of derivatives and a great many other forms of fictive wealth.

Subtract those from the national and global balance sheet, and the result is an economy in contraction. The intractable rise in the permanently jobless, the epidemic of malign neglect affecting even the most crucial elements of America's infrastructure, and the ongoing decline in income and living standards among all those classes that lack access to fictive wealth, among many other things, all tell the same story. Thus it's far from surprising that all the people whose jobs depend on intermediation, all the way up the corporate food chain to the corner offices, are increasingly worried about the number of people who are trying to engage in disintermediation—to buy food, health care, and other goods and services directly from the producers.

Their worries are entirely rational. One of the results of the contraction of the real economy is that the costs of intermediation, financial and otherwise, have not merely gone through the roof but zoomed off into the stratosphere, with low Earth orbit the next logical stop. Health care, again, is among the most obvious examples. In most parts of the United States, for instance, a visit to the acupuncturist for some ordinary health condition will typically set you back rather less than $100, while if you go to an MD for the same condition, you'll be lucky to get away for under $1,000, counting lab work and other costs—and you can typically count on thirty or forty minutes of personal attention from the acupuncturist, as compared to five or ten minutes with a harried and distracted MD. It's therefore no surprise that more and more Americans are turning their backs on the officially sanctioned health care industry and seeking out alternative health care instead.

They'd probably be just as happy to go to an ordinary MD who offered medical care on the same terms as the acupuncturist, which happen to be the same terms that were standard a century ago for every kind of health care. As matters stand, though, physicians are dependent on the system as it presently exists; their standing with their peers, and even their legal right to practice medicine, depends on their willingness to play by the rules of intermediation—and of course, it's also true that acupuncturists don't generally make the six-figure salaries that so many physicians do in America. A hundred years ago, the average American doctor didn't make that much more than the average American plumber. Many of the changes in the US health care system since that time were quite openly intended to change that fact.

A hundred years ago, as the United States moved through the early stages of its age of imperial excess, that was something the nation could afford. Equally, all the other modes of profiteering, intermediation, and other maneuvers aimed at maximizing the take of assorted economic sectors were viable then, since a growing economy provides plenty of slack for such projects. As the economics of growth gave way to the economics of stagnation in the last quarter of the twentieth century, such things became considerably more burdensome. As stagnation gives way to contraction, and the negative returns on excess complexity combine with the impact of depleting nonrenewable resources, the burden is rapidly becoming more than the US economy or the wider society can bear.

The result, in one way or another, will be disintermediation: the dissolution of the complex relations and institutions that currently come between the producer and the consumer of goods and services, and their replacement by something much less costly to maintain. "In one way or another," though, covers a great deal of ground, and it's far from easy to predict exactly how the current system will come unglued in the United States or, for that matter, anywhere else.

Disintermediation might happen quickly, if a major crisis shatters some central element of the US economic system—for example, the financial sector—and forces the entire economy to regroup around less abstract and more local systems of exchange. It might happen slowly, as more and more of the population can no longer afford to participate in the intermediated economy at all, and have to craft their own localized economies from the bottom up, while the narrowing circle of the well-to-do continue to make use of some equivalent of the current system for a long time to come. It might happen at different rates in different geographical areas—for example, cities and their suburbs might keep the intermediated economy going long after rural areas have abandoned it, or what have you.

Plenty of people these days like to look forward to some such transformation, and not without reason. Complexity has long since passed the point of negative returns in the US economy, as in most other aspects of American society, and the coming of disintermediation across a wide range of economic activities will arguably lead to significant improvements in many aspects of our collective life. That said, it's not all roses and affordable health care. The extravagant rates of energy per capita that made today's absurdly complex economy possible also made it possible for millions of Americans to make their living working in offices and other relatively comfortable settings, rather than standing hip-deep in hog manure with a shovel in their hands, and it also allowed them to earn what currently passes for a normal income, rather than the bare subsistence that's actually normal in societies that haven't had their economies inflated to the bursting point by a temporary glut of cheap energy.

It was popular a number of years back for the urban and suburban middle classes, most of whom work in jobs that exist only due to intermediation, to go in for "voluntary simplicity"—at best a pallid half-equivalent of Thoreau's far more challenging concept of voluntary poverty, at worst a marketing gimmick for the consumption of round after round of overpriced "simple" products.[10] For all its more embarrassing features, the voluntary simplicity movement was at least occasionally motivated by an honest recognition of the immediate personal implications of Tainter's fundamental point—that complexity taken past the point of diminishing returns becomes a burden rather than a benefit.

In the years ahead of us, a great many of these same people are going to experience what might best be called involuntary simplicity: the disintermediation of most aspects of economic life, the departure of lifestyles that can be supported only by the cheap abundant energy of the recent past, and a transition to the much less complex—and often, much less comfortable—lifestyles that are possible in a deindustrial world. There may be a certain entertainment value in watching those who praised voluntary simplicity to the skies deal with the realities of simple living when it's no longer voluntary, and there's no way back to the comforts of a bygone era.

That said, the impact of involuntary simplicity on the economic sphere won't be limited to the lifestyles of the formerly privileged. It promises to bring an end to certain features of economic life that contemporary thought assumes are fixed in place forever: among them, the market economy itself. Unthinkable as the concept may be, the end of the market economy will be a central feature of the coming of America's deindustrial dark ages.

⚏

One of the factors that makes it difficult to think through the economic consequences of the end of the industrial age is that we've all grown up in a world where every form of economic activity has been channeled through certain familiar forms for so long that very few people remember that things could be any other way. Another of the factors that make the same effort of thinking difficult is that the conventional economic thought of our time has invested immense effort and oceans of verbiage into obscuring the fact that things could be any other way.

Those are formidable obstacles. We're going to have to confront them, though, because one of the core features of the decline and fall of civilizations is that most of the habits of everyday life that are standard practice when civilizations are at zenith get chucked into the recycle bin as decline picks up speed. That's true across the whole spectrum of cultural phenomena, and it's especially true of economics, since the economic institutions and habits of a civilization in full flower are too complex for the same civilization to support once it's gone to seed.

The institutions and habits that contemporary industrial civilization uses to structure its economic life make up that tangled realm of supposedly voluntary exchanges we call "the market." Back when the United States was still contending with the Soviet Union, that almost always got rephrased as "the free market"; the adjective still gets some use among ideologues, but by and large it's dropped out of use elsewhere. This is a good thing, at least from the perspective of honest speaking, because the "free" market is, of course, nothing of the kind. It's unfree in at least two crucial senses: first, in that it's compulsory; second, in that it's expensive.

"The law in its majestic equality," Anatole France once noted drolly, "forbids rich and poor alike to sleep under bridges, beg in the streets, or steal bread."[11] In much the same sense, no one is actually forced to participate in the market economy in the modern industrial world. Those who want to abstain are perfectly free to go looking for some other way to keep themselves fed, clothed, housed, and supplied with the other necessities of life, and the fact that every option outside of the market has been hedged around with impenetrable legal prohibitions if it hasn't simply been annihilated by legal fiat or brute force is just one of those minor details that make life so interesting.

Historically speaking, there are a vast number of ways to handle exchanges of goods and services between people. In modern industrial societies, on the other hand, outside of the occasional vestige of an older tradition here and there, there's only one. Exchanging some form of labor for money, on whatever terms an employer chooses to offer, and then exchanging money for goods and services, on whatever terms the seller chooses to offer, is the only game in town. There's nothing free about either exchange, other than the aforesaid freedom to starve in the gutter. The further up you go in the social hierarchy, to be sure, the less burdensome the conditions on the exchanges generally turn out to be—here as elsewhere, privilege has its advantages—but unless you happen to have inherited wealth or can find some other way to parasitize the market economy without having to sell your own labor, you're going to participate if you like to eat.

Your participation in the market, furthermore, doesn't come cheap. Every exchange you make, whether it's selling your labor or buying goods and services with the proceeds, takes place within a system that has been subjected to the process of intermediation. Thus, in most cases, you can't simply sell your labor directly to individuals who want to buy it or its products. Instead, you are expected to sell your labor to an employer, who then sells it or its product to others, gives you part of the proceeds, and pockets the rest. Plenty of other people are lined up for their share of the value of your labor: bankers, landlords, government officials, and the list goes on. When you go to exchange money for goods and services, the same principle applies; how much of the value of your labor you get to keep for your own purposes varies from case to case, but it's always less than the whole sum, and sometimes a great deal less.

Karl Marx performed a valuable service to political economy by pointing out these facts and giving them the stress they deserve, in the teeth of savage opposition from the cheerleaders of the status quo who, then as now, dominated economic thought.[12] His proposed solution to the pervasive problems of the (un)free market was another matter. Like most of his generation of European intellectuals, Marx was dazzled by the swamp-gas luminescence of Hegelian philosophy, and he followed Hegel's verbose and vaporous trail into a morass of circular reasoning and false prophecy from which few of his remaining followers have yet managed to extract themselves.

It's from Hegel that Marx got the enticing but mistaken notion that history consists of a sequence of stages that move in a predetermined direction toward some as-perfect-as-possible state: the same idea, please note, that Francis Fukuyama used to justify his risible vision of the first Bush administration as the glorious fulfillment of human history.[13] (To borrow a bit of old-fashioned European political jargon, there are right-Hegelians and left-Hegelians; Fukuyama was an example of the former, Marx of the latter.) I'll leave such claims and the theories founded on them to the true believers, alongside such equally plausible claims as the Singularity, the Rapture, and the visionary fantasies of Charles Fourier, who believed that the oceans would turn into lemonade once enough people adopted his sociopolitical theories. What history itself shows is something rather different.

What history shows, as already noted, is that the complex systems that emerge during the heyday of a civilization are inevitably scrapped on the way back down. Market economies are among those complex systems. Not all civilizations have market economies—some develop other ways to handle the complicated process of allocating goods and services in a society with many different social classes and occupational specialties—but those that do set up market economies inevitably load them with as many intermediaries as the overall complexity of their economies can support.

It's when decline sets in and maintaining the existing level of complexity becomes a problem that the trouble begins. Under some conditions, intermediation can benefit the productive economy, but in a complex economy, more and more of the intermediation over time amounts to finding ways to game the system, profiting off economic activity without actually providing any benefit to anyone else. A complex society at or after its zenith thus typically ends up with a huge burden of unproductive intermediaries supported by an increasingly fragile foundation of productive activity.

All the intermediaries, no matter how wholly parasitic their function, expect to be maintained in the style to which they're accustomed, and since they typically have more wealth and influence than the producers and consumers who support them, they can usually stop moves to block their access to the feed trough. Economic contraction, however, makes it hard to support business as usual on the shrinking supply of real wealth. The intermediaries thus end up competing with the actual producers and consumers of goods and services, and since the intermediaries typically have the support of governments and institutional forms, more often than not it's the intermediaries who win that competition.

It's not at all hard to see that process at work; all it takes is a stroll down the main street of the old red brick mill town where I live. Here, as in thousands of other towns and cities in today's America, there are empty storefronts all through downtown, and empty buildings well suited to any other kind of economic activity you care to name there and elsewhere in town. There are plenty of people who want to work; wage and benefit expectations are modest; and there are plenty of goods and services that people would buy if they had the chance. Yet the storefronts stay empty, the workers stay unemployed, the goods and services remain unavailable. Why?

The reason is intermediation. Start a business in this town, or anywhere else in America, and the intermediaries all come running to line up in front of you with their hands out. Local, state, and federal bureaucrats all want their cut. So do the bankers, the landlords, the construction firms, and so on down the long list of businesses that feed on other businesses, and can't be dispensed with because this or that law or regulation requires them to be paid their share. The resulting burden is far too large for most businesses to meet. Thus businesses don't get started, and those that do start up generally go under in short order. It's the same problem faced by every parasite that becomes too successful: it kills the host on which its own survival depends.

That's the usual outcome when a heavily intermediated market economy slams face-first into the hard realities of decline. Theoretically, it would be possible to respond to the resulting crisis by forcing disintermediation, and thus salvaging the market economy. Practically, that's usually not an option, because the disintermediation requires dragging a great many influential economic and political sectors away from their accustomed feed trough. Far more often than not, declining societies with heavily intermediated market economies respond to the crisis just described by trying to force the buyers and sellers of goods and services to participate in the market even at the cost of their own economic survival, so that some semblance of business as usual can proceed.

That's why the late Roman Empire, for example, passed laws requiring that each male Roman citizen take up the same profession as his father, whether he could survive that way or not.[14] That's also why, as already noted, so many American jurisdictions are cracking down on people who try to buy and sell food, medical care, and the like outside the corporate economy. In the Roman case, the attempt to keep the market economy fully intermediated ended up killing the market economy altogether, and in most of the post-Roman world—interestingly, this was as true across much of the Byzantine empire as it was in the barbarian West—the complex money-mediated market economy of the old Roman world went away, and centuries passed before anything of the kind reappeared.[15]

What replaced it is what always replaces the complex economic systems of fallen civilizations: a system that systematically chucks the intermediaries out of economic activity and replaces them with personal commitments set up to block any attempt to game the system; that is to say, feudalism.

Enough confusion hovers around that last word these days that a concrete example is probably needed here. I'll borrow a minor character from a favorite book of my childhood, therefore, and introduce you to Higg, son of Snell. His name could just as well be Michio, Chung-Wan, Devadatta, Hafiz, Diocles, Bel-Nasir-Apal, Mentu-hetep, or any of a score or more of other names, because the feudalisms that evolve in the wake of societal collapse are re-markably similar around the world and throughout time, but we'll stick with Higg for now. On the off chance that the name hasn't clued you in, Higg is a peasant—a free peasant, he'll tell you with some pride, and *not* a mere serf. His father died a little while back of what people call "elf-stroke" in his time and we've shortened to "stroke" in ours, and he's come in the best of his two woolen tunics to the court of the local baron to take part in the ceremony at the heart of the feudal system.

It's a verbal contract performed in the presence of witnesses: in this case, the baron, the village priest, a couple of elderly knights who serve the baron as advisers, and a gaggle of village elders who remember every detail of the local customary law with the verbal exactness common to learned people among the illiterate. Higg places his hands between the baron's and repeats the traditional pledge of loyalty, coached as needed by the priest; the baron replies in equally formal words, and the two of them are bound for life in the relationship of liegeman to liege lord.

What this means in practice is anything but vague. As the baron's man, Higg has the lifelong right to dwell in his father's house and make use of the garden and pigpen; to farm a certain precisely specified portion of the village farmland; to pasture one milch cow and its calf, one ox, and twelve sheep on the village commons; to gather, on fourteen specified saint's days, as much wood as he can carry on his back in a single trip from the forest north of the village, but only limbwood and fallen wood; to catch each year two dozen adult rabbits from the warren on the near side of the stream, being strictly forbidden to catch any from the warren on the far side of the millpond; and, as a reward for a service his great-grandfather once performed for the baron's great-grandfather during a boar hunt, to take anything that washes up on the weir across the stream between the first sound of the matin bell and the last of the vespers bell on the day of St. Ethelfrith each year.

In exchange for these benefits, Higg is bound to an equally specific set of duties. He will labor in the baron's fields, as well as his own and his neighbors', at seedtime and harvest; his son will help tend the baron's cattle and sheep along with the rest of the village herd; he will give a tenth of his crop at harvest each year for the support of the village church; he will provide the baron with unpaid labor in the fields or on the great stone keep rising next to the old manorial hall for three weeks each year; if the baron goes to war, whether he's staging a raid on the next barony over or answering the summons of that half-mythical being, the king, in the distant town of London, Higg will put on a leather jerkin and an old iron helmet, take a stout knife and the billhook he normally uses to harvest wood on those fourteen saint's days, and follow the baron in the field for up to forty days. None of these benefits and duties are negotiable. All Higg's paternal ancestors have held their land on these terms since time out of mind, and each of his neighbors holds some equivalent set of feudal rights from the baron for some similar set of duties.

Higg has heard of markets. One is held annually every St. Audrey's day at the king's town of Norbury, twenty-seven miles away, but he's never been there and may well never travel that far from home in his life. He also knows about money, and has even seen a silver penny once, but he will live out his entire life without ever buying or selling something for money, or engaging in any economic transaction governed by the law of supply and demand. Not until centuries later, when the feudal economy begins to break down and intermediaries once again begin to insert themselves between producer and consumer, will that change—and that's precisely the point, because feudal economics are what emerge in a society that has learned about the dangers of intermediation the hard way and sets out to build an economy where that doesn't happen.

There are good reasons, in other words, why medieval European economic theory focused on the concept of the just price, which is not set by supply and demand, and why medieval European economic practice included a galaxy of carefully designed measures meant to prevent supply and demand from influencing prices, wages, or anything else.[16] There are equally good reasons why lending money at interest was considered a sufficiently heinous sin in the Middle Ages that Dante, in *The Inferno*, put lenders at the bottom of the seventh circle of hell, below mass murderers, heretics, and fallen angels.[17] The only sinners who go further down than lenders were the practitioners of fraud, in the eighth circle, and traitors, in the ninth: here again, this was a straightforward literary reflection of everyday reality in a society that depended on the sanctity of verbal contracts and the mutual personal obligations that structure feudal relationships.

(It's probably necessary at this point to note that yes, I'm quite aware that European feudalism had its downsides—that it was rigidly caste-bound, brutally violent, and generally unjust. So is the system under which you live, dear reader, and it's worth noting that the average medieval peasant worked fewer hours and had more days off than you do. Medieval societies also valued stability or, as today's economists like to call it, stagnation, rather than economic growth and technological progress. Whether that's a good thing or not probably ought to be left to be decided in the far future, when the long-term consequences of our system can be judged against the long-term consequences of Higg's.)

A fully developed feudal system takes several centuries to emerge. The first stirrings of one, however, begin to take shape as soon as people in a declining civilization start to realize that the economic system under which they live is stacked against them and benefits, at their expense, whatever class of parasitic intermediaries their society happens to have spawned. That's when people begin looking for ways to meet their own economic needs outside the existing system, and certain things reliably follow. The replacement of temporary economic transactions with enduring personal relationships is one of these; so is the primacy of farmland and other productive property to the economic system—this is why land and the like are still referred to legally as "real property," as though all other forms of property are somehow unreal—as indeed they are, in the times of crisis that give rise to feudal systems.

A third consequence of the shift of economic activity away from the institutions and forms of a failing civilization has already been mentioned: the abandonment of money as an abstract intermediary in economic activity. That's a crucial element of the process, and it has even more crucial implications, but those are sweeping enough that the end of money will require an extended discussion of its own.

⚛️

Of all the differences that separate the feudal economy just sketched out from the market economy most of us inhabit today, the one that tends to throw people for a loop is the near-total absence of money in everyday medieval life. Money is so central to current notions of economics that getting by without it is all but unthinkable these days. The fact—and, of course, it is a fact—that the vast majority of human societies, including complex civilizations, have gotten by just fine without money of any kind barely registers in our collective imagination.

One source of this curious blindness, I've come to think, is the way that the logic of money is presented in school. Those of my readers who sat through an Economics 101 class will no doubt recall the sort of narrative that inevitably pops up in textbooks when this point is raised. You have, let's say, a pig farmer who has bad teeth, but the only dentist in the village is Jewish, so the pig farmer can't simply swap pork chops and bacon for dental work. Barter might be an option, but according to the usual textbook narrative, that would end up requiring some sort of complicated multiparty deal whereby the pig farmer gives pork to the carpenter, who builds a garage for the auto repairman, who fixes the hairdresser's car, and eventually things get back around to the dentist. Once money enters the picture, by contrast, the pig farmer sells bacon and pork chops to all and sundry, uses the proceeds to pay the dentist, and everyone's happy. Right?

Well, maybe. Let's stop right there for a moment, and take a look at the presuppositions hardwired into this little story. First of all, the narrative assumes that *participants have a single rigidly defined economic role*: the pig farmer can only raise pigs, the dentist can only fix teeth, and so on. Furthermore, it assumes that *participants can't anticipate needs and adapt to them*: even though he knows the only dentist in town is Jewish, the pig farmer can't do the logical thing and start raising lambs for Passover on the side, or what have you. Finally, the narrative assumes that *participants can interact economically only through market exchanges*: there are no other options for meeting needs for goods and services, no other way to arrange exchanges between people other than market transactions driven by the law of supply and demand.

Even in modern industrial societies, these three presuppositions are rarely true. I happen to know several pig farmers, for example, and none of them are so hyperspecialized that their contributions to economic exchanges are limited to pork products; garden truck, fresh eggs, venison, moonshine, and a good many other things could come into the equation as well. For that matter, outside the bizarre feedlot landscape of industrial agriculture, mixed farms raising a variety of crops and livestock are far more resilient than single-crop farms, and thus considerably more common in societies that haven't shoved every economic activity into the procrustean bed of the money economy.

As for the second point raised above, the law of supply and demand works just as effectively in a barter economy as in a money economy, and successful participants are always on the lookout for a good or service that's in short supply relative to potential demand, and so can be bartered with advantage. It's no accident that traditional village economies tend to be exquisitely adapted to produce exactly that mix of goods and services the inhabitants of the village need and want.

Finally, of course, there are many ways of handling the production and distribution of goods and services without participating in market exchanges. The household economy, in which people produce goods and services that they themselves consume, is the basis of economic activity in most human societies, and still accounted for the majority of economic value produced in the United States until not much more than a century ago. The gift economy, in which members of a community give their excess production to other members of the same community in the expectation that the gift will be reciprocated, is immensely common; so is the feudal economy delineated above, with its systematic exclusion of market forces from the economic sphere. There are others, plenty of them, and none of them require money at all.

Thus the logic behind money pretty clearly isn't what the textbook story claims it is. That doesn't mean that there's no logic to it at all. What it means, rather, is that nobody wants to talk about what it is that money is actually meant to do. Fortunately, we've already discussed the relevant issues, so I can sum up the matter here in a single sentence: the point of money is that it makes intermediation easy.

Intermediation is very easy to do in a money economy, because— as we all know from personal experience—the intermediaries can simply charge fees for whatever service they claim to provide, and then cash in those fees for whatever goods and services they happen

to want. By way of contrast, imagine the predicament of an intermediary who wanted to insert himself into, and take a cut out of,
a money-free transaction between the pig farmer and the dentist.
We'll suppose that the arrangement the two of them have worked
out is that the pig farmer raises enough lambs each year that all
the Jewish families in town can have a proper Passover seder, the
dentist takes care of the dental needs of the pig farmer and his
family, and the other families in the Jewish community work things
out with the dentist in exchange for their lambs—a type of arrangement, half barter and half gift economy, that's tolerably common in
close-knit communities.

Intermediation works by taking a cut from each transaction.
The cut may be described as a tax, a fee, an interest payment, a
service charge, or what have you, but it amounts to the same thing:
whenever money changes hands, part of it gets siphoned off for the
benefit of the intermediaries. The same thing can be done in some
money-free transactions, but not all. Our intermediary might be
able to demand a certain amount of meat from each Passover lamb,
or require the pig farmer to raise one lamb for the intermediary per
six lambs raised for the local Jewish families, though this assumes
that he either likes lamb chops or can swap the lamb to someone
else for something he wants.

What on Earth, though, is he going to do to take a cut from
the dentist's side of the transaction? There wouldn't be much point
in demanding one tooth out of every six the dentist extracts, for
example, and requiring the dentist to fill one of the intermediary's
teeth for every twenty other teeth he fills would be awkward at
best—what if the intermediary doesn't happen to need any teeth
filled this year? What's more, once intermediation is reduced to
such crassly physical terms, it's hard to pretend that it's anything
but a parasitic relationship that benefits the intermediary at everyone else's expense.

What makes intermediation seem to make sense in a money
economy is that *money is the primary intermediation*. Money is a

system of arbitrary tokens used to facilitate exchange, but it's also a good deal more than that. It's the framework of laws, institutions, and power relationships that creates the tokens, defines their official value, and mandates that they be used for certain classes of economic exchange. Once the use of money is required for any purpose, the people who control the framework get to decide the terms on which everyone else gets access to money, which amounts to effective economic control over everyone else. That is to say, they become the primary intermediaries, and every other intermediation depends on them and the money system they control.

This is why, to cite only one example, British colonial administrators in Africa imposed a hut tax on the native population, even though the cost of administering and collecting the tax was more than the revenue the tax brought in.[18] By requiring the tax to be paid in money rather than in kind, the colonial government forced the natives to participate in the money economy, on terms that were, of course, set by the colonial administration and British business interests. The money economy is the basis on which nearly all other forms of intermediation rest, and forcing the native peoples to work for money instead of allowing them to meet their economic needs in some less easily exploited fashion was an essential part of the mechanism that pumped wealth out of the colonies for Britain's benefit.

Watch the way that the money economy has insinuated itself into every dimension of modern life in an industrial society, and you've got a ringside seat from which to observe the metastasis of intermediation in recent decades. Where money goes, intermediation follows: that's one of the unmentionable realities of political economy, the science that Adam Smith actually founded but which was gutted, stuffed, and mounted on the wall—turned, that is, into the contemporary pseudoscience of economics—once it became painfully clear just what kind of trouble got stirred up when people got to talking about the implications of the links between political power and economic wealth.

There's another side to the metastasis just mentioned, though, and it has to do with the habits of thought that the money economy both requires and reinforces. At the heart of the entire system of money is the concept of abstract value, the idea that goods and services share a common, objective attribute called "value" that can be gauged according to the one-dimensional measurement of price.

It's an astonishingly complex concept, and so needs unpacking here. Philosophers generally recognize a crucial distinction between facts and values; there are various ways of distinguishing them, but the one that matters for our present purposes is that facts are collective and values are individual. Consider the statement "It rained here last night." Given agreed-upon definitions of "here" and "last night," that's a statement about fact—in this case, the fact that all those who stood outside last night in the town where I live and looked up at the sky got raindrops on their faces. In the strict sense of the word, facts are objective—that is, they deal with the properties of objects of perception, such as raindrops and nights.

Values, by contrast, are subjective—that is, they deal with the properties of perceiving subjects, such as people who look up at the sky and notice wetness on their faces. One person is annoyed by the rain, another is pleased, another is completely indifferent to it, and these value judgments are irreducibly personal; it's not that the rain is annoying, pleasant, or indifferent; it's the individuals who are affected in these ways. Nor are these personal valuations easy to sort out along a linear scale without drastic distortion. The human experience of value is a richly multidimensional thing; even in a language as poorly furnished with descriptive terms for emotion as English is, there are countless shades of meaning available for talking about positive valuations, and at least as many more for negative ones.

From that vast universe of human experience, the concept of abstract value extracts a single variable—"How much will you give for it?"—and reduces the answer to a numerical scale denominated in dollars and cents or the local equivalent. Like any other act of reductive abstraction, it has its uses, but the benefits of any such act always have to be measured against the blind spots generated by reductive modes of thinking, and the consequences of that induced blindness must either be guarded against or paid in full. The latter is far and away the more common of the two, and it's certainly the option that modern industrial society has enthusiastically chosen.

Those of my readers who want to see the blindness just mentioned in full spate need only turn to any of the popular cornucopian economic theorists of our time. The fond and fatuous insistence that resource depletion can't possibly be a problem, because investing additional capital will inevitably turn up new supplies—precisely the same logic, by the way, that appears in the legendary utterance "I can't be overdrawn, I still have checks left!"—unfolds precisely from the flattening out of qualitative value into quantitative price just discussed. The habit of reducing every kind of value to bare price is profitable in a money economy, because it facilitates ignoring every variable that might get in the way of making money off transactions. Unfortunately it misses a minor but crucial fact, which is that the laws of physics and ecology trump the laws of economics and can neither be bribed nor bought.

The contemporary fixation on abstract value isn't limited to economists and those who believe them, nor is this fixation's potential for catastrophic consequences. I'm thinking here specifically of those people who have grasped the fact that industrial civilization is picking up speed on the downslope of its decline but whose response to it consists of trying to find some way to stash away as much abstract value as possible now so that it will be available to them in the future. Far more often than not, gold plays a central role in that strategy, though there are a variety of less popular vehicles that play starring roles the same sort of plan.

Now, of course, it was probably inevitable in a consumer society like ours that even the downfall of industrial civilization would be turned promptly into yet another reason to go shopping. Still, there's another difficulty here, and that's that the same strategy has been tried before, many times, in the last years of other civilizations. There's an ample body of historical evidence that can be used to see just how well it works. The short form? Don't go there.

It so happens, for example, that in there among the sagas and songs of early medieval Europe are a handful that deal with historical events in the years right after the fall of Rome: the *Nibelungenlied*, *Beowulf*, the oldest strata of Norse saga, and some others. Now, of course, all these started out as oral traditions, and finally found their way into written form centuries after the events they chronicle, when their compilers had no way to check their facts; they also include plenty of folktale and myth, as oral traditions generally do. Still, they describe events and social customs that have been confirmed by surviving records and archeological evidence and offer one of the best glimpses we've got into the lived experience of descent into a dark age.

Precious metals played an important part in the political economy of that age—no surprises there, as the Roman world had a precious-metal currency, and since banks had not been invented yet, portable objects of gold and silver were the most common way that the Roman world's well-off classes stashed their personal wealth. As the Western Empire foundered in the fifth century CE and its market economy came apart, hoarding precious metals became standard practice, and rural villas, the doomsteads of the day, popped up all over. When archeologists excavate those villas, they routinely find evidence that they were looted and burned when the empire fell, and tolerably often a hobbyist with a metal detector has located the buried stash of precious metals somewhere nearby, an expressive reminder of just how much benefit that store of abstract wealth actually provided to its owner.

That's the same story you get from all the old legends: when treasure turns up, a lot of people are about to die. The *Volsunga saga* and the *Nibelungenlied*, for example, are versions of the same story, based on dim memories of events in the Rhine valley in the century or so after Rome's fall.[19] The primary plot engine of those events is a hoard of the usual late Roman kind, which passes from hand to hand by way of murder, torture, betrayal, vengeance, and the annihilation of entire dynasties. For that matter, when Beowulf dies after slaying his dragon, and his people discover that the dragon was guarding a treasure, do they rejoice? Not at all; they take it for granted that the kings and warriors of every neighboring kingdom are going to come and slaughter them to get it—and in fact that's what happens.[20] That's business as usual in a dark age society.

The problem with stockpiling gold on the brink of a dark age is thus simply another dimension, if a more extreme one, of the broader problem with intermediation. It bears remembering that gold is not wealth; it's simply a durable form of money, and thus, like every other form of money, an arbitrary token embodying a claim to real wealth—that is, goods and services—that other people produce. If the goods and services aren't available, a basement safe full of gold coins won't change that fact, and if the people who have the goods and services need them more than they want gold, the same is true. Even if the goods and services are to be had, if everyone with gold is bidding for the same diminished supply, that gold isn't going to buy anything close to what it does today. What's more, tokens of abstract value have another disadvantage in a society where the rule of law has broken down: they attract violence the way a dead rat draws flies.

The fetish for stockpiling gold has always struck me, in fact, as the best possible proof that most of the people who think they are preparing for total social collapse haven't actually thought the matter through and considered the conditions that will obtain after the rubble stops bouncing. Let's say industrial civilization comes apart, quickly or slowly, and you have gold. In that case, either you spend it to purchase goods and services after the collapse, or you don't. If you do, everyone in your vicinity will soon know that you have gold; the rule of law no longer discourages people from killing you and taking it in the best *Nibelungenlied* fashion; and sooner or later you'll run out of ammo. If you don't, what good will the gold do you?

The era when *Nibelungenlied* conditions apply—when, for example, armed gangs move from one doomstead to another, annihilating the people holed up there, living for a while on what they find, and then moving on to the next, or when local governments round up the families of those believed to have gold and torture them to death, starting with the children, until someone breaks—is a common stage of dark ages. It's a self-terminating one, since sooner or later the available supply of precious metals or other carriers of abstract wealth are spread thin across the available supply of warlords. This can take anything up to a century or two before we reach the stage commemorated in the Anglo-Saxon poem "The Seafarer": *Nearon nú cyningas ne cáseras, ne goldgiefan swylce iú wáeron* (No more are there kings or caesars, or gold-givers as once there were).[21]

That's when things begin settling down and the sort of feudal arrangement sketched out above begins to emerge, when money and the market play little role in most people's lives and labor and land become the foundation of a new, impoverished but relatively stable society where the rule of law again becomes a reality. From there, the slow growth of economic complexity will proceed as it has in the past and eventually bring North America out of the deindustrial dark age into whatever new economic arrangements emerge on its far side.

6

THE SUICIDE OF SCIENCE

EVERY HUMAN SOCIETY LIKES TO THINK THAT ITS CORE CUL-
tural and intellectual projects, whatever those happen to be, are
the be-all and end-all of human existence. As each society rounds
out its trajectory through time with the normal process of decline
and fall, in turn, its intellectuals face the dismaying experience
of watching those projects fail and betray the hopes that were so
fondly confided to them.

It's important not to underestimate the shattering force of this
experience. The plays of Euripides offer cogent testimony of the
despair felt by ancient Greek thinkers as their grand project of
reducing the world to rational order dissolved in a chaos of competing ideologies and brutal warfare. Fast-forward most of a millennium, and Augustine's *The City of God* anatomized the comparable
despair of Roman intellectuals at the failure of their dream of a
civilized world at peace under the rule of law.

Skip another millennium and a bit, and the collapse of the imagined unity of Christendom into a welter of contending sects and
warring nationalities had a similar impact on cultural productions
of all kinds as the Middle Ages gave way to the era of the Reforma-
tion. No doubt when people a millennium or so from now assess
the legacies of the twenty-first century, they'll have no trouble
tracing a similar tone of despair in our arts and literature, driven
by the failure of science and technology to live up to the messianic

fantasies of perpetual progress that have been loaded onto them since Francis Bacon's time.

There are several reasons why such projects so reliably fail. To begin with, of course, the grand designs of intellectuals in a mature society normally presuppose access to the kind and scale of resources that such a society supplies to its more privileged inmates. When the resource needs of an intellectual project can no longer be met, it doesn't matter how useful it would be if it could be pursued further, much less how closely aligned it might happen to be to somebody's notion of the meaning and purpose of human existence.

Furthermore, as a society begins its one-way trip down the slippery chute labeled "Decline and Fall," and its ability to find and distribute resources starts to falter, its priorities necessarily shift. Triage becomes the order of the day, and projects that might ordinarily get funding end up out of luck so that more immediate needs can get as much of the available resource base as possible. A society's core intellectual projects tend to face this fate a good deal sooner than other more pragmatic concerns. When the barbarians are at the gates, funds that might otherwise be used to pay for schools of philosophy tend to get spent hiring soldiers instead.

Modern science, the core intellectual project of the contemporary industrial world, and technological complexity, its core cultural project, are as subject to these same two vulnerabilities as were the corresponding projects of other civilizations. Yes, I'm aware that this is a controversial claim, but I'd argue that it follows necessarily from the nature of both projects. Scientific research, like most things in life, is subject to the law of diminishing returns; what this means in practice is that the more research has been done in any field, the greater an investment is needed on average to make the next round of discoveries. Consider the difference between the absurdly cheap hardware that was used in the late nineteenth century to detect the electron and the fantastically expensive facility that had to be built to detect the Higgs boson; that's the sort of shift in the cost-benefit ratio of research that I have in mind.

A civilization with ample resources and a thriving economy can afford to ignore the rising cost of research and can gamble that new discoveries will be valuable enough to cover the costs. A civilization facing resource shortages and economic contraction can't. If the cost of new discoveries in particle physics continues to rise along the same curve that gave us the Higgs boson's multibillion-Euro price tag, for example, the next round of experiments, or the one after that, could easily rise to the point that, in an era of resource depletion, economic turmoil, and environmental payback, no consortium of nations on the planet will be able to spare the resources for the project. Even if the resources could theoretically be spared, furthermore, there will be many other projects begging for them, and it's far from certain that another round of research into particle physics would be the best available option.

The project of technological complexification is even more vulnerable to the same effect. Though true believers in progress like to think of new technologies as replacements for older ones, it's actually more common for new technologies to be layered over existing ones. Consider, as one example out of many, the US transportation grid, in which airlanes, freeways, railroads, local roads, and navigable waterways are all still in use, reflecting most of the history of transport on this continent from colonial times to the present. The more recent the transport mode, by and large, the more expensive it is to maintain and operate, and the exotic new transportation schemes floated in recent years are no exception to that rule.

Now factor in economic contraction and resource shortages. The most complex and expensive parts of the technostructure tend also to be the most prestigious and politically influential, and so the logical strategy of a phased withdrawal from unaffordable complexity—for example, shutting down airports and using the proceeds to make good some of the impact of decades of malign neglect on the nation's rail network—is rarely if ever a politically viable option. As contraction accelerates, the available resources come to be distributed by way of a political free-for-all in which rational strategies for the future play no significant role. In such a setting, will new technological projects be able to get the kind of ample funding they've gotten in the past? Let's be charitable and simply say that this isn't likely.

Thus the end of the age of fossil-fueled extravagance means the coming of a period in which science and technology will have a very hard row to hoe, with each existing or proposed project having to compete for a slice of a shrinking pie of resources against many other equally urgent needs. That in itself would be a huge challenge. What makes it much worse is that many scientists, technologists, and their supporters in the lay community are currently behaving in ways that all but guarantee that when the resources are divided up, science and technology will draw the short sticks.

It has to be remembered that science and technology are social enterprises. They don't happen by themselves in some sort of abstract space insulated from the grubby realities of human collective life. Laboratories, institutes, and university departments are social constructs, funded and supported by the wider society. That funding and support doesn't happen by accident; it exists because people outside the scientific community believe that the labors of scientists and engineers will benefit the rest of society to a degree that outweighs the costs.

Historically speaking, it's only in exceptional circumstances that something like scientific research gets as large a cut of a society's total budget as it does today.[1] As recently as a century ago, the sciences received only a tiny fraction of the support they currently receive; a modest number of university positions with limited resources provided most of what institutional backing the sciences got, and technological progress was largely a matter of individual inventors pursuing projects on their own nickel in their off hours—consider the Wright brothers, who carried out the research that led to the first successful airplane in between waiting on customers in their bicycle shop, and without benefit of research grants.

The transformation of scientific research and technological progress from the part-time activity of an enthusiastic fringe culture to its present role as a massively funded institutional process took place over the course of the twentieth century. Plenty of things drove that transformation, but among the critical factors were the successful efforts of scientists, engineers, and the patrons and publicists of science and technology to make a case for science and technology as forces for good in society, producing benefits that would someday be extended to all. In the boom times that followed the Second World War, it was arguably easier to make that case than it had ever been before, but it took a great deal of work—not merely propaganda but actual changes in the way that scientists and engineers interacted with the public and met their concerns—to overcome the public wariness toward science and technology that made the mad scientist such a stock figure in the popular media of the time.

These days, the economic largesse that made it possible for the latest products of industry to reach most American households is increasingly a fading memory, and that's made life rather more difficult for those who argue for science and technology as forces for good. Still, there's another factor, which is the increasing failure of the proponents of institutional science and technology to make that case in any way that convinces the general public.

Here's a homely example. I have a friend who suffered from severe asthma. She was on four asthma medications, each accompanied by its own bevy of nasty side effects, which more or less kept the asthma under control without curing it. After many years of this, she happened to learn that another health problem she had was associated with a dietary allergy, cut the offending food out of her diet, and was startled and delighted to find that her asthma cleared up as well.

After a year with no asthma symptoms, she went to her physician, who expressed surprise that she hadn't had to come in for asthma treatment in the meantime. She explained what had happened. The doctor admitted that the role of that allergy as a cause of severe asthma was well-known. When she asked the doctor why she hadn't been told this, so she could make an informed decision, the only response she got was, and I quote, "We prefer to medicate for that condition."

Most of the people I know have at least one such story to tell about their interactions with the medical industry, in which the convenience and profit of the industry took precedence over the well-being of the patient. Quite a few have simply stopped going to physicians, since the side effects from the medications they received have been reliably worse than the illness they had when they went in. Since today's mainstream medical industry founds its publicity on its claims to a scientific basis, the growing public unease with mainstream industrial medicine splashes over onto science in general. For that matter, whenever some technology seems to be harming people, it's a safe bet that somebody in a lab coat with a prestigious title will appear on the media insisting that everything's all right. Some of the time, the person in the lab coat is correct, but it's happened often enough that everything was *not* all right that the trust once reposed in scientific experts is getting noticeably threadbare these days.

Public trust in scientists has taken a beating for several other reasons as well. One of the more awkward of these is the way that the vagaries of scientific opinion concerning climate change have been erased from our collective memory by one side in the current climate debate. It's probably necessary for me to note here that I find the arguments for disastrous anthropogenic climate change far stronger than the arguments against it, and I have discussed the likely consequences of our civilization's maltreatment of the atmosphere repeatedly in my books, as well as in an earlier chapter of this one. The fact remains that in my teen years, in the 1970s and 1980s, scientific opinion was still sharply divided on the subject of future climates, and a significant number of experts believed that the descent into a new ice age was likely.

I would encourage anyone who doubts that claim to get past the shouting and obtain copies of the following books, which document that fact: *The Weather Machine* by Nigel Calder, *After the*

Ice Age by E. C. Pielou, and *Ice Ages* by Windsor Chorlton, which was part of Time Life's *Planet Earth* series. (There are many others, but these are still readily available on the used-book market.) The authors were by no means nonentities. Nigel Calder was a highly respected science writer and media personality, and E. C. Pielou is still one of the most respected Canadian ecologists. Windsor Chorlton occupied a less exalted station in the food chain of science writers, but all the volumes in the *Planet Earth* series were written in consultation with acknowledged experts and summarized the state of the art in the earth sciences at the time of publication.

Because certain science fiction writers have been among the most vitriolic figures denouncing those who remember the warnings of an imminent ice age, I'd also encourage readers who have their doubts to pick up copies of *The Winter of the World* by Poul Anderson and *The Time of the Great Freeze* by Robert Silverberg, both of which are set in an ice age future. My younger readers may not remember these authors; those who do will know that both of them were respected, competent SF writers who paid close attention to the scientific thought of their time and wrote about futures defined by an ice age at the time when this was still a legitimate scientific extrapolation

These books exist. I still own copies of most of them. Those of my readers who take the time to find and read them will discover, in each nonfiction volume, a thoughtfully developed argument suggesting that the Earth would soon descend into a new ice age, and in each of the novels, a lively story set in a future shaped by the new ice age in question. Those arguments turned out to be wrong, no question. They were made by qualified experts, at a time when the evidence concerning climate change was a good deal more equivocal than it's become since that time, and the more complete evidence that was gathered later settled the matter; but the arguments and the books existed, many people alive today know that they existed, and when scientists associated with climate activism insist that they didn't, the result is a body blow to public trust in science.

It's far from the only example of the same kind. Many of my readers will remember the days when all cholesterol was bad and polyunsaturated fats were good for you. Most of my readers will recall drugs that were introduced to the market with loud assurances of safety and efficacy, and then withdrawn in a hurry when those assurances turned out to be dead wrong. Those readers who are old enough may even remember when continental drift was being denounced as the last word in pseudoscience, a bit of history that a number of science writers these days claim never happened.[2] Support for science depends on trust in scientists, and that's become increasingly hard to maintain at a time when it's unpleasantly easy to point to straightforward falsifications of the kind just outlined.

On top of all this, there's the impact of the atheist movement on public debates concerning science. I hasten to say that I know quite a few atheists, and the great majority of them are decent, compassionate people who have no trouble with the fact that their beliefs aren't shared by everyone around them. Unfortunately, the atheists who have managed to seize the public limelight rarely merit description in those terms. Most of my readers will be wearily familiar with the sneering bullies who so often claim to speak for atheism these days; I can promise you that as a public figure in a minority faith, I get to hear from them far too often for my taste.

Mind you, there's a certain wry amusement in the way that the resulting disputes are playing out in contemporary culture. Even diehard atheists have begun to notice that every time Richard Dawkins opens his mouth, a couple of dozen people decide to give God a second chance. Still, the dubious behavior of the "angry atheist" crowd affects the subject of this chapter at least as powerfully as it does the field of popular religion. A great many of today's atheists claim the support of scientific materialism for their beliefs, and no small number of the most prominent figures in the atheist movement hold down day jobs as scientists or science educators. In the popular mind, as a result, these people, their beliefs, and their behavior are quite generally conflated with science as a whole.

The implications of all these factors are best explored by way of a simple thought experiment. Let's say, dear reader, that you're an ordinary American citizen. Over the last month, you've heard one scientific expert insist that the latest fashionable heart drug is safe and effective, while two of your drinking buddies have told you in detail about the ghastly side effects it gave them and three people you know have died from the side effects of other drugs similarly pronounced safe and effective. You've heard another scientific expert denounce acupuncture as crackpot pseudoscience, while your Uncle Jeff, who messed up his back in Iraq, got more relief from three visits to an acupuncturist than he got from six years of conventional treatment. You've heard still another scientific expert claim yet again that nobody ever said back in the 1970s that the world was headed for a new ice age, and you read the same books I did when you were in high school and know the expert is either misinformed or lying. Finally, you've been on the receiving end of yet another diatribe by yet another atheist of the sneering-bully type just mentioned, who vilified your religious beliefs in terms that would count as hate speech in most other contexts and used the prestige of science to justify his views and excuse his behavior.

Given all this, will you vote for a candidate who says that you have to accept a cut in your standard of living in order to keep laboratories and university science departments fully funded?

No, I didn't think so.

In miniature, that's the crisis faced by science as we move into the endgame of industrial civilization, just as comparable crises challenged Greek philosophy, Roman jurisprudence, and medieval theology in the endgames of their own societies. When a society assigns one of its core intellectual or cultural projects to a community of specialists, those specialists need to think—and think hard—about the way their words and actions will come across to those outside that community. That's important enough when the society is still in a phase of expansion; when it tips over its historic peak

and begins the long road down, it becomes an absolute necessity—
but it's a necessity that, very often, the specialists in question never
get around to recognizing until it's far too late.

For all the reasons just surveyed, it's unlikely that science as a
living tradition will be able to survive in its current institutional
framework as the Long Descent picks up speed around us. It's by
no means certain that it will survive at all. The abstract conviction
that science is humanity's best hope for the future, even if it were
more broadly held than it is, offers little protection against the
consequences of popular revulsion driven by the corruptions, falsifications, and abusive behaviors sketched out above, especially when
this is added to the hard economic realities that beset any civilization's core intellectual projects in its twilight years. The resurgence
of religion in the declining years of a culture, a commonplace of
history in the run-up to previous dark ages, could have taken many
forms in the historical trajectory of industrial society; at this point
I think it's all too likely to contain a very large dollop of hostility
toward science and complex technology.

꼛ꕤꖀ

It's important, in order to make sense of the fate of science and
technology in the impending dark age, to recall that these things
function as social phenomena, and fill social roles, in ways that
have more than a little in common with the intellectual activities of
civilizations of the past. That doesn't mean, as some postmodern
theorists have argued, that science and technology are *purely* social
phenomena;[3] both of them have to take the natural world into
account, and so have an important dimension that transcends the
social. That said, the social dimension also exists, and since human
beings are social mammals, that dimension has an immense impact on the way that science and technology function in this or any
other human society.

From a social standpoint, it's thus not actually all that relevant
that that the scientists and engineers of contemporary industrial

society can accomplish things with matter and energy that weren't within the capacities of Babylonian astrologer-priests, Hindu gurus, Chinese literati, or village elders in New Guinea. Each of these groups has been assigned a particular social role, the role of interpreter of nature, by their respective societies, and each of them is accorded substantial privileges for fulfilling the requirements of that role. It's therefore possible to draw precise and pointed comparisons between the different bodies of people filling that very common social role in different societies.

The exercise is worth doing, not least because it helps sort out the far-from-meaningless distinction between the aspects of modern science and technology that unfold from their considerable capacities for doing things with matter and energy, on the one hand, and the aspects of modern science and technology that unfold from the normal dynamics of social privilege, on the other. What's more, since modern science and technology weren't around in previous eras of decline and fall, but privileged intellectual castes certainly were, recognizing the common features that unite today's scientists, engineers, and promoters of scientific and technological progress with equivalent groups in past civilizations makes it a good deal easier to anticipate the fate of science and technology in the decades and centuries to come.

A specific example will be more useful here than any number of generalizations, so let's consider the fate of philosophy in the waning years of the Roman world. The extraordinary intellectual adventure we call classical philosophy began in the Greek colonial cities of Ionia around 585 BCE, when Thales of Miletus first proposed a logical rather than a mythical explanation for the universe, and proceeded through three broad stages from there. The first stage, that of the so-called Presocratics, focused on the natural world, and the questions it asked and tried to answer can more or less be summed up as "What exists?" Its failures and equivocal successes led the second stage, which extended from Socrates through Plato and Aristotle to the Old Academy and its rivals, to focus attention on different questions, which can be summed up just as neatly as "How can we know what exists?"

That was an immensely fruitful shift in focus. It led to the creation of classical logic—one of the great achievements of the human mind—and it also drove the transformations that turned mathematics from an assortment of rules of thumb to an architecture of logical proofs and thus laid the foundations on which Newtonian physics and other quantitative sciences eventually built. Like every other great intellectual adventure of our species, though, it never managed to fulfill all the hopes that had been loaded onto it. The philosopher's dream of human society made wholly subject to reason turned out to be just as unreachable as the scientist's dream of the universe made wholly subject to the human will. As that failure became impossible to ignore, classical philosophy shifted focus again, to a series of questions and attempted answers that amounted to "Given what we know about what exists, how should we live?"

That's the question that drove the last great age of classical philosophy, the age of the Epicureans, the Stoics, and the Neoplatonists. At first these and other schools carried on lively and far-reaching debates, but as the Roman world stumbled toward its end under the burden of its unsolved problems, the philosophers closed ranks. Debates continued, but they focused more and more tightly on narrow technical issues within individual schools. What's more, the schools themselves closed ranks; pure Stoic, Aristotelian, and Epicurean philosophy gradually dropped out of fashion, and by the fourth century CE, a Neoplatonism enriched with bits and pieces of all the other schools stood effectively alone, the last school standing in the long struggle Thales had kicked off ten centuries before.

Now, I have to confess to a strong personal partiality for the Neoplatonists. It was from Plotinus and Proclus, respectively the first and last great figures of classical Neoplatonism, that I first grasped why philosophy matters and what it can accomplish, and for all its problems—like every philosophical account of the world, it has its share—Neoplatonism still makes intuitive sense to me in a way that few other philosophies do. What's more, the men and women who defended classical Neoplatonism in its final years were people of great intellectual and personal dignity, committed to proclaiming the truth as they knew it in the face of intolerance and persecution that ended up costing no few of them their lives.[4]

The awkward fact remains that classical philosophy, like modern science, functioned as a social phenomenon and filled certain social roles. The intellectual power of the final Neoplatonist synthesis and the personal virtues of its last proponents have to be balanced against its blind support of a deeply troubled social order. In all the long history of classical philosophy, it never seems to have occurred to anyone that debates about the nature of justice might reasonably address, say, the ethics of slavery. While a stonecutter like Socrates could take an active role in philosophical debate in Athens in the fourth century BCE, furthermore, the institutionalization of philosophy meant that by the last years of classical Neoplatonism, its practice was restricted to those with ample income and leisure, and its values inevitably became more and more closely tied to the social class of its practitioners.

That's the thing that drove the ferocious rejection of philosophy by the underclass of the age, the slaves and urban poor who made up the vast majority of the population throughout the Roman Empire and who received little if any benefit from the intellectual achievements of their society. To them, the subtleties of Neoplatonist thought were irrelevant to the increasingly difficult realities of life on the lower end of the social pyramid in a brutally hierarchical and increasingly dysfunctional world. That's one important reason—there were others, some of which will be considered in a later chapter—why so many of them turned for solace to a new religious movement from the eastern fringes of the empire, a despised sect that claimed that God had been born on Earth as a mere carpenter's son and communicated through his life and death a way of salvation that privileged the poor and downtrodden above the rich and well-educated.

It was as a social phenomenon, filling certain social roles, that Christianity attracted persecution from the imperial government, and it was in response to Christianity's significance as a social phenomenon that the imperial government executed an about-face under Constantine and took the new religion under its protection. Like plenty of autocrats before and since, Constantine clearly grasped that the real threat to his position and power came from other members of his own class—in his case, the patrician elite of the Roman world—and saw that he could undercut those threats and counter potential rivals through an alliance of convenience with the leaders of the underclass. That's the political subtext of the Edict of Milan, which legalized Christianity throughout the empire and brought it imperial patronage.

The patrician class of late Roman times, like its equivalent today, exercised power through a system of interlocking institutions from which outsiders were carefully excluded, and it maintained a prickly independence from the central government. By the fourth century, tensions between the bureaucratic imperial state and the patrician class, with its local power bases and local loyalties, were rising toward a flashpoint. The rise of Christianity thus gave Constantine and his successors an extraordinary opportunity.

Most of the institutions that undergirded patrician power were linked to Pagan religion. Local senates, temple priesthoods, philosophical schools, and other elements of elite culture normally involved duties drawn from the traditional faith. A religious pretext to strike at those institutions must have seemed as good as any other, and the Christian underclass offered one other useful feature: mobs capable of horrific acts of violence against prominent defenders of the patrician order.

That was why, for example, a Christian mob in 415 CE dragged the Neoplatonist philosopher Hypatia from her chariot as she rode home from her teaching gig at the Academy in Alexandria, cudgeled her to death, cut the flesh from her bones with sharpened oyster shells—the cheap pocketknives of the day—and burned the bloody gobbets to ashes. What doomed Hypatia was not only her defense of the old philosophical traditions but also her connection to Alexandria's patrician class. Her ghastly fate was as much the vengeance of the underclass against the elite as it was an act of religious persecution. She was far from the only victim of violence driven by those paired motives. It was as a result of such pressures that, by the time the emperor Justinian ordered the last academies closed in 529 CE, the classical philosophical tradition was essentially dead.

That's the sort of thing that happens when an intellectual tradition becomes too closely affiliated with the institutions, ideologies, and interests of a social elite. If the elite falls, so does the tradition—and if it becomes advantageous for anyone else to target the elite, the tradition can be a convenient target, especially if it's succeeded in alienating most of the population outside the elite in question.

Modern science is extremely vulnerable to such a turn of events. There was a time when the benefits of scientific research and technological development routinely reached the poor as well as the privileged, but that time has long since passed. These days, the benefits of research and development move up the social ladder, while the costs and negative consequences move down. Nearly all the jobs eliminated by automation, globalization, and the computer revolution, for example, used to hire from the bottom end of the job market, and what replaced them was a handful of jobs that require far more extensive (and expensive) education. In the same way, changes in US health care in recent decades have disproportionately benefited the privileged, while subjecting most others to substandard care at prices so high that medical bills are the leading cause of bankruptcy in the US today.[5]

It's all very well for the promoters of progress to gabble on about science as the key to humanity's destiny, but the poor know from hard experience that the destiny thus marketed isn't for them. To the poor, progress means fewer jobs with lower pay and worse conditions, more surveillance and impersonal violence carried out by governments that show less and less interest in paying even lip service to the concept of civil rights, a rising tide of illnesses caused by environmental degradation and industrial effluents, and glimpses from afar of an endless stream of lavishly advertised tech-derived trinkets, perks and privileges that they will never have. Between the poor and any appreciation for modern science stands a wall made of failed schools, defunded libraries, denied opportunities, and the systematic use of science and technology to benefit other people at their expense. Such a wall, it probably bears noting, makes a good surface against which to sharpen oyster shells.

It seems improbable that anything significant will be done to change this picture until it's far too late for such changes to have any meaningful effect. Barring dramatic transformations in the distribution of wealth, the conduct of public education, the funding for such basic social amenities as public libraries, and a great deal more, the underclass of the modern industrial world can be expected to grow more and more disenchanted with science as a social phenomenon in our culture, and to turn instead—as their equivalents in the Roman world and so many other civilizations did—to some tradition from the fringes that places itself in stark opposition to everything modern scientific culture stands for. Once that process gets under way, it's simply a matter of waiting until the corporate elite that funds science, defines its values, and manipulates it for PR purposes becomes sufficiently vulnerable that some other power center decides to take it out, using institutional science as a convenient point of attack.

Saving anything from the resulting wreck will be a tall order. Still, the same historical parallel discussed above offers some degree of hope. The narrowing focus of classical philosophy in its last years meant, among other things, that a substantial body of knowledge that had once been part of the philosophical movement was no longer identified with it by the time the cudgels and shells came out, and much of it was promptly adopted by Christian clerics and monastics as useful for the Church. That's how classical astronomy, music theory, and agronomy, among other things, found their way into the educational repertoire of Christian monasteries and nunneries in the dark ages. What's more, once the power of the patrician class was broken, a carefully sanitized version of Neoplatonist philosophy found its way into Christianity, where it's still a living presence in some denominations today.

Something along the same lines may well happen again as the impending deindustrial dark age grows closer. Certainly today's defenders of science are doing their best to shove a range of scientific viewpoints out the door. There's an interesting distinction between the sciences that get this treatment and those that don't: on the one hand, those that are being flung aside are those that focus on observation of natural systems rather than control of artificial ones; on the other, any science that raises doubts about the possibility or desirability of infinite technological expansion can expect to find itself shivering in the dark outside in very short order.

Thus it's entirely possible that observational sciences, if they can squeeze through the bottleneck imposed by the loss of funding and prestige, will be able to find a new home in whatever intellectual tradition replaces modern scientific rationalism in the deindustrial future. It's at least as likely that such dissident sciences as ecology, which has always raised challenging questions about the fantasies of the manipulative sciences, may find themselves eagerly embraced by a future intellectual culture that has no trouble at all recognizing the futility of those fantasies. That said, it's still going to take some hard work to preserve what's been learned in those fields—and it's also going to take more than the usual amount of prudence and plain dumb luck not to get caught up in the conflict when the sharp edge of the shell gets turned on modern science.

꼃꼶꼃

All the factors already discussed feed into the widening chasm between the sciences and the rest of human culture that C. P. Snow discussed in his famous work *The Two Cultures*.[6] That chasm has opened up a good deal further since Snow's time, and its impact on the future deserves discussion here, not least because it's starting to become impossible to ignore, even among those who accept the vision of the universe presented by contemporary scientific thought.

The driving force here is the extreme mismatch between the way science works and the way scientists expect their claims to be received by the general public. Within the community of researchers, the conclusions of the moment are, at least in theory, open to constant challenge, but only from within the scientific community. The general public is not invited to take part in those challenges. Quite the contrary; it's supposed to treat the latest authoritative pronouncement as truth pure and simple, even when that contradicts the authoritative pronouncements of six months before.

That the authoritative pronouncements of science do contradict themselves on a regular basis will be obvious, as already noted, to anyone who remembers the days when polyunsaturated fats were supposed to be good for you and all cholesterol was bad—but woe betide anyone outside the scientific community who mentions this when a scientist trots out the latest authoritative pronouncement. The reaction is as predictable as it is counterproductive: how *dare* ordinary citizens express an opinion on the subject!

Now, of course, there are reasons why scientists might not want to field a constant stream of suggestions and challenges from people who don't have training in relevant disciplines. The fact remains that expecting people to blindly accept whatever scientists say, when scientific opinion on so many subjects has been whirling around like a weathercock for decades now, is not a strategy with a long shelf life. Sooner or later people start asking why they should take anything a scientist says on faith, and for many people in North America today, "sooner or later" has already arrived.

There's another, darker, reason why such questions are increasingly common just now. I'm thinking here of the recent revelation that the British scientists tasked by the government with making dietary recommendations have been taking payola of various kinds from the sugar industry.[7] That's hardly a new thing these days. Especially but not only in those branches of science concerned with medicine, pharmacology, and nutrition, the prostitution of the scientific process by business interests has become an open scandal. When a scientist gets behind a podium and makes a statement about the safety or efficacy of a drug, a medical treatment, or what have you, the first question asked by an ever-increasing number of people outside the scientific community these days is "Who's paying him?"

It would be bad enough if that question were being asked because of scurrilous rumors or hostile propaganda. Unfortunately, it's being asked because there's nothing particularly unusual about the behavior of the British scientists mentioned above.[8] These days, in any field where science comes into contact with serious money, scientific studies are increasingly just another dimension of marketing. From influential researchers being paid to put their names on dubious studies to give them unearned credibility, to the systematic concealment of "outlying" data that doesn't support the claims made for this or that lucrative product, the corruption of science is an ongoing reality, and one that existing safeguards within the scientific community are not effectively countering.

Scientists have by and large treated the collapse in scientific ethics as an internal matter. That's a lethal mistake, because the view that matters here is the view from outside. What looks to insiders like a manageable problem that will sort itself out in time, looks from outside the laboratory and the faculty lounge like institutionalized corruption on the part of a self-proclaimed elite whose members cover for each other and are accountable to no one. It doesn't matter, by the way, how inaccurate that view is in specific cases, how many honest men and women are laboring at lab benches, or how overwhelming the pressure to monetize research that's brought to bear on scientists by university administrations and corporate sponsors. None of that finds its way into the view from outside, and in the long run, the view from outside is the one that counts.

The corruption of science by self-interest is an old story, and unfortunately it's most intense in those fields where science impacts the lives of nonscientists most directly: medicine, pharmacology, and nutrition. I mentioned earlier a friend whose lifelong asthma, which landed her in the hospital repeatedly and nearly killed her twice, was cured at once by removing a common allergen from her diet. The physician's comment, "We prefer to medicate for that," makes perfect sense from a financial perspective, since a patient who's cured of an ailment is a good deal less lucrative for the doctor and the rest of the medical profession than one who has to keep on receiving regular treatments and prescriptions. As a result of that interaction among others, though, the friend in question has lost most of what respect she once had for mainstream medicine, and is now using herbalism to meet her health care needs.

It's an increasingly common story these days, and plenty of other accounts could be added here. The point I want to make, though, is that it's painfully obvious that the physician who preferred to medicate never thought about the view from outside. I have no way of knowing what combination of external pressures and personal failings led that physician to conceal a less costly cure from my friend and keep her on expensive and ineffective drugs with a gallery of noxious side effects instead, but from outside the walls of the office, it certainly looked like a callous betrayal of whatever ethics the medical profession might still have left—and again, the view from outside is the one that counts.

It counts because institutional science has the authority and prestige it possesses today only because enough of those outside the scientific community accept its claim to speak the truth about nature. Not that many years ago, all things considered, scientists didn't have that authority or prestige, and no law of nature or of society guarantees that they'll keep either one indefinitely. Every doctor who would rather medicate than cure, every researcher who treats conflicts of interest as just another detail of business as usual, every scientist who insists in angry tones that nobody without a

PhD in this or that discipline is entitled to ask why this week's pronouncement should be taken any more seriously than the one it just disproved—and let's not even talk about the increasing, and increasingly public, problem of overt scientific fraud in the pharmaceutical field among others—is hastening the day when modern science is taken no more seriously by the general public than, say, academic philosophy is today.

That day may not be all that far away. That's the message that should be read, and is far too rarely read, in the accelerating emergence of countercultures that reject the authority of science in one field. As a thoughtful essay in *Salon*[9] pointed out, that crisis of authority is what gives credibility to such movements as climate denialists and "anti-vaxxers" (the growing number of parents who refuse to have their children vaccinated). A good many people these days, when the official voices of the scientific community say this or that, respond by asking "Why should we believe you?"—and too many of them don't get a straightforward answer that addresses their concerns.

A bit of personal experience from a different field may be relevant here. Back in the late 1980s and early 1990s, when I lived in Seattle, I put a fair amount of time into collecting local folklore concerning ghosts and other paranormal phenomena. I wasn't doing this out of any particular belief, or for that matter any particular unbelief; instead, I was seeking a sense of the mythic terrain of the Puget Sound region, the landscapes of belief and imagination that emerged from the experiences of people on the land, with an eye toward the career in writing fiction that I then hoped to launch. While I was doing this research, when something paranormal was reported anywhere in the region, I generally got to hear about it fairly quickly, and in the process I got to watch a remarkable sequence of events that repeated itself like a broken record more often than I can count.

Whether the phenomenon that was witnessed was an unusual light in the sky, a seven-foot-tall hairy biped in the woods, a visit from a relative who happened to be dead at the time, or what have you, two things followed promptly once the witness went public. The first was the arrival of a self-proclaimed skeptic, usually a member of CSICOP (the Committee for Scientific Investigation of Claims of the Paranormal), who treated the witness with scorn and condescension, made dogmatic claims about what must have happened, and responded to any disagreement with bullying and verbal abuse. The other thing that followed was the arrival of an investigator from one of the local organizations of believers in the paranormal, who was invariably friendly and supportive, listened closely to the account of the witness, and took the incident seriously. I'll let you guess which of the proposed explanations the witness usually ended up embracing, not to mention which organization he or she often joined.

The same process on a larger and far more dangerous scale is shaping attitudes toward science across a wide and growing sector of American society. Notice that, unlike climate denialism, the anti-vaxxer movement isn't powered by billions of dollars of grant money, but it's getting increasing traction. The reason is as simple as it is painful: parents are asking physicians and scientists, "How do I know this substance you want to put into my child is safe?"— and the answers they're getting are not providing them with the reassurance they need.

It's probably necessary here to point out that I'm no fan of the anti-vaxxer movement. Since epidemic diseases are likely to play a massive role in the future ahead of us, I've looked into anti-vaxxer arguments with some care, and they don't convince me at all. It's clear from the evidence that vaccines do, far more often than not, provide protection against dangerous diseases. While some children are harmed by the side effects of vaccination, that's true of every medical procedure, and the toll from side effects is orders of magnitude smaller than the annual burden of deaths from these same diseases in the pre-vaccination era. Nor does the anti-vaxxer claim that vaccines cause autism hold water; the epidemiology of autism spectrum disorders simply doesn't support that claim.

That is to say, I don't share the beliefs that drive the anti-vaxxer movement. Similarly, I'm sufficiently familiar with the laws of thermodynamics and the chemistry of the atmosphere to know that when the climate denialists insist that dumping billions of tons of carbon dioxide into the atmosphere can't change its capacity to retain heat, they're smoking their shorts. I've retained enough of a childhood interest in paleontology, and studied enough of biology and genetics since then, to be able to follow the debates between evolutionary biology and so-called creation science, and I'm solidly on Darwin's side of the bleachers. I could go on; I have my doubts about a few corners of contemporary scientific theory, but then so do plenty of scientists.

That is to say, I don't agree with the anti-vaxxers, the climate denialists, the creationists, or their equivalents, but I understand why they've rejected the authority of science, and it's not just because they're ignorant cretins. It's because they've seen far too much of the view from outside. Parents who encounter a medical industry that would rather medicate than heal are more likely to listen to anti-vaxxers; Americans who watch climate change activists demand that the rest of the world cut its carbon footprint, while the activists themselves get to keep cozy middle-class lifestyles, are more likely to believe that global warming is a politically motivated hoax; Christians who see atheists using evolution as a stalking horse for their ideology are more likely to turn to creation science—and all three, and others, are not going to listen to scientists who insist that they're wrong, until and unless the scientists stop and take a good hard look at how they and their proclamations look when viewed from outside.

I'm far from sure that anybody in the scientific community is willing to take that hard look. It's possible. The arrogant bullying that has long been standard practice among the self-proclaimed skeptics and "angry atheists" has taken on a sullen and defensive tone recently, as though it's started to sink in that yelling hate speech at people who disagree with you might not be the best way to win their hearts and minds. Still, for that same act of reflection to get any traction in the scientific community, a great many people in that community are going to have to rethink the way they handle dealing with the public, especially when science, technology, and medicine cause harm. That, in turn, is going to happen only if enough of today's scientists remember the importance of the view from outside.

That view has another dimension, and it's a considerably harsher one. Among the outsiders whose opinion of contemporary science matters most are some who haven't been born yet: our descendants, who will inhabit a world shaped by science and the technologies that have resulted from scientific research. The most likely futures for our descendants are those in which the burdens left behind by today's science and technology are much more significant than the benefits. Those most likely futures, as noted in previous chapters, will be battered by unstable climate and rising oceans due to anthropogenic climate change; stripped of most of their topsoil, natural resources, and ecosystems; and strewn with the radioactive and chemical trash that our era produced in such abundance and couldn't be bothered to store safely—and most of today's advanced technologies will have long since rusted into uselessness, because the cheap abundant energy and other nonrenewable resources that were needed to keep them running all got used up in our time.

People living in such a future aren't likely to remember that a modest number of scientists signed petitions and wrote position papers protesting some of these things. They're even less likely to recall the utopian daydreams of perpetual progress and limitless abundance that encouraged so many other people in the scientific community to tell themselves that these things didn't really matter—and if by chance they do remember those daydreams, their reaction to them won't be pretty. That science today, like every other human institution in every age, combines high ideals and petty motives in the usual proportions will not matter to them in the least.

Unless something changes sharply very soon, their view from outside may well see modern science—all of it, from the first gray dawn of the scientific revolution straight through to the flame-lit midnight when the last laboratory was sacked and burned by a furious mob—as a wicked dabbling in accursed powers that eventually brought down just retribution upon a corrupt and arrogant age. So long as the proponents and propagandists of science ignore the view from outside, and blind themselves to the ways that their own defense of science is feeding the forces that are rising against it, that's far more likely to become the default belief system of the deindustrial dark ages than the comfortable fantasies of perpetual scientific advancement cherished by so many people today.

7

THE TWILIGHT OF
TECHNOLOGY

It's probably inevitable that the previous chapter, with its discussion of the ways that contemporary science is offering itself up as a sacrifice on the altar of corporate greed and institutional arrogance, will convince at least some readers that I must hate science. This is all the more ironic in that the shoddy logic involved in that claim also undergirded George W. Bush's famous and fatuous insistence that the Muslim world is riled at the United States because "they hate our freedom."

In point of fact, the animosity that many Muslims feel toward the United States is based on specific grievances concerning specific acts of US foreign policy. Whether or not those grievances are justified is a matter I don't propose to discuss here. The point that's relevant here is that the grievances exist; they relate to identifiable actions on the part of the US government; and insisting that the animosity in question is aimed at an abstraction instead is simply one of the ways that Bush, like his successor, tried to sidestep any discussion of the means, ends, and cascading failures of US policy toward the Middle East and the rest of the Muslim world.

In the same way, it's convenient to insist that people who ask hard questions about the way that contemporary science has whored itself out to economic and political interests, or who have noticed gaps between the claims about reality made by the voices of the scientific mainstream and their own lived experience of the world, just hate science. That evasive strategy makes it easy to brush aside questions about the more problematic dimensions of science as currently practiced. This isn't a strategy with a long shelf life. Responding to a rising spiral of problems by insisting that the problems don't exist, and denouncing those who demur, is one of history's all-time bad choices. Even so, intellectuals in falling civilizations all too often try to shore up the crumbling foundations of their social prestige and privilege via that foredoomed approach.

Central to the entire rhetorical strategy behind the claim "They just hate science" is a bit of obfuscation that treats "science" as a monolithic unity, rather than the complex and rather ramshackle grab bag of fields of study, methods of inquiry, and theories about how different departments of nature appear to work that it actually is. There's no particular correlation between, let's say, the claims made for the latest heavily marketed and dubiously researched pharmaceutical, on the one hand, and the facts of astronomy, evolutionary biology, or agronomy on the other; and someone can quite readily find it impossible to place blind faith in the pharmaceutical and the doctor who's pushing it on her, while enjoying long nights observing the heavens through a telescope, delighting in the elegant prose and even more elegant logic of Darwin's *The Origin of Species*, or running controlled experiments in her backyard on the effectiveness of compost as a soil amendment. To say that such a person "hates science" is to descend from meaningful discourse to thought-stopping noise.

The habit of insisting that science is a single package, take it or leave it, is paralleled by the equivalent and equally specious insistence that there is this single thing called "technology," that objecting to any single component of that alleged unity amounts to rejecting all of it, and that you're not allowed to pick and choose among technologies—you have to take all of it or reject it all. I field this sort of nonsense all the time. It so happens, for example, that I have no interest in owning a cell phone, never got around to playing video games, and have a sufficiently intense fondness for books printed on actual paper that I've never given more than a passing thought to the current fad for e-books.

I rarely mention these facts to those who don't already know them, because it's a foregone conclusion that if I do so, someone will ask me whether I hate technology. *Au contraire*, I'm fond of slide rules, love rail travel, cherish an as yet unfulfilled ambition to get deep into letterpress printing, and have an Amateur Extra class amateur radio license. All these things entail enthusiastic involvement with specific technologies, and indeed affection for them, but if I mention these points in response to the claim that I must hate technology, the responses I get range from baffled incomprehension to angry dismissal.

"Technology," in the mind of those who make such claims, clearly doesn't mean what the dictionary says it means. To some extent, of course, it amounts to whatever an assortment of corporate and political marketing firms want you to buy this week, but there's more to it than that. Like the word "science," "technology" has become a buzzword freighted with a vast cargo of emotional, cultural, and (whisper this) political meanings. It's so densely entangled with passionately felt emotions, vast and vague abstractions, and frankly mythic imagery that many of those who use the word can't explain what they mean by it—and get angry if you ask them to try.

The flattening out of the vast diversity of technologies, in the plural, into a single monolithic shape guarded by unreasoning emotions would be problematic under any conditions. When a civilization that depends on the breakneck exploitation of non-renewable resources is running up against the unyielding limits of a finite planet, with resource depletion and pollution in a neck-and-neck race to see which one gets to bring the industrial project to an end first, it's a recipe for disaster. A sane response to the predicament of our time would have to start by identifying the technological suites that will still be viable in a resource-constrained and pollution-damaged environment, and then shift as much vital infrastructure to those as possible with the sharply limited resources we have left. Our collective thinking about technology is so muddled by unexamined emotions, though, that it doesn't matter now obviously necessary such a project might be: it remains unthinkable.

Willy-nilly, though, the imaginary monolith of "technology" is going to crumble, because different technologies have wildly varying resource requirements, and they vary just as drastically in terms of their importance to the existing order of society. As resource depletion and economic contraction tighten their grip on the industrial world, the stock of existing and proposed technologies face triage in a continuum defined by two axes—the utility of the technology, on the one hand, and its cost in real (i.e., nonfinancial) terms on the other. A chart may help show how this works.

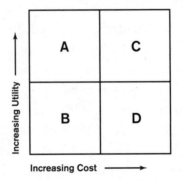

This is a very simplified representation of the frame in which decisions about technology are made. Every kind of utility, from the demands of bare survival to the whims of fashion, is lumped in together and measured on the vertical axis; and every kind of nonfinancial cost, from energy and materials straight through to such intangibles as opportunity cost, is lumped in together and measured on the horizontal axis. In an actual analysis, of course, these variables would be broken out and considered separately. The point of a more schematic view of the frame, like this one, is that it allows the basic concepts to be grasped more easily.

The vertical and horizontal lines that intersect in the middle of the graph are similarly abstractions from a complex reality. The horizontal line represents the boundary between those technologies that have enough utility to be worth building and maintaining, which are above the line, and those that have too little utility to be worth the trouble, which are below it. The vertical line represents the boundary between those technologies that are affordable and those that are not. In the real world, those aren't sharp boundaries but zones of transition, with complex feedback loops weaving back and forth among them, but again, this is a broad conceptual model.

The intersection of the lines divides the whole range of technology into four categories, which I've somewhat unoriginally marked with the first four letters of the alphabet. Category A consists of things that are both affordable and useful, such as indoor plumbing. Category B consists of things that are affordable but useless, such as electrically heated underwear for chickens. Category C consists of things that are useful but unaffordable, such as worldwide 30-minute pizza delivery from low Earth orbit. Category D, rounding out the set, consists of things that are neither useful nor affordable, such as building a mile-high statue of Richard Nixon on Mars.

Now, of course, the horizontal and vertical lines aren't fixed; they change position from one society to another, from one historical period to another, and indeed from one community, family, or individual to another. (To me, for example, cell phones belong in category B, right next to the electrically heated chicken underwear; other people would doubtless put them in somewhere else on the chart.) Every society, though, has a broad general consensus about what goes in which category, which is heavily influenced by but by no means entirely controlled by the society's political class. That consensus is what guides its collective decisions about funding or defunding technologies.

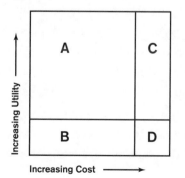

With the coming of the industrial revolution, both lines shifted substantially from their previous position, as shown in the second chart. Obviously, the torrent of cheap abundant energy gave the world's industrial nations access to an unparalleled wealth of resources, and this pushed the dividing line between what was affordable and what was unaffordable quite a ways over toward the right-hand side of the chart. A great many things that had been desirable but unaffordable to previous civilizations swung over from category C into category A as fossil fuels came on line. This has been discussed at great length in my blog and elsewhere in the peak oil blogosphere.

Less obviously, the dividing line between what was useful and what was useless also shifted quite a bit toward the bottom of the chart, moving a great many things from category B into category A. To follow this, it's necessary to grasp the concept of *technological suites*. A technological suite is a set of interdependent technologies that work together to achieve a common purpose. Think of the relationship between cars and petroleum drilling, computer chips and the clean-room filtration systems required for their manufacture, or commercial airliners and ground control radar. What connects each pair of technologies is that they belong to the same technological suite. If you want to have the suite, you must either have all the elements of the suite in place or be ready to replace any absent element with something else that can serve the same purpose.

For the purpose of our present analysis, we can sort out the component technologies of a technological suite into three very rough categories. There are *interface technologies*, which are the things with which the end user interacts—in the three examples just listed, those would be private cars, personal computers, and commercial flights to wherever you happen to be going. There are *support technologies*, which are needed to produce, maintain, and operate the output technologies; they make up far and away the majority of technologies in a technological suite—consider the extraordinary range of technologies it takes to manufacture a car from raw materials, maintain it, fuel it, provide it with roads on which to drive, and so on. Some interface technologies and most support technologies can be replaced with other technologies as needed, but some of both categories can't; we can put those that can't be replaced into a third category, *bottleneck technologies*, for reasons that will become clear shortly.

What makes this relevant to the charts we've been examining is that most support technologies have no value aside from the technological suites to which they belong and the interface technologies they serve. Without commercial air travel, for example, most of the specialized technologies found at airports are unnecessary. Thus a great many things that once belonged in category B—say, automated baggage carousels—shifted into category A with the emergence of the technological suite that gave them utility. Thus category A ballooned with the coming of industrialization, and it kept getting bigger as long as energy and resource use per capita in the industrial nations kept on increasing.

Once energy and resource use per capita peak and begin their decline, though, a different reality comes into play, leading over time to the situation shown in the third chart.

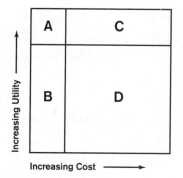

As cheap abundant energy runs short, and it and all its products become expensive, scarce, or both, the vertical line slides inexorably toward the left. That's obvious enough. Less obviously, the horizontal line also slides upwards. The reason, here again, is the interrelationship of individual technologies into technological suites. If commercial air travel stops being economically viable, the support technologies that belong to that suite are no longer needed. Even if they're affordable enough to stay on the left-hand side of the vertical line, the technologies needed to run automated baggage carousels thus no longer have enough utility to keep them above the horizontal line, and down they drop into category B.

That's one way that a technology can drop out of use. It's just as possible, of course, for something that would still have ample utility to cost too much in terms of real wealth to be an option in a contracting society, and slide across the border into category C. Finally, it's possible for something to do both at once—to become useless and unaffordable at something like the same time, as economic contraction takes away the ability to pay for the technology and the ability to make use of it at the same time.

It's also possible for a technology that remains affordable, and participates in a technological suite that's still capable of meeting genuine needs, to tumble out of category A into one of the others. This can happen because the costs of different technologies differ qualitatively, and not just quantitatively. If you need small amounts of unobtainium for the manufacture of blivets, and the handful of unobtainium mines around the world stop production—whether this happens because the ore has run out or for some other reason, environmental, political, economic, cultural, or what have you— you aren't going to be able to make blivets any more. That's one kind of difficulty if it's possible to replace blivets with something else; it's quite another, and much more challenging, if blivets made with unobtainium are the only thing that will work for certain purposes, or the only thing that makes those purposes economically viable.

It's habitual in modern economics to insist that such bottlenecks don't exist, because there's always a viable alternative. That sort of thinking made a certain degree of sense back when energy per capita was still rising, because the standard way to get around material shortages for a century now has been to throw more energy, more technology, and more complexity into the mix. That's how low-grade taconite ores with scarcely a trace of iron in them have become the mainstay of today's iron and steel industry; all you have to do is add fantastic amounts of cheap energy, soaring technological complexity, and an assortment of supply and resource chains reaching around the world and then some, and diminishing ore quality is no problem at all.

It's when you don't have access to as much cheap energy, technological complexity, and baroque supply chains as you want that this sort of logic becomes impossible to sustain. Once this point is reached, bottlenecks become an inescapable feature of life. The bottlenecks, as already suggested, don't have to be technological in nature—a bottleneck technology essential to a given technological suite can be perfectly feasible yet still out of reach for other reasons—but whatever generates them, they throw a wild card into the process of technological decline that shapes the last years of a civilization on its way out and the first few centuries of the dark age that follows.

The crucial point to keep in mind here is that one bottleneck technology, if it becomes inaccessible for any reason, can render an entire technological suite useless and compromise other technological suites that depend on the one directly affected. Consider the twilight of ceramics in the late Roman Empire. Rome's ceramic industry operated on as close to an industrial scale as you can get without torrents of cheap abundant energy; regional factories in various places, where high-quality clay existed, produced ceramic goods in vast amounts and distributed them over Roman roads and sea lanes to the far corners of the empire and beyond it. The technological suite that supported Roman dishes and roof tiles thus included transport technologies, and those turned out to be the bottleneck: as long-distance transport went away, the huge ceramic factories could no longer market their products, and they shut down, taking with them every element of their technological suite that couldn't be repurposed in a hurry.[1]

The same process affected many other technologies that played a significant role in the Roman world, and for that matter in the decline and fall of every other civilization in history. The end result can best be described as technological fragmentation: what had been a more or less integrated whole system of technology, composed of many technological suites working together more or less smoothly, became a jumble of disconnected technological suites, nearly all of them drastically simplified compared to their pre-decline state, and many of them jury-rigged to make use of still-viable fragments of technological suites whose other parts didn't survive their encounter with one bottleneck or another. In places where circumstances permit, relatively advanced technological suites can remain in working order long after the civilization that created them has perished—consider the medieval cities that got their water from carefully maintained Roman aqueducts a millennium after Rome's fall—while other systems operate at far simpler levels, and other regions and communities get by with much simpler technological suites.

All this has immediate practical importance for those of us who happen to live in a civilization that's skidding down the curve of its decline and fall. In such a time, as noted above, one critical task is to identify the technological suites that will still be viable in the aftermath of the decline, and shift as much vital infrastructure as possible over to depend on those suites rather than on those that won't survive the decline. In terms of the charts above, that involves identifying those technological suites that will still be in category A when the lines stop shifting up and to the left, figuring out how to work around any bottleneck technologies that might otherwise cripple them, and get the necessary knowledge into circulation among those who might be able to use it, so that access to information doesn't become a bottleneck of its own.

That sort of analysis, triage, and salvage is among the most necessary tasks of our time, especially for those who want to see viable technologies survive the end of our civilization, and it's being actively hindered by the insistence that the only possible positive attitude toward technology is sheer blind faith. For connoisseurs of irony, it's hard to think of a more intriguing spectacle.

ৎ৪ৎ

The blind faith in technology just anatomized has any number of odd effects in today's culture, but one of the strangest is the blindness to the downside that clamps down on the collective imagination of our time once people become convinced that something or other is the wave of the future. It doesn't matter in the least how many or obvious the warning signs are, or how many times the same tawdry drama has been enacted. Once some shiny new gimmick gets accepted as the next glorious step in the invincible march of progress, most people lose the ability to imagine that the wave of the future might just do what waves generally do: that is to say, crest, break, and flow back out to sea, leaving debris scattered on the beach in its wake.

It so happens that I grew up in the middle of just such a temporary wave of the future, in the south Seattle suburbs in the 1960s, where every third breadwinner worked for Boeing. The wave in question was the supersonic transport, SST for short: a jetliner that would fly faster than sound, cutting hours off long flights. The inevitability of the SST was an article of faith locally, and not just because Boeing was building one; an Anglo-French consortium was in the lead with the Concorde, and the Soviets were working on the Tu-144, but the Boeing 2707 was expected to be the biggest and baddest of them all, a 300-seat swing-wing plane that was going to make commercial supersonic flight an everyday reality.

Long before the 2707 had even the most ghostly sort of reality, you could buy model kits of the plane, complete with Pan Am decals, at every hobby store in the greater Seattle area. For that matter, if you took Interstate 5 south from downtown Seattle past the sprawling Boeing plant just outside of town during those years, you'd see the image of the 2707 on the wall of one of the huge assembly buildings, a big delta-winged shape in white and gold winging its way through the imagined air toward the gleaming future in which so many people believed back then.

There was, as it happened, a small problem with the 2707, a problem it shared with all the other SST projects; it made no economic sense at all. It was technically feasible but economically impractical, and it existed mostly as a way to pump government subsidies into Boeing's coffers. Come 1971, the well ran dry. Faced with gloomy numbers from the economists, worried calculations from environmental scientists, and a public not exactly enthusiastic about dozens of sonic booms a day rattling plates and cracking windows around major airports, Congress cut the project's funding.

That happened right when the US economy generally, and the notoriously cyclical airplane industry in particular, were hitting downturns. Boeing was Seattle's biggest employer in those days, and when it laid off employees en masse, the result was a local depression of legendary severity. You heard a lot of people in those days insisting that the US had missed out on the next aviation boom and Congress would have to hang its head in shame once Concordes and Tu-144s were hauling passengers all over the globe. Of course, that's not what happened; the Tu-144 flew a handful of commercial flights and then was grounded for safety reasons, and the Concorde lingered on, a technical triumph but an economic white elephant, until the last plane retired from service in 2003.

The same logic may well apply to the most loudly ballyhooed of the current round of waves of the future, the internet. The comparison may seem far-fetched, but then that's what supporters of the SST would have said if anyone had compared the Boeing 2707 to, say, the Zeppelin, another wave of the future that turned out to make too little economic sense to matter. Granted, the internet isn't currently supported by overt government subsidies, and it's also much more complex than the SST; if anything, it might be compared to the entire system of commercial air travel, which we still have with us for the moment. Nonetheless, a strong case can be made that the internet, like the SST, doesn't actually make economic sense. It's being propped up by a set of financial gimmickry with a distinct resemblance to smoke and mirrors, and when those go away—and they will—much of what makes the internet so central a part of pop culture will go away as well.

It's probably necessary to repeat here that the reasons for this are economic, not technical. Those of my readers who have tried to discuss the hard economic realities that will affect the internet in an age of economic contraction and environmental blowback, as I have, will have noticed that nearly everybody else wants to talk about issues of technical feasibility instead. Those issues are beside the point. No doubt it would be possible to make something like the internet technically feasible in a society on the far side of the Long Descent, but that doesn't matter. What matters is that the internet has to cover its operating costs, and it also has to compete with other ways of doing the things that the internet currently does.

It's a source of wry amusement to me that so many people seem to have forgotten that the internet doesn't actually do very much that's new. Long before the internet, people were reading the news, publishing essays and stories, navigating through unfamiliar neighborhoods, sharing images of kittens with their friends, ordering products from faraway stores for home delivery, looking at pictures of people with their clothes off, sending anonymous hate-filled messages to unsuspecting recipients, and doing pretty much everything else that they do on the internet today. For the moment, doing these things on the internet is cheaper and more convenient than the alternatives, and that's what makes the internet so popular. If that changes—if the internet becomes more costly and less convenient than other options—its current popularity will not last.

Let's start by looking at the costs. The price of monthly internet service, it probably needs to be pointed out, is not a reasonable measure of the cost of the internet as a whole. Talk to people who work in data centers, and you'll hear about trucks pulling up to the loading dock every single day to offload pallet after pallet of brand-new hard drives and other components, to replace those that will burn out that same day. You'll hear about power bills that would easily cover the electricity costs of a small city. You'll hear about many other costs as well. Data centers are not cheap to run, there are many thousands of them, and they're only one part of the vast infrastructure we call the internet—by many measures, the most gargantuan technological project in the history of our species.

Your monthly fee for internet service covers only a small portion of what the internet costs. Where does the rest come from? That depends on which part of the net we're discussing. The basic structure is paid for by internet service providers (ISPs), who recoup part of the costs from your monthly fee, part from the much larger fees paid by big users, and part from advertising. Content providers use some mix of advertising, pay-to-play service fees, sales of goods and services, packaging and selling your personal data to advertisers and government agencies, and new money from investors and loans to meet their costs. The ISPs routinely make a modest profit on the deal, but many of the content providers do not. Amazon may be the biggest retailer on the planet, for example, and its cash flow has soared in recent years, but its expenses have risen just as fast, and it rarely makes a profit. Many other content provider firms, including fish as big as Twitter, rack up big losses year after year.

How do they stay in business? A combination of vast amounts of investment money and ultracheap debt. That's very common in the early decades of a new industry, though it's been made a good deal easier by the Fed's policy of next-to-zero interest rates. Investors who dream of buying stock in the next Microsoft provide venture capital for internet startups, banks provide lines of credit for existing firms, the stock and bond markets snap up paper of various kinds churned out by internet businesses, and all that money goes to pay the bills. It's a reasonable gamble for the investors; they know perfectly well that a great many of the firms they're funding will go belly up within a few years, but the few that don't either will be bought up at inflated prices by one of the big dogs of the online world or will figure out how to make money and then become big dogs themselves.

Notice, though, that this process has an unexpected benefit for ordinary internet users: a great many services are available for free because venture-capital investors and lines of credit are footing the bill for the time being. Boosting the number of page views and click-throughs is far more important for the future of an internet company these days than making a profit, and so the usual business plan is to provide plenty of free goodies to the public without worrying about the financial end of things. That's very convenient just now for internet users, but it fosters the illusion that the internet costs nothing.

As mentioned earlier, this sort of thing is very common in the early decades of a new industry. As the industry matures, markets become saturated, startups become considerably riskier, and venture capital heads for greener pastures. Once this happens, the companies that dominate the industry have to stay in business the old-fashioned way, by earning a profit, and that means charging as much as the market will bear, monetizing services that are currently free, and cutting service to the lowest level that customers will tolerate. That's business as usual, and it means the end of most of the noncommercial content that gives the internet so much of its current role in popular culture.

All other things being equal, in other words, the internet can be expected to follow the usual trajectory of a maturing industry, becoming more expensive, less convenient, and more tightly focused on making a quick buck with each passing year. Governments have already begun to tax internet sales, removing one of the core "stealth subsidies" that boosted the internet at the expense of other retail sectors, and taxation of the internet will only increase as cash-starved officials contemplate the tidal waves of money sloshing back and forth online. None of these changes will kill the internet, but they'll slap limits on the more utopian fantasies currently burbling about the web and provide major incentives for individuals and businesses to back away from the internet and do things in the real world instead.

Then there's the increasingly murky world of online crime, espionage, and warfare, which promises to push very hard in the same direction in the years ahead.[2] I think most people are starting to realize that on the internet, there's no such thing as secure data, and the costs of conducting business online these days include a growing risk of having your credit cards stolen, your bank accounts looted, your identity borrowed for any number of dubious purposes, and the files on your computer encrypted without your knowledge, so that you can be forced to pay a ransom for their release, or what have you.

Online crime is one of the few fields of criminal endeavor in which raw cleverness is all you need to make out, as the saying goes, like a bandit. In the years ahead, as a result, the internet may look less like an information superhighway and more like one of those grim inner city streets where not even the muggers go alone. Trends in online espionage and warfare are harder to track, but either or both could become a serious burden on the internet as well.

Online crime, espionage, and warfare aren't going to kill the internet, any more than the ordinary maturing of the industry will. Rather, they'll lead to a future in which costs of being online are very often greater than the benefits, and the internet is by and large endured rather than enjoyed. They'll also help drive the inevitable rebound away from the net. That's one of those things that always happens and always blindsides the cheerleaders of the latest technology: a few decades into its lifespan, people start to realize that they liked the old technology better, thank you very much, and go back to it. The rebound away from the internet has already begun, and will only become more visible as time goes on, making a great many claims about the future of the internet look as absurd as those 1950s articles insisting that, in the future, every restaurant would inevitably be a drive-in.

To be sure, the resurgence of live theater in the wake of the golden age of movie theaters didn't end cinema, and the revival of bicycling in the aftermath of the automobile didn't make cars go away. In the same way, the renewal of interest in offline practices and technologies isn't going to make the internet go away. It's simply going to accelerate the shift of avant-garde culture away from an increasingly bleak, bland, unsafe, and corporate- and government-controlled internet and into alternative venues. That won't kill the internet, though once again it will put a stone marked R.I.P. atop the grave of the giddier fantasies that have clustered around today's net culture.

All other things being equal, in fact, there's no reason why the internet couldn't keep on its present course for years to come. Under those circumstances, it would shed most of the features that make it popular with today's avant-garde and become one more centralized, regulated, vacuous mass medium, packed to the bursting point with corporate advertising and lowest-common-denominator content, with dissenting voices and alternative culture shut out or shoved into corners where nobody ever looks. That's the normal trajectory of an information technology in today's industrial civilization, after all; it's what happened with radio and television in their day, as the gaudy and grandiose claims of the early years gave way to the crass commercial realities of the mature forms of each medium.

But all other things aren't equal, of course.

Radio and television, like most of the other familiar technologies that define life in a modern industrial society, were born and grew to maturity in an expanding economy. The internet, by contrast, was born during the last great blowoff of the petroleum age—the last decades of the twentieth century, during which the world's industrial nations took the oil reserves that might have cushioned the transition to sustainability and blew them instead on one last orgy of over-the-top conspicuous consumption. It's coming to maturity, in turn, in the early years of an age of economic contraction and ecological blowback.

The rising prices, falling service quality, and relentless monetization of a maturing industry, together with the increasing burden of online crime and the inevitable rebound away from internet culture, will thus be hitting the internet in a time when the global economy no longer has the slack it once did, and the immense costs of running the internet in anything like its present form will have to be drawn from a pool of real wealth that has many other demands on it. What's more, quite a few of those other demands will be far more urgent than the need to provide consumers with a convenient way to send pictures of kittens to their friends. That stark reality will add to the pressure to monetize internet services and will provide incentives to those who choose to send their kitten pictures by other means.

It's crucial to remember here, as noted above, that the internet is simply a cheaper and more convenient way of doing things that people were doing long before the first website went live, and a big part of the reason why it's cheaper and more convenient right now is that internet users are being subsidized by the investors and venture capitalists who are funding the internet industry. That's not the only subsidy on which the internet depends, though. Along with the rest of industrial society, it's also subsidized by half a billion years of concentrated solar energy in the form of fossil fuels. As those dwindle, the vast inputs of energy, labor, raw materials, industrial products, and other forms of wealth that sustain the internet will become increasingly expensive to provide, and ways of distributing kitten pictures that don't require the same inputs will prosper in the resulting competition.

There are also crucial issues of scale. Most pre-internet communications and information technologies scale down extremely well. A community of relatively modest size can have its own public library, its own small press, its own newspaper, and its own radio station running local programming, and could conceivably keep all of these functioning and useful even if the rest of humanity suddenly vanished from the map. Internet technology doesn't have that advantage.

Internet fans boast about the net's scalability, but that analysis makes sense only if you ignore the constellations of server farms needed to keep it supplied with the content that makes it popular and the archipelagoes of mines and factories that supply its insatiable appetite for hardware. Take those into account, and the internet makes sense only if you've got a modern global economy to back it up. A simple radio transmitter and receiver can be built by any competent hobbyist in a basement workshop out of readily available raw materials, and the fourteenth-century technology of printing presses and card catalogs needed for print media is even more accessible to local-scale manufacture; try making a memory chip or a central processing unit under the same conditions. On the scale of a small community, the benefits of using internet technology instead of simpler equivalents wouldn't come close to justifying the vast additional cost.

Now, of course, the world of the future isn't going to consist of a single community surrounded by desolate wasteland. That's one of the reasons why the demise of the internet won't happen all at once. Telecommunications companies serving some of the more impoverished parts of rural America are already letting their networks in those areas degrade, since income from customers doesn't cover the costs of maintenance. That's a harbinger of the internet's future—an uneven decline punctuated by local and regional breakdowns, some of which will be fixed for a while.

That said, it's quite possible that there will still be an internet of some sort fifty years from now. It will connect government agencies, military units, defense contractors, and the handful of universities that survive the approaching implosion of the academic industry here in the US, and it may provide email and a few other services to the very rich, but it will otherwise have a lot more in common with the original DARPAnet than with the 24/7 virtual cosmos imagined by today's more gullible netheads.

Unless you're one of the very rich or an employee of one of the institutions just named, furthermore, you won't have access to the internet of 2065. You might be able to hack into it, if you have the necessary skills and are willing to risk a long stint in a labor camp, but unless you're a criminal or a spy working for the insurgencies flaring in the South or the mountain West, there's not much point to the stunt. If you're like most Americans in 2065, you'll likely live in Third World conditions without regular access to electricity or running water, and you've got other ways to buy things, find out what's going on in the world, find out how to get to the next town, and, yes, share kitten pictures with your friends. What's more, in a deindustrializing world, those other ways of doing things will be cheaper, more resilient, and more useful than reliance on the baroque intricacies of a vast computer net.

Exactly when the last vestiges of the internet will sputter to silence is a harder question to answer. Long before that happens, though, it will have lost its current role as one of the poster children of the myth of perpetual progress and turned back into what it really was all the time: a preposterously complex way to do things most people have always done by much simpler means, which only seemed to make sense during that very brief interval of human history when fossil fuels were abundant and cheap.

❦

The trajectory of the internet on the way to the deindustrial dark ages is by no means unique, any more than the internet is. A great many other elements of everyday life in today's North America will fade out in the same uneven but relentless way, and these include such essential services as electricity and running water.

The electrical grid and the assorted systems that send potable water flowing out of faucets are so basic to the rituals of everyday life in today's America that their continued presence is taken for granted. At most, it's conceivable that individuals might choose not to connect to them; there's a certain amount of talk about off-grid living here and there in the alternative media, for example. That people who want these things might not have access to them, though, is pretty much unthinkable.

Meanwhile, as I write these words, tens of thousands of residents of Detroit and Baltimore are in the process of losing their access to water and electricity.[3]

The situation in both cities is much the same, and there's every reason to think that identical headlines will shortly reference other cities around the nation. Not that many decades ago, Detroit and Baltimore were important industrial centers with thriving economies. Along with more than a hundred other cities in America's Rust Belt, they were thrown under the bus with the first wave of industrial offshoring in the 1970s. The situation for both cities has only gotten worse since that time, as the United States completed its long transition from a manufacturing economy producing goods and services to a bubble economy that mostly produces unpayable IOUs.

These days, the middle-class families whose tax payments propped up the expansive urban systems of an earlier day have long since moved out of town. Most of the remaining residents are poor, and the ongoing redistribution of wealth in America toward the very rich and away from everyone else has driven down the income of the urban poor to the point that many of them can no longer afford to pay their water and power bills. City utilities in Detroit and Baltimore have been sufficiently sensitive to political pressures that large-scale utility shutoffs have been delayed, but shifts in the political climate in both cities are bringing the delays to an end; water bills have increased steadily, more and more people have been unable to pay them, and the result is as predictable as it is brutal.

The debate over the Detroit and Baltimore shutoffs has followed the usual pattern, as one side wallows in bash-the-poor rhetoric while the other side insists plaintively that access to utilities is a human right. Neither side seems to be interested in talking about the broader context in which these disputes take shape. There are two aspects to that broader context, and it's a toss-up which is the more threatening.

The first aspect is the failure of the US economy to recover in any meaningful sense from the financial crisis of 2008. Now, of course, politicians from Obama on down have gone overtime grandstanding about the alleged recovery we're in. I invite any of my readers who bought into that rhetoric to try the following simple experiment. Go to your favorite internet search engine and look up how much the fracking industry has added to the US gross domestic product each year from 2009 to 2014. Now subtract that figure from the US gross domestic product for each of those years, and see how much growth there's actually been in the rest of the economy since the real estate bubble imploded.

What you'll find, if you take the time to do that, is that the rest of the US economy has been flat on its back gasping for air for the past five years. What makes this even more problematic is that the great fracking boom about which we've heard so much was never actually the game-changing energy revolution that its promoters claimed. It was simply another installment in the series of speculative bubbles that has largely replaced constructive economic activity in this country over the two decades or so just past.[4]

What's more, it's not the only bubble currently being blown, and it may not even be the largest. We've also got a second tech-stock bubble, with money-losing internet corporations racking up absurd valuations in the stock market while they burn through millions of dollars of venture capital; we've got a student loan bubble, in which billions of dollars of loans that will never be paid back have been bundled, packaged, and sold to investors just like all those no-doc mortgages were a decade ago; car loans are getting the same treatment; the real estate market is fizzing again in many urban areas as investors pile into another round of lavishly marketed property investments—well, I could go on for some time. It's entirely possible that if all the bubble activity were to be subtracted from the past five years or so of GDP, the result would show an economy in freefall.

Certainly that's the impression that emerges if you take the time to check out those economic statistics that aren't being systematically jiggered by the US government for PR purposes. The number of long-term unemployed in America is at an all-time high; roads, bridges, and other basic infrastructure is falling to pieces; measurements of US public health—generally considered a good proxy for the real economic condition of the population—are well below those of other industrial countries, heading toward Third World levels; abandoned shopping malls litter the landscape while major retailers announce one round of store closures after another. These are not things you see in an era of economic expansion, or even one of relative stability; they're markers of decline.

The utility shutoffs in Detroit and Baltimore are further symptoms of the same broad process of economic unraveling. It's true, as pundits in the media have been insisting since the story broke, that utilities get shut off for nonpayment of bills all the time. It's equally true that shutting off the water supply of 20,000 or 30,000 people all at once is pretty much unprecedented. Both cities, please note, have had very large populations of poor people for many decades now. Those who like to blame a "culture of poverty" for the tangled relationship between US governments and the American poor— and of course, that trope has been rehashed by some of the pundits just mentioned—haven't yet gotten around to explaining how the culture of poverty all at once inspired tens of thousands of people who had been paying their utility bills to stop doing so.

There are plenty of good reasons, after all, why poor people who used to pay their bills can't do so any more. Standard business models in the United States used to take it for granted that the best way to run the staffing dimensions of any company, large or small, was to have as many full-time positions as possible and to use raises and other practical incentives to encourage employees who were good at their jobs to stay with the company. That approach has been increasingly unfashionable in today's America, partly due to perverse regulatory incentives that penalize employers for offering full-time positions, partly to the emergence of attitudes in corner offices that treat employees as just another commodity. (I doubt it's any kind of accident that most corporations nowadays refer to their employment offices as "human resource departments." What do you do with a resource? You exploit it.)

These days, most of the jobs available to the poor are part-time, pay very little, and include nasty little clawbacks in the form of requirements that employees pay out of pocket for uniforms, equipment, and other things that employers used to provide as a matter of course. Meanwhile housing prices and rents are rising well above their post-2008 dip, and a great many other necessities are becoming more costly—inflation may be under control, or so the official statistics say, but anyone who's been shopping at the same grocery store for the past eight years knows perfectly well that prices kept on rising anyway.

So you've got falling incomes running up against rising costs for food, rent, and utilities, among other things. In the resulting collision, something's got to give, and for tens of thousands of poor Detroiters and Baltimoreans, what gave first was the ability to keep current on their water bills. Expect to see the same story playing out across the country as more people on the bottom of the income pyramid find themselves in the same situation. What you won't hear in the media, though it's visible enough if you know where to look and are willing to do so, is that people above the bottom of the income pyramid are also losing ground, being forced down toward economic nonpersonhood. From the middle classes down, everyone's losing ground.

That process doesn't continue much higher on the economic ladder than the upper middle class, to be sure. It's been pointed out repeatedly that over the past four decades or so, the distribution of wealth in America has skewed further and further out of balance, with the top twenty percent of incomes taking a larger and larger share at the expense of everybody else.[5] That's an important factor in bringing about the collision just described. Some thinkers on the radical fringes of society, which is the only place in the US you can talk about such things these days, have argued that the raw greed of the well-to-do is the sole reason why so many people lower down the ladder are being pushed further down still.

Scapegoating rhetoric of that sort is always comforting, because it holds out the promise—theoretically, if not practically—that something can be done about the situation. If only the thieving rich could be lined up against a convenient brick wall and removed from the equation in the time-honored fashion, the logic goes, people in Detroit and Baltimore could afford to pay their water bills! I suspect we'll hear such claims increasingly often as the years pass and more and more Americans find their access to familiar comforts and necessities slipping away. Simple answers are always popular in such times, not least when the people being scapegoated go as far out of their way to make themselves good targets for such exercises as the American rich have done in recent decades.

John Kenneth Galbraith's equation of the current US political and economic elite with the French aristocracy on the eve of revolution rings even more true than it did when he wrote it back in 1992, in the pages of *The Culture of Contentment*. The unthinking extravagances, the casual dismissal of the last shreds of *noblesse oblige*, the obsessive pursuit of personal advantages and private feuds without the least thought of the potential consequences, the bland inability to recognize that the power, privilege, wealth, and sheer survival of the aristocracy depended on the system that the aristocrats themselves were destabilizing by their actions—it's all there, complete with sprawling overpriced mansions that could just about double for Versailles. The urban mobs that played so large a role back in 1789 are warming up for their performances as I write these words. The only thing left to complete the picture is a few tumbrils and a guillotine, and those will doubtless arrive on cue.

The senility of the current US elite, as noted earlier, is a massive political fact in today's America. Still, it's not the only factor in play here. Previous generations of wealthy Americans recognized without too much difficulty that their power, prosperity, and survival depended on the willingness of the rest of the population to put up with their antics. Several times already in America's history, elite groups have allied with populist forces to push through reforms that sharply weakened the power of the wealthy elite, because they recognized that the alternative was a social explosion even more destructive to the system on which elite power depends.

I suppose it's possible that the people currently occupying the upper ranks of the political and economic pyramid in today's America are just that much more stupid than their equivalents in the Jacksonian, Progressive, and New Deal eras. Still, there's at least one other explanation to hand, and it's the second of the two threatening contextual issues mentioned earlier.

Until the nineteenth century, fresh running water piped into homes for everyday use was purely an affectation of the very rich in a few very wealthy and technologically adept societies. Sewer pipes to take dirty water and human wastes out of the house belonged in the same category. This wasn't because nobody knew how plumbing works—the Romans had competent plumbers, for example, and water faucets and flush toilets were to be found in Roman mansions of the imperial age. The reason those same things weren't found in every Roman house was economic, not technical.

Behind that economic issue lay an ecological reality. White's law, as already noted, states that economic development is a function of energy per capita. For a society before the industrial age, the Roman Empire had an impressive amount of energy per capita to expend; control over the agricultural economy of the Mediterranean basin; modest inputs from sunlight, water, and wind; and a thriving slave industry fed by the expansion of Roman military power all boosted the capacity of Roman society to develop itself economically and technically. That's why rich Romans had running water and iced drinks in summer, while their equivalents in ancient Greece a few centuries earlier had to make do without either one.

Fossil fuels gave industrial civilization a supply of energy many orders of magnitude greater than any previous human civilization has had: a supply vast enough that the difference remains huge even after the vast expansion of population that followed the Industrial Revolution. As already noted, though, there are two difficulties with this otherwise sanguine picture. To begin with, fossil fuels are finite, nonrenewable resources; no matter how much handwaving is employed in the attempt to obscure this point, every barrel of oil, ton of coal, or cubic foot of natural gas that's burned takes the world one step closer to the point at which there will be no economically extractable reserves of oil, coal, or natural gas at all.

That's catch #1. Catch #2 is subtler, and considerably more dangerous. Oil, coal, and natural gas don't leap out of the ground on command. They have to be extracted and processed, and this takes energy. Companies in the fossil fuel industries have always targeted the deposits that cost less to extract and process, for obvious economic reasons. What this means, though, is that over time, a larger and larger fraction of the energy yield of oil, coal, and natural gas has to be put right back into extracting and processing oil, coal, and natural gas—and this leaves less and less for all other uses.

That's the vise that's tightening around the American economy these days. The great fracking boom, to the extent that it wasn't simply one more speculative gimmick aimed at the pocketbooks of chumps, was an attempt to make up for the ongoing decline of America's conventional oilfields by going after oil that was far more expensive to extract. The fact that none of the companies at the heart of the fracking boom ever turned a profit, even when oil brought more than $100 a barrel, gives some sense of just how costly shale oil is to get out of the ground.[6] The financial cost of extraction, though, is a proxy for the energy cost of extraction—the amount of energy, and of the products of energy, that had to be thrown into the task of getting a little extra oil out of marginal source rock.

Energy needed to extract energy, again, can't be used for any other purpose. It doesn't contribute to the energy surplus that makes economic development possible. As the energy industry itself takes a bigger bite out of each year's energy production, every other economic activity loses part of the fuel that makes it run. That, in turn, is the core reason why the American economy is on the ropes, America's infrastructure is falling to bits, and Americans in Detroit and Baltimore are facing a transition to Third World conditions, without electricity or running water.

I suspect, for what it's worth, that the shutoff notices being mailed to tens of thousands of poor families in those two cities are a good working model for the way that industrial civilization itself will wind down. It won't be sudden; for decades to come, there will still be people who have access to what Americans today consider the ordinary necessities and comforts of everyday life; there will just be fewer of them each year. Outside that narrowing circle, the number of economic nonpersons will grow steadily, one shutoff notice at a time.

As noted earlier in this book, the line of fracture between the senile elite and the internal proletariat—the people who live within a failing civilization's borders but receive essentially none of its benefits—eventually opens into a chasm that swallows what's left of the civilization. Sometimes the tectonic processes that pull the chasm open are hard to miss, but there are times when they're a good deal more difficult to sense in action, and this is one of these latter times. Listen to the whisper of the shutoff valve, and you'll hear tens of thousands of Americans being cut off from basic services the rest of us, for the time being, still take for granted.

8

THE DISSOLUTION
OF CULTURE

ALL THE CONVERGING CRISES TRACED OUT SO FAR IN THIS
book—the environmental disasters, the coming demographic
collapse, the implosion of political and economic institutions, the
failure of science and technology—have another kind of impact,
which focuses on culture. Sociologists argue about what culture is
and isn't, and a variety of competing definitions have been proposed
over the years. For the purposes of this exploration, though, a relatively simple definition will be most useful: a culture is the set of
narratives, concepts, and interpretations of the world that make a
given society make sense to the people who live in it.

Cultures, that is, are the inward dimension of a society, the
structures of the mind that define (and are defined by) the structures of matter that give a society its outward expression. A house,
let's say, is a particular kind of material object, but it's also a particular set of concepts with its own distinctive emotional loading.
Since that set of concepts differs from culture to culture, and even
among subgroups within a culture, what counts as a house depends
very much on who's doing the counting, and on what cultural and
subcultural frameworks they're bringing to the task.

Broadly speaking, a culture is viable when it succeeds in giving
meaning and direction to a society in the context of its environment.

A culture fails when it fails to do this. Any number of anthropological studies have sketched out what happens when a culture is unable to adapt to changed conditions; the short form is that the results are never good and can quite readily plunge into the extremes of human ghastliness. This is uncomfortably relevant to the theme of this book, because the major cultures of North America today are showing many of the signs of the failure to adapt just noted, and potent forces hardwired into today's industrial societies are pushing them steadily in that unwelcome direction.

To a remarkable extent, even the privileged classes of today's North American societies find their lives empty of meaning, and the stories our culture provides to make sense of their experiences simply aren't up to the task. What's more, the products and lifestyles our culture labels "more advanced," "more progressive," and the like are very often less satisfactory and less effective at meeting human needs than the allegedly more primitive products and lifestyles they replaced. To an extent not always recognized, today's technology fails systematically at meeting certain human needs, and that failure isn't due to a lack of complexity but an excess of it. The peak of technological complexity in our time thus might also be described as peak meaninglessness.

I'd like to take the time to unpack that phrase. In the most general sense, technologies can be divided into two broad classes, which we can respectively call tools and prosthetics. The difference is a matter of function. A tool expands human potential, giving people the ability to do things they couldn't otherwise do. A prosthetic, on the other hand, replaces human potential, doing something that under normal circumstances, people can do just as well for themselves. Most discussions of technology these days focus on tools, but the vast majority of technologies that shape the lives of people in a modern industrial society are not tools but prosthetics.

Prosthetics have a definite value, to be sure. Consider an artificial limb, the sort of thing on which the concept of technology-as-prosthetic is modeled. If you've lost a leg in an accident, say, an artificial leg is well worth having; it replaces a part of ordinary human potential that you don't happen to have any more, and enables you to do things that other people can do with their own legs. Imagine, though, that some clever marketer were to convince people to have their legs cut off so that they could be fitted for artificial legs. Imagine, furthermore, that the advertising for artificial legs became so pervasive, and so successful, that nearly everybody became convinced that human legs were hopelessly old-fashioned and ugly, and they rushed out to get their legs amputated so they could walk around on artificial legs.

Then, of course, the manufacturers of artificial arms got into the same sort of marketing, followed by the makers of sex toys. Before long you'd have a society in which most people were gelded quadruple amputees fitted with artificial limbs and rubber genitals, who spent all their time talking about the wonderful things they could do with their prostheses. Only in the darkest hours of the night, when the TV was turned off, might some of them wonder why it was that a certain hard-to-define numbness had crept into all their interactions with other people and the rest of the world.

In a very real sense, that's the way modern industrial society has reshaped and deformed human life for its more privileged inmates. Take any human activity, however humble or profound, and some clever marketer has found a way to insert a piece of technology in between the person and the activity, in a mode of intermediation that goes far beyond the merely financial. You can't simply bake bread—a simple, homely, pleasant activity that people have done themselves for thousands of years using their hands and a few simple handmade tools. No, you have to have a bread machine, into which you dump a prepackaged mix and some liquid, push a button, and stand there being bored while it does the work for you, if you don't farm out the task entirely to a bakery and get the half-stale industrially extruded product that passes for bread these days.

Of course, the bread machine manufacturers and the bakeries pitch their products to the clueless masses by insisting that nobody has time to bake their own bread any more. Ivan Illich pointed out a long time ago in *Energy and Equity* the logical fallacy here, which is that using a bread machine or buying from a bakery is faster only if you don't count the time you have to spend earning the money needed to pay for it, power it, provide it with overpriced prepackaged mixes, repair it, clean it, etc., etc., etc. Illich's discussion focused on automobiles rather than bread machines. He pointed out that if you take the distance traveled by the average American auto in a year, and divide that by the total amount of time spent earning the money to pay for the auto, fuel, maintenance, insurance, etc., plus all the other time eaten up by tending to the auto in various ways, the average American car goes about 3.5 miles an hour: about the same pace, that is, that an ordinary human being can walk.

If this seems reminiscent of the concept of externalities introduced earlier in this book, dear reader, it should. The claim that technology saves time and labor seems to make sense only if you ignore a whole series of externalities. In this case, the time you have to put into earning the money to pay for the technology, and into coping with whatever requirements, maintenance needs, and side effects the technology has, is an important externality that's carefully excluded from discussions of the value of technology. Have you ever noticed that the more "time-saving technologies" you bring into your life, the less free time you have? This is why—and it's also why the average medieval peasant worked shorter hours, had more days off, and kept a larger fraction of the value of his labor than you do.

Something else is being externalized by prosthetic technology, though. What are you doing, really, when you use a bread machine? To begin with, you're not baking bread. The machine is doing that. You're dumping a prepackaged mix and some water into a machine, closing the lid, pushing a button, and going away to do something else. Fair enough, but what is this "something else" that you're doing? In today's industrial societies, odds are you're going to go use another piece of prosthetic technology, which means that once again, you're not actually doing anything. A machine is doing something for you. You can push that button and walk away, but again, what are you going to do with your time? Use another machine?

The machines that industrial society uses to give this infinite regress somewhere to stop—televisions, video games, and computers hooked up to the internet—simply take the same process to its ultimate extreme. Whatever you think you're doing when you're sitting in front of one of these things, you're actually staring at little colored pictures on a screen and maybe pushing some buttons as well. All things considered, this is a profoundly boring activity, which is why the little colored pictures jump around all the time. That's to keep your nervous system so far off balance that you don't notice just how boring it is to spend hours at a time staring at little colored pictures on a screen.

I can't help but laugh when people insist that the internet is an information-rich environment. It's quite the opposite, actually. All you get from it is the very narrow trickle of verbal, visual, and auditory information that can squeeze through the digital bottleneck and turn into little colored pictures on a screen. The best way to experience this is to engage in a media fast—a period in which you deliberately cut yourself off from all electronic media for a week or more, preferably in a quiet natural environment. If you do that, you'll find that it can take two or three days, or even more, before your nervous system recovers far enough from the narrowing effects of the digital bottleneck that you can begin to tap in to the ocean of sensory information and sensual delight that surrounds you at every moment. It's only then, furthermore, that you can start to think your own thoughts and dream your own dreams, instead of just rehashing whatever the little colored pictures tell you.

A movement of radical French philosophers back in the 1960s, the Situationists, argued that modern industrial society is basically a scheme to convince people to hand over their own human capabilities to the industrial machine, so that imitations of those capabilities can be sold back to them at premium prices.[1] It was a useful analysis then, and it's even more useful now, when the gap between realities and representations has become even more drastic than it was. These days, as often as not, what gets sold to people isn't even an imitation of some human capability but an abstract representation of it, an arbitrary marker with only the most symbolic connection to what it represents.

This is one of the reasons why I think it's deeply mistaken to claim that Americans are materialistic. Americans are arguably the least materialistic people in the world. No actual materialist—no one who had the least appreciation for actual physical matter and its sensory and sensuous qualities—could stand the vile plastic tackiness of America's built environment and consumer economy for a fraction of a second. Americans don't care in the least about matter. They're happy to buy even the most ugly, uncomfortable, shoddily made, and absurdly overpriced consumer products you care to imagine, so long as they've been convinced that having those products symbolizes some abstract quality they want, such as happiness, freedom, sexual pleasure, or what have you.

Then they wonder in the darkest hours of the night, when the TV is off, why all the things that are supposed to make them happy and satisfied somehow never manage to do anything of the kind. Of course, there's a reason for that, too, which is that happy and satisfied people don't keep on frantically buying products in a quest for happiness and satisfaction. Still, the little colored pictures keep showing them images of people who are happy and satisfied because they guzzle the right brand of tasteless fizzy sugar water, and pay for the right brand of shoddily made half-disposable clothing, and keep watching the little colored pictures: that last above all else. "Tune in tomorrow" is the most important product that every media outlet sells, and they push it every minute of every day on every stop and key.

That is to say, between my fantasy of voluntary amputees eagerly handing over the cash for the latest models of prosthetic limbs, and the reality of life in a modern industrial society, the difference is simply in the less permanent nature of the alterations imposed on people here and now. It's easier to talk people into amputating their imaginations than it is to convince them to amputate their limbs. Fortunately, it's also a good deal easier to reverse the surgery.

What gives this even more importance than it would otherwise have, in turn, is that all this is happening in a society that's hopelessly out of touch with the realities that support its existence, and that relies on bookkeeping tricks and sheer fantasy to prop up the belief that it's headed somewhere other than history's well-used compost bin. The externalization of the mind and the imagination plays just as important a role in maintaining that fantasy as the externalization of costs—and the cold mechanical heart of the externalization of the mind and imagination is the mode of intermediation discussed here, the insertion of technological prosthetics into the space between the individual and the world.

⚛

Technology is not the only thing that slips into that vulnerable space, though. Abstract concepts have the same function. In both cases, that process of insertion begins with sheer necessity—human beings use abstractions to understand the world in much the same way they use tools to shape the world, and much of what counts as being human can be traced back to one or the other of these two deeply ingrained habits—but both processes can become pathological when they are used not to adapt to reality but to evade it.

Let's start with the basics. Human beings everywhere use abstract categories and the words that denote them as handles by which to grab hold of unruly bundles of experience. We do it far more often, and far more automatically, than most of us ever notice. It's only under special circumstances—waking up at night in an unfamiliar room, for example, and finding that the vague somethings around us take a noticeable amount of time to coalesce into ordinary furniture—that the mind's role in assembling the fragmentary data of sensation into the objects of our experience comes to light.[2]

When you look at a tree, for example, it's common sense to think that the tree is sitting out there and your eyes and mind are just passively receiving a picture of it, in much the same sense that it's common sense to think that the sun revolves around the Earth. In fact, as philosophers and researchers into the psychophysics of sensation both showed a long time ago, what happens is that you get a flurry of fragmentary sense data—green, brown, line, shape, high contrast, low contrast—and your mind constructs a tree out of it, using your subjective tree concept (as well as a flurry of related concepts such as "leaf," "branch," "bark," and so on) as a template. You do that with everything you see. The reason you don't notice yourself doing it is that it was the very first thing you learned how to do, as a newborn infant, and you've practiced it so often you don't have to think about it anymore.

You do the same thing with every representation of a sensory object. Let's take visual art for an example. Back in the 1880s, when the Impressionists first started displaying their paintings, it took many people a real effort to learn how to look at them, and a great many never managed the trick at all. Among those who did, though, it was quite common to hear comments about how this or that painting had taught them to see a landscape, or what have you, in a completely different way. That wasn't just hyperbole: the Impressionists had learned how to look at things in a way that brought out features of their subjects that other people in late-nineteenth-century Europe and America had never gotten around to noticing, and they highlighted those things in their paintings so forcefully that the viewer had to notice them.[3]

The relation between words and the things they denote is thus much more complex, and much more subjective, than most people ever quite get around to realizing. That's challenging enough when we're talking about objects of immediate experience, where the concept in the observer's mind has the job of fitting fragmentary sense data into a pattern that can be verified by other forms of sense data:

in the example of the tree, by walking up to it and confirming by touch that the trunk is in fact where the sense of sight said it was. It gets far more difficult when the raw material that's being assembled by the mind consists of concepts rather than sensory data: when, let's say, you move away from your neighbor Joe, who can't find a job and is about to lose his house, start thinking about all the people in town who are in a similar predicament, and end up dealing with abstract concepts such as unemployment, poverty, distribution of wealth, and so on.

Difficult or not, we all do this, all the time. There's a common notion that dealing in abstractions is the hallmark of the intellectual, but that puts things almost exactly backwards. It's the ordinary unreflective person who thinks in vague abstract generalizations most of the time, while the serious thinker's task is to work back from the abstract category to the raw sensory data on which it's based. That's what the Impressionists did: staring at a snowbank as Monet did until he could see the rainbow play of colors behind the surface impression of featureless white, and then painting the colors into the representation of the snowbank so that the viewer was shaken out of the trance of abstraction ("snow" = "white") and saw the colors too—first in the painting and then when looking at actual snow.

Human thinking, and human culture, thus dance constantly between the concrete and the abstract, or to use a slightly different terminology, between immediate experience and a galaxy of forms that reflect experience back in mediated form. It's a delicate balance: too far into the immediate and experience disintegrates into fragmentary sensation; too far from the immediate and experience vanishes into an echo chamber of abstractions mediating one another. The most successful and enduring creations of human culture have tended to be those that maintain the balance. Representational painting is one of those; another is literature. Read the following passage closely:

Eastward the Barrow-downs rose, ridge behind ridge into the morning, and vanished out of eyesight into a guess: it was no more than a guess of blue and a remote white glimmer blending with the hem of the sky, but it spoke to them, out of memory and old tales, of the high and distant mountains.[4]

By the time you finished reading it, you likely had a very clear sense of what Frodo Baggins and his friends were seeing as they looked off to the east from the hilltop behind Tom Bombadil's house. So did I, as I copied the sentence, and so do most people who read that passage—but no two people see the same image, because the image each of us sees is compounded out of bits of our own remembered experiences. For me, the image that comes to mind has always drawn heavily on the view eastwards from the suburban Seattle neighborhoods where I grew up, across the rumpled landscape to the stark white-topped rampart of the Cascade Mountains. I know for a fact that that wasn't the view that Tolkien himself had in mind when he penned that sentence. I suspect he was thinking of the view across the West Midlands toward the Welsh mountains, which I've never seen, and I wonder what it must be like for someone to read that passage whose concept of ridges and mountains draws on childhood memories of the Urals, the Andes, or Australia's Great Dividing Range instead.

That's one of the ways that literature takes the reader through the mediation of abstractions back around to immediate experience. If I ever do have the chance to stand on a hill in the West Midlands and look off toward the Welsh mountains, Tolkien's words are going to be there with me, pointing me toward certain aspects of the view I might not otherwise have noticed, just as they shaped my childhood sense of the hills and mountains of Washington State. It's the same trick the Impressionists managed with a different medium: stretching the possibilities of experience by representing (literally re-presenting) the immediate in a mediated form.

Now think about what happens when that same process is hijacked, using modern technology, for the purpose of marketing.

That's what advertising does, and more generally what the mass media do. Think about the fast-food company that markets its product under the slogan "I'm loving it," complete with all those images of people sighing with post-orgasmic bliss as they ingest some artificially flavored and colored gobbet of processed pseudo-food. Are they actually loving it? Of course not. They're hack actors being paid to go through the motions of loving it, so that the imagery can be drummed into your brain, where it drowns out your own recollection of the experience of not loving it. The goal of the operation is to keep you away from immediate experience, in a haze of abstractions, so that a deliberately distorted mediation can be put in its place.

You can do that with literature and painting, by the way. You can do it with any form of mediation, but it's a great deal more effective with modern visual media because those latter short-circuit the journey back to immediate experience. You see the person leaning back with the sigh of bliss after he takes a bite of pasty bland bun and tasteless gray mystery-meat patty, and you see it over and over and over again. If you're like most Americans, and spend four or five hours a day staring blankly at little colored images on a glass screen, a very large fraction of your total experience of the world consists of this sort of thing: distorted imitations of immediate experience, intended to get you to think about the world in ways that immediate experience won't justify.

The externalization of the human mind and imagination via the modern mass media has no shortage of problematic features, but the one I want to talk about here is the way that it feeds the habit, pervasive in modern industrial societies just now, of responding to serious crises by manipulating abstractions to make them invisible. That kind of thing is commonplace in civilizations on their way out history's exit door, but modern visual media make it an even greater problem in the present instance. These latter function as a prosthetic for the imagination, a device for replacing the normal image-making functions of the human mind with electromechanical equivalents. What's more, you don't control the prosthetic imagination. Governments and corporations control it, and use it to shape your thoughts and behavior in ways that aren't necessarily in your best interests.

The impact of the prosthetic imagination on the crisis of our time is almost impossible to overstate. I wonder, for example, how many of my readers have noticed just how pervasive references to science fiction movies and TV shows have become in discussions of the future of technology. My favorite example just now is the replicator, a convenient gimmick from the *Star Trek* mass media franchise: you walk up to it and order something, and the replicator pops what you want into being out of nothing.

It's hard to think of a better metaphor for the way that people in the privileged classes of today's industrial societies like to think of the consumer economy. It's also hard to think of anything that's further removed from the realities of the consumer economy. The replicator is the ultimate wet dream of externalization: it has no supply chains, no factories, no smokestacks, no toxic wastes, just whatever product you want any time you happen to want it. It's probably no accident that inevitably, whenever I've had conversations with people who think that 3-D printers are the solution to everything, they've dragged *Star Trek* replicators into the discussion.

3-D printers are not replicators. Their supply chains and manufacturing costs include smokestacks, outflow pipes, toxic-waste dumps, sweatshopped factories, and open-pit mines worked by slave labor, and the social impacts of their widespread adoption would include another wave of mass technological unemployment—remember, it's only in the imaginary world of economic propaganda that people who lose their jobs due to automation automatically get new jobs in some other field. In the immediate world, the one we actually inhabit, that's become vanishingly rare. As long as people look at 3-D printers through minds full of little pictures of *Star*

Trek replicators, though, those externalized ecological and social costs are going to be invisible to them.

That, in turn, defines the problem with the externalization of the human mind and imagination: no matter how frantically you manipulate abstractions, the immediate world is still what it is, and it can still clobber you. Externalizing something doesn't make it go away. It just guarantees that you won't see it in time to do anything but suffer the head-on impact. A culture that shoves all its problems out of sight by way of various modes of externalization and intermediation thus guarantees that those problems will not be solved. The question that remains is what will replace the culture of externalization as it finally collapses, and what kind of narratives will appeal to those who have finally gotten around to realizing that they aren't loving it and never were.

༺☯༻

One uncommonly clear glimpse at the narratives that may shape meaning in the impending dark age appeared in a news story from 1997 about the spread of secret stories among homeless children in Florida's Dade County.[5] These aren't your ordinary children's stories: they're myths in the making, a bricolage of images from popular religion and folklore torn from their original contexts and pressed into the service of a harsh new vision of reality.

God, according to Dade County's homeless children, is missing in action. Demons stormed heaven a while back, and God hasn't been seen since. The mother of Christ murdered her son and morphed into the terrifying Bloody Mary, a nightmare being who weeps blood from eyeless sockets and seeks out children to kill them. Opposing her is a mysterious spirit from the ocean who takes the form of a blue-skinned woman and who can protect children who know her secret name. The angels, though driven out of heaven, haven't given up; they carry on their fight against the demons from a hidden camp in the jungle somewhere outside Miami, guarded by friendly alligators who devour hostile intruders. The spirits of children who die in Dade County's pervasive gang warfare can go to the camp and join the war against the demons, so long as someone who knows the stories puts a leaf on their graves.

This isn't the sort of worldview you'd expect from people living in a prosperous, scientifically literate industrial society, but then the children in Dade County's homeless shelters don't fit that description in any meaningful sense. They live in conditions indistinguishable from those in the Third World's more hazardous regions, leading lives defined by poverty, hunger, substance abuse, shattered families, constant uncertainty, and lethal violence dispensed at random. If, as William Gibson suggested, the future is already here, just not evenly distributed, they're the involuntary early adopters of a future very few people want to think about just now.[6]

The transformations that inspired the "secret stories," after all, have uncomfortable parallels in the processes that unfold as a civilization descends into a dark age. Over and over again, in the twilight of one civilization after another, something snaps the thread that connects past to present, and allows the accumulated knowledge of an entire civilization to fall into oblivion. That failure of transmission can be seen at work in those homeless children of Dade County, whispering strange stories to one another in the night.

Arnold Toynbee, whose ideas have been cited repeatedly in this book, proposed that the most important factor that makes a rising civilization work is mimesis—the universal human habit by which people imitate the behavior and attitudes of those they admire.[7] As long as the political class of a civilization can inspire admiration and affection from those below it, the civilization thrives, because the shared sense of values and purpose generated by mimesis keeps the pressures of competing class interests from tearing it apart.

Civilizations fail, in turn, because their political classes lose the ability to inspire mimesis, and this happens in turn because members of the elite become so fixated on maintaining their own power and privilege that they stop doing an adequate job of addressing the problems facing their society. As those problems spin out of control, the political class loses the ability to inspire and settles instead for the ability to dominate. This in turn becomes one of the forces that drives the emergence of the internal proletariat, the increasingly sullen underclass that still provides the political class with its cannon fodder and labor force but no longer sees anything to admire or emulate in those who order it around.

It can be an unsettling experience to read American newspapers or wide-circulation magazines from before 1960 or so with eyes sharpened by Toynbee's analysis. Most newspapers in those days included a feature known as the society pages, which chronicled the social and business activities of the well-to-do, and those were read, with a sort of fascinated envy, very far down the social pyramid. Established figures of the political and business world were treated with a degree of effusive respect you won't find in today's media, and even those who hoped to shoulder aside this politician or that businessman rarely dreamed of anything more radical than filling the same positions themselves. Nowadays? Watching politicians, businesspeople, and celebrities get dragged down by some wretched scandal or other is this nation's most popular spectator sport.

That's what happens when mimesis breaks down. The failure to inspire has disastrous consequences for the political class—when the only things left that motivate people to seek political office are cravings for power or money, you've pretty much guaranteed that the only leaders you'll get are the sort of incompetent hacks who dominate today's political scene in the United States and elsewhere—but I want to concentrate for a moment on the effects on the other end of the spectrum. The failure of the political class to inspire mimesis in the rest of society doesn't mean that mimesis goes away. The habit of imitation is as universal among humans as it is among other social primates. The question becomes this: what will inspire mimesis among the internal proletariat? What will they use as the templates for their choices and their lives?

That's a crucial question, because it's not just social cohesion that depends on mimesis. The survival of the collective knowledge of a society—the thread connecting past with present I mentioned earlier—also depends on the innate habit of imitation. In most human societies, children learn most of what they need to know about the world by imitating parents, older siblings, and the like, and in the process the skills and knowledge base of the society are passed on to each new generation. Complex societies like ours do the same thing in a less straightforward way, but the principle is still the same. Back in the day, what motivated so many young people to fiddle with chemistry sets? More often than not, mimesis—the desire to be just like a real scientist, making real discoveries—and that was reasonable in the days when a significant fraction of those young people could expect to grow up to be real scientists.

That still happens, but it's less and less common these days, and for those who belong to the rapidly expanding underclass of American society, the sort of mimesis that might lead to a career in science isn't even an option. A great many of the children in Dade County's homeless shelters won't live to reach adulthood, and they know it. Those who do manage to dodge the stray bullets and the impact of collapsing public health, by and large, will spend their days in the crumbling, crowded warehouse facilities that substitute for schools in this country's poorer neighborhoods, where maybe half of each graduating high-school class comes out functionally illiterate. Their chances of getting a decent job of any kind weren't good even before the global economy started unraveling, and let's not even talk about those chances now.

When imitating the examples offered by the privileged becomes a dead end, in other words, people find other examples to imitate. That's one of the core factors, I'm convinced, behind the collapse of the reputation of the sciences in contemporary American society, which is so often bemoaned by scientists and science educators, and has been analyzed from a different angle in a previous chapter. Neil DeGrasse Tyson, say, may rhapsodize about the glories of science, but what exactly do those glories have to offer children huddling in an abandoned house in some down-at-heels Miami suburb, whose main concerns are finding ways to get enough to eat and stay out of the way of the latest turf war between the local drug gangs?

Now, of course, there's been a standard knee-jerk answer to such questions for the past century or so. That answer was that science and technology would eventually create such abundance that everyone in the world would be able to enjoy a middle-class lifestyle and its attendant opportunities. That same claim can still be heard nowadays, though it's grown shrill of late after repeated disconfirmation. In point of fact, for the lower eighty percent of Americans by income, the zenith of prosperity was reached in the third quarter of the twentieth century, and it's all been downhill from there.[8] This isn't an accident. What the rhetoric of progress through science misses is that the advance of science may have been a necessary condition for the boom times of the industrial age, but it was never a sufficient condition in itself.

The other half of the equation, of course, was the resource base on which industrial civilization depended. Three centuries ago, as industrialism got under way, it could draw on vast amounts of cheap, concentrated energy in the form of fossil fuels, which had been stored up in the Earth's crust over the previous half billion years or so. It could draw on equally huge stocks of raw materials of various kinds, and it could also make use of a biosphere whose capacity to absorb pollutants and other environmental insults hadn't yet been overloaded to the breaking point by human activity. None of those conditions still obtain, and the popular insistence that the economic abundance of the recent past must inevitably be maintained in the absence of the material conditions that made it possible—well, let's just say that makes a tolerably good example of faith-based thinking.

Thus Tyson is on one side of the schism Toynbee traced out, and the homeless children of Dade County and their peers and soon-to-be-peers elsewhere in America and the world are on the other. He may denounce superstition and praise reason and science until the cows come home, but again, what possible relevance does that have for those children? His promises are for the privileged, not for them. Whatever benefits further advances in technology might still have to offer will go to the dwindling circle of those who can still afford such things, not to the poor and desperate. Of course, that simply points out another way of talking about Toynbee's schism. Tyson thinks he lives in a progressing society, while the homeless children of Dade County know that they live in a collapsing one.

As the numbers shift toward the far side of that dividing line, and more and more Americans find themselves struggling to cope with a new and unwelcome existence in which talk about progress and prosperity amounts to a bad joke, the failure of mimesis—as in the fallen civilizations of the past—will become a massive social force. If the usual patterns play themselves out, there will be a phase when the leaders of successful drug gangs, the barbarian warbands of our decline and fall, will attract the same rock-star charisma that clung to Attila, Alaric, Genseric, and their peers. The first traces of that process are already visible. Just as young Romans in the fourth century adopted the clothes and manners of Visigoths,[9] it's not unusual to see the children of white families in the suburban upper middle class copying the clothing and culture of inner city gang members.

Eventually, to judge by past examples, this particular mimesis is likely to extend a great deal further than it has so far. It's when the internal proletariat turns on the failed dominant minority and makes common cause with the external proletariat—the people who live just beyond the borders of the falling civilization, who have been shut out from its benefits but burdened with many of its costs, and who will eventually tear the corpse of the civilization to bloody shreds—that civilizations make the harsh transition from decline to fall. That transition hasn't arrived yet for our civilization, and exactly when it will arrive is by no means a simple question, but the first whispers of its approach are already audible for those who know what to listen for and are willing to hear.

The age of charismatic warlords, though, is an epoch of transition rather than an enduring reality. The most colorful figures of that age, remade by the workings of the popular imagination, become the focus of folk memories and epic poetry in the ages that follow; Theodoric the Ostrogoth becomes Dietrich von Bern, and the war leader Artorius becomes the courtly King Arthur, taking their place alongside Gilgamesh, Arjuna, Achilles, Yoshitsune, and their many equivalents. In their new form as heroes of romance, they have a significant role to play as objects of mimesis, but it tends to be restricted to specific classes and finds a place within broader patterns of mimesis that draw from other sources.

And those other sources? What evidence we have—for the early stages of their emergence are rarely well-documented—suggests that they begin as strange stories whispered in the night, stories that deliberately devalue the most basic images and assumptions of a dying civilization to find meaning in a world those images and assumptions no longer explain.

Two millennia ago, to return to a familiar and useful example, the classical Greco-Roman world imagined itself seated comfortably at the summit of history. Religious people in that culture gloried in gods that had reduced primal chaos to permanent order and exercised a calm rulership over the cosmos. Those who rejected traditional religion in favor of rationalism—and there was no shortage of those, any more than there is today, because it's a common stage in the life of every civilization—rewrote the same story in secular terms, invoking various philosophical principles of order to fill the role of the gods of Olympus. Political thinkers defined history in the same terms, with the Roman Empire standing in for Jupiter Optimus Maximus. It was a very comforting way of thinking about the world, if you happened to be a member of the gradually narrowing circle of those who benefited from the existing order of society.

To those who formed the nucleus of the Roman Empire's internal proletariat, though, to slaves and the urban poor, that way of thinking communicated no meaning and offered no hope. The scraps of evidence that survived the fall of the Roman world suggest that a great many different stories got whispered in the darkness, but those stories increasingly came to center around a single narrative: a story in which the God who created everything came down to walk the Earth as a man, was condemned by a Roman court as a common criminal, and was nailed to a cross and left hanging there to die.

That's not the sort of worldview you'd expect from people living in a prosperous, philosophically literate classical society, but then the internal proletariat of the Roman world increasingly didn't fit that description. They were the involuntary early adopters of the post-Roman future, and they needed stories that would give meaning to lives defined by poverty, brutal injustice, uncertainty, and violence. That's what they found in Christianity, which denied the most basic assumptions of Greco-Roman culture in order to give value to the lived experience of those for whom the Roman world offered least.

This is what the internal proletariat of every collapsing civilization finds in whatever stories become central to the faith of the dark age to come. It's what Egyptians in the last years of the Old Kingdom found by abandoning the official Horus-cult in favor of the worship of Osiris, who walked the Earth as a man and suffered a brutal death; it's what many Indians in the twilight of the Guptas and many Chinese in the aftermath of the Han dynasty found by rejecting their traditional faiths in favor of reverence for the Buddha, who walked away from a royal lifestyle to live by his begging bowl and search for a way to leave the miseries of existence behind forever. Those and the many more examples like them inspired mimesis among those for whom the official beliefs of their civilizations had become a closed book, and they became the core around which new societies emerged.

The stories being whispered from one homeless Dade County child to another probably aren't the stories that will serve that same function as our civilization follows the familiar trajectory of decline and fall. That's my guess, at least, though, of course, I could be wrong. What those whispers in the night seem to be telling me is that the trajectory in question is unfolding in the usual way—that those who benefit least from modern industrial civilization are already finding meaning and hope in narratives that deliberately reject our culture's traditional faiths and overturn the most fundamental presuppositions of our age. As more and more people find themselves in similar straits, in turn, what are whispers in the night just now will take on greater and greater volume until they drown out the stories that most people take on faith today.

9

THE ROAD TO A RENAISSANCE

ALL THE POINTS COVERED IN THE FIRST EIGHT CHAPTERS OF this book point to a single hard conclusion: as industrial civilization heads out through history's exit turnstile, most of the world we know is going with it. It doesn't require any particular genius or prescience to grasp this, merely the willingness to recognize that if something is unsustainable, sooner or later it won't be sustained. Of course, that's the sticking point, because what can't be sustained at this point is the collection of wildly extravagant energy- and resource-intensive habits that used to pass for a normal lifestyle in the world's industrial nations and has recently become just a little less normal than it used to be.

Those lifestyles, and nearly all of what goes with them, existed in the first place only because a handful of the world's nations burned through half a billion years of fossil sunlight in a few short centuries, and stripped the planet of most of its other concentrated resource stocks into the bargain. That's the unpalatable reality of the industrial era. Despite the rhetoric of universal betterment that was brandished about so enthusiastically by the propagandists of the industrial order, there were never enough of any of the necessary resources to make that possible for more than a small fraction of the world's population or for more than a handful of generations.

Nearly all the members of our species who lived outside the industrial nations, and a tolerably large number who resided within them, were expected to carry most of the costs of reckless resource extraction and ecosystem disruption while receiving few if any of the benefits. They'll have plenty of company shortly. Industrial civilization is winding down, but its consequences are not, and people around the world for centuries and millennia to come will have to deal with the depleted and damaged planet our actions have left them. That's a bitter pill to swallow, and the likely aftermath of the industrial age won't do anything to improve the taste.

In this book, I've drawn on the downside trajectories of other failed civilizations to sketch out how that aftermath will probably play out here in North America. It's an ugly picture, and the only excuse I have for that unwelcome fact is that falling civilizations look like that. The question that remains, though, is what we're going to do about it all.

I should say up front that by "we" I don't mean some suitably photogenic collection of Hollywood heroes and heroines who just happen to have limitless resources and a bag of improbable inventions at their disposal. I don't mean a US government that has somehow shaken off the senility that affects all great powers in their last days and is prepared to fling everything it has into the quest for a sustainable future. Nor do I mean a coterie of gray-skinned aliens from Zeta Reticuli, square-jawed rapists out of Ayn Rand novels, or some other source of allegedly superior beings who can be counted upon to come swaggering onto the scene to bail us out of the consequences of our own stupidity. They aren't part of this conversation; the only people who are, just now, are the writer and the readers of this book.

One of the things that gives the question just raised an ironic flavor is that quite a few people are making what amounts to the same claim in far more grandiose terms than mine. I'm thinking here of the various proposals for a Great Transition of one kind or another being hawked at various points along the social and political spectrum these days. I suspect we're going to be hearing a lot more of those in the months and years immediately ahead, as the steady unraveling of the industrial age encourages people who want to maintain their current lifestyles to insist that they can have their planet and eat it too.

Part of the motivation behind the grand plans just mentioned is straightforwardly financial. One part of what drives the current unwillingness to deal with the future actually facing us is a panicked conviction on the part of a great many people that some way has to be found to keep living the same lifestyles they're living today. Another part of it, though, is the recognition on the part of a somewhat smaller but more pragmatic group of people that the panicked conviction in question could be turned into a sales pitch. Plenty of things have been put to work in the time-honored process of proving Ben Franklin's proverb about a fool and his money; hydrofracturing ("fracking") oil shales, tar sands, fuel ethanol, biodiesel, and large-scale wind power had their promoters and sucked up their share of government subsidies and private investment.

Now that most of these have fallen by the wayside, there'll likely be a wild scramble to replace them in the public eye with some other ghost of energy future. The nuclear industry will doubtless be in there. Nuclear power is one of the most durable subsidy dumpsters in modern economic life, and the nuclear industry has had to become highly skilled at slurping from the government teat, since nuclear power isn't economically viable otherwise; as already mentioned, no nation on Earth has been able to create or maintain a nuclear power program without massive ongoing government subsidies. No doubt we'll get plenty of cheerleading for fusion, satellite-based solar power, and other bits of high-end vaporware, too.

Still, I suspect the next big energy bubble is probably going to come from the green end of things. Over the past few years, there's been no shortage of claims that renewable resources can pick right up where fossil fuels leave off and keep the lifestyles of today's privileged middle classes intact. Those claims tend to be long on enthusiasm and cooked numbers and short on meaningful assessment, but then that same habit hasn't slowed up any of the previous bubbles. We can therefore expect to see a renewed flurry of claims that solar power must be sustainable because the sticker price has gone down, and similar logical non sequiturs. By the same logic, the internet must be sustainable if you can pay your monthly ISP bill by selling cute kitten photos on eBay. In both cases, the sprawling and almost entirely fossil-fueled infrastructure of mines, factories, supply chains, power grids, and the like has been left out of the equation, as though those don't have to be accounted for: typical of the blindness to whole systems that pervades so much of contemporary culture.

It's not enough for an energy technology to be green, in other words; it also has to work. It's probably safe to assume that that point is going to be finessed over and over again, in a galaxy of inventive ways, in the years immediately ahead. The point that next to nobody wants to confront is simple enough: if something is unsustainable, sooner or later it won't be sustained, and what's unsustainable in this case isn't simply fossil fuel production and consumption, it's the lifestyles that were made possible by the immensely abundant and highly concentrated energy supply we got from fossil fuels.

You can't be part of the solution if your lifestyle is part of the problem. I know that those words are guaranteed to make the environmental equivalent of limousine liberals gasp and clutch their pearls or their Gucci ties, take your pick, but there it is; it really is as simple as that. There are at least two reasons why that maxim needs to be taken seriously. On the one hand, if you're clinging to an unsustainable lifestyle in the teeth of increasingly strong economic and environmental headwinds, you're not likely to be able to spare the money, the free time, or any of the other resources you would need to contribute to a solution; on the other, if you're emotionally and financially invested in keeping an unsustainable lifestyle, you're likely to put preserving that lifestyle ahead of things that arguably matter more, like leaving a livable planet for future generations.

Is letting go of unsustainable lifestyles the only thing that needs to be done? Of course not. I'd like to suggest, though, that it's the touchstone or, if you will, the boundary that divides those choices that might actually do some good from those that are pretty much guaranteed to do no good at all. That's useful when considering the choices before us as individuals; it's at least as useful, if not more so, when considering the collective options we'll be facing in the months and years ahead, among them the flurry of campaigns, movements, and organizations that are already gearing up to exploit the crisis of our time in one way or another—and with one agenda or another.

An acronym that might well be worth using here is LESS, which stands for "Less Energy, Stuff, and Stimulation." That's a convenient summary of the changes that have to be made to move from today's unsustainable lifestyles to ways of living that will be viable when today's habits of absurd extravagance are fading memories. It's worth taking a moment to unpack the acronym a little further, and see what it implies.

"Less energy" might seem self-evident, but there's more involved here than just turning off unneeded lights and weatherstripping your windows and doors—though those are admittedly good places to start. A huge fraction of the energy consumed by a modern industrial society is used indirectly to produce, supply, and transport goods and services; an allegedly "green" technological device that's made from petroleum-based plastics and exotic metals taken from an open-pit mine in a Third World country, then shipped halfway around the planet to the air-conditioned shopping mall where you bought it, can easily have a carbon footprint substantially bigger than some simpler item that does the same thing in a less immediately efficient way. The blindness to whole systems mentioned earlier has to be overcome in order to make any kind of meaningful sense of energy issues.

"Less stuff" is equally straightforward on the surface, equally subtle in its ramifications. Now, of course, it's hardly irrelevant that ours is the first civilization in the history of the planet to have to create an entire industry of storage facilities to store the personal possessions that won't fit into homes that are also bigger than any other in history. That said, "stuff" includes a great deal more than the contents of your closets and storage lockers. It also includes infrastructure—the almost unimaginably vast assortment of technological systems on which the privileged classes of the industrial world rely for most of the activities of their daily lives. That infrastructure was made possible only by the deluge of cheap abundant energy our species briefly accessed from fossil fuels. As what's left of the world's fossil fuel supply moves deeper into depletion, the infrastructure that it created has been caught in an accelerating spiral of deferred maintenance and malign neglect; the less dependent you are on what remains, the less vulnerable you are to further systems degradation, and the more of what's left can go to those who actually need it.

"Less stimulation" may seem like the least important part of the acronym, but in many ways it's the most crucial point of all. These days most people in the industrial world flood their nervous systems with a torrent of electronic noise. As already noted, much of this is quite openly intended to manipulate their thoughts and feelings by economic and political interests. A great deal more has that effect, if only by drowning out any channel of communication that doesn't conform to the increasingly narrow intellectual tunnel vision of late industrial society. If you've ever noticed how much of what passes for thinking these days amounts to the mindless regurgitation of sound bites from the media, dear reader, that's why. What comes through the media—any media—is inevitably prechewed and predigested according to someone else's agenda. Those who are interested in thinking their own thoughts and making their own decisions, rather than bleating in perfect unison with the rest of the herd, might want to keep this in mind.

It probably needs to be said that very few of us are in a position to go whole hog with LESS all at once, though it's also relevant that all of us will end up there willy-nilly in due time, and depending on the rate at which the economic unraveling proceeds, that time may come a good deal sooner for some of us than for others. Outside of that grim possibility, "less" doesn't have to mean "none at all"—certainly not at first; for those who aren't caught in the crash, at least, there may yet be time to make a gradual transition toward a future of scarce energy and scarce resources. Still, I'd like to suggest that any proposed response to the crisis of our time that doesn't start with LESS simply isn't serious.

As already noted, I expect to see a great many nonserious proposals in the months and years ahead. Those who put maintaining their comfortable lifestyles ahead of other goals will doubtless have no trouble coming up with enthusiastic rhetoric and canned numbers to support their case. Not too far in the future, something or other will have been anointed as the shiny new technological wonder that will save us all, or more precisely, that will give the privileged classes of the industrial world a new set of excuses for clinging to some semblance of their current lifestyles for a little while longer. Mention the growing list of things that have previously occupied that hallowed but inevitably temporary status, and you can count on either busy silence or a flustered explanation why it really is different this time.

There may not be that many of us who get past the nonserious proposals, ask the necessary but unwelcome questions about the technosavior du jour, and embrace LESS while there's still time to do so a step at a time. I'm convinced, though, that those who manage these things are going to be the ones who make a difference in the shape the future will have on the far side of the crisis years ahead. Let go of the futile struggle to sustain the unsustainable, take the time and money and other resources that might be wasted in that cause and do something less foredoomed with them, and there's a lot that can still be done, even in the confused and calamitous time that's breaking over us right now.

᪥᪥᪥

Beyond LESS, the available paths diverge rapidly, and once again there are many serious options and many more nonserious ones. A great many people, for example, are interested only in answers that will allow them to keep on enjoying the absurd extravagance that passed, not too long ago, for an ordinary lifestyle among the industrial world's privileged classes. To such people I have nothing to say. Those lifestyles were possible only because the world's industrial nations burned through half a billion years of stored sunlight in a few short centuries and gave most of the benefits of that orgy of consumption to a relatively small fraction of their populations; now that easily accessible reserves of fossil fuels are running short, the party's over.

Yes, I'm quite aware that that's a controversial statement. Anyone who says that in public can count on fielding heated denunciations on a regular basis insisting that it just ain't so, that solar energy or fission or perpetual motion or *something* will allow the industrial world's privileged classes to keep on living the high life they're used to. Printer's ink being unfashionable these days, a great many electrons have been inconvenienced on the internet to proclaim that this or that technology must surely allow the comfortable to remain comfortable, no matter what the laws of physics, geology, or economics have to say. Of course, the only alternative energy sources that have been able to stay in business even in a time of sky-high oil prices are those that can count on gargantuan government subsidies to pay their operating expenses. Equally, the alternatives receive an even more gigantic "energy subsidy" from fossil fuels, which make them look much more economical than they otherwise would. Such reflections carry no weight with those whose sense of entitlement makes living with less unthinkable.

I'm glad to say that there's a fair number of people who've gotten past that unproductive attitude, who have grasped the severity of the crisis of our time and are ready to accept unwelcome change in order to secure a livable future for our descendants. They want to know how we can pull modern civilization out of its current power dive and perpetuate it into the centuries ahead. I have no answers for them, either, because that's not an option at this stage of the game. We're long past the point at which decline and fall can be avoided, or even ameliorated on any large scale.

A decade ago, a team headed by Robert Hirsch and funded by the Department of Energy released a study outlining what would have to be done in order to transition away from fossil fuels before they transitioned away from us.[1] What they found, to sketch out too briefly the findings of a long and carefully worded study, is that in order to avoid massive disruption, the transition would have to begin twenty years before conventional petroleum production peaked and plateaued. There's a certain irony in the fact that 2005, the year this study was published, was also the year when conventional petroleum production reached its current plateau; the transition would thus have had to begin in 1985—right about the time, that is, that the Reagan administration in the US and its clones overseas were scrapping the promising steps toward just such a transition.

A transition that got under way in 2005, in other words, would have been too late, and given the political climate, it probably would have been too little as well. Even so, it would have been a much better outcome than the one we got, in which politicians have spent the last eleven years insisting that we don't have to worry about depleting oilfields because fracking or tar sands or some other petroleum source is going to save us all. At this point, thirty years after the point at which we would have had to get started, it's all very well to talk about some sort of grand transition to sustainability, but the time when such a thing would have been possible came and went decades ago. We could have chosen that path, but we didn't, and insisting thirty-one years after the fact that we've changed our minds and want a different future than the one we chose isn't likely to make any kind of difference that matters.

So what options does that leave? In the minds of a great many people in North America, the option that comes reflexively to mind involves buying farmland in some isolated rural area and setting up a homestead in the traditional style. Many of the people who talk enthusiastically about this option, to be sure, have never grown any-thing more demanding than a potted petunia, know nothing about the complex and demanding arts of farming and livestock raising, and aren't in the sort of robust physical condition needed to handle the unremitting hard work of raising food without benefit of fossil fuels. Thus it's a safe guess that in most of these cases, heading out to the country is simply a comforting daydream that serves to distract attention from the increasingly bleak prospects so many people are facing in the age of unraveling upon us.

There's a long history behind such daydreams. Since colonial times, the lure of the frontier has played a huge role in the North American imagination, providing any number of colorful inkblots onto which fantasies of a better life could be projected. Those of my readers who are old enough to remember the aftermath of the Sixties counterculture, when a great many young people followed that dream to an assortment of hastily created rural communes, will also recall the head-on collision between middle-class fantasies of entitlement and the hard realities of rural subsistence farming that generally resulted. Some of the communes survived, though many more did not. That I know of, none of the surviving ones made it without a long and difficult period of readjustment in which romantic notions of easy living in the lap of nature got chucked in favor of a more realistic awareness of just how little in the way of goods and services a bunch of untrained ex-suburbanites can actually produce by their own labor.

In theory, that process of reassessment is still open. In practice, given the rising spiral of converging crises bearing down on indus-trial society right now, I'm far from sure it's an option for anyone who's not already out there on their own parcel of rural farmland. If you're already there, there's good reason to pursue the strategy that put you there. If your plans to get the necessary property, equipment, and skills are well advanced at this point, you may still be able to make it, but you'd probably better hustle. On the other hand, dear reader, if your rural retreat is still off there in the realm of daydreams and good intentions, it's almost certainly too late to do much about it, and where you are right now is probably where you'll be when the onrushing waves of crisis come surging up and break over your head.

That being the case, are there any options left other than hiding under the bed and hoping that the end will be relatively painless? As it happens, there are.

The point that has to be understood to make sense of those options is that in the real world, as distinct from Hollywood-style disaster fantasies, the impacts of decline and fall aren't uniform. They vary in intensity over space and time, and they impact particular systems of a falling civilization at different times and in different ways. If you're in the wrong place at the wrong time, and depend on the wrong systems to support you, your chances aren't good, but the places, times, and systems that take the brunt of the collapse aren't random. To some extent, those can be anticipated, and some of them can also be avoided.

Here's an obvious example. Right now, if your livelihood depends on the fracking industry, the tar sands industry, or any of the subsidiary industries that feed into those, your chances of getting through the next few years with your income intact are pretty minimal. As I write this, the layoffs and bankruptcies have already started, and can be expected to accelerate in the years ahead.[2] People in those industries who got to witness earlier booms and busts know this, and a good many of them are paying off their debts, settling any unfinished business they might have, and making sure they can cover a tank of gas or a plane ticket to get back home when the bottom falls out. People in those industries who don't have that experience to guide them and are convinced that nothing bad can actually happen to them are not doing these things and are likely to end up in a world of hurt when their turn comes.

They're not the only ones who would benefit right now from taking such steps. Most of North America's banking and finance industry has been flying high on bloated profits from an assortment of dubious fracking-related speculations, ranging from junk bonds through derivatives to exotic financial fauna such as volumetric production payments. Now that the goose that laid the golden eggs is bobbing feet upwards in a pond of used fracking fluid, the good times are coming to a sudden stop, and that means sharply reduced income for those junior bankers, brokers, and salespeople who can keep their jobs, and even more sharply reduced prospects for those who don't.

They've got plenty of company on the chopping block. The entire retail sector in the United States is already in trouble, with big-box stores struggling for survival and shopping malls being abandoned, and the future ahead promises more of the same, varying in intensity by region and a galaxy of other factors. Those who brace themselves for a hard landing now are a good deal more likely to make it than those who don't, and those who have the chance to jump to something more stable now would be well advised to make the leap.

For another example, the climate changes covered in Chapter Two are highly relevant to the shape of the immediate future. One thing that's been learned from the past few years of climate vagaries is that North America, at least, is shifting in exactly the way paleo-climatic data would suggest—that is to say, more or less the same way it did during warm periods over the past ten or twenty million years. The short form is that the Southwest and mountain West are getting baked to a crackly crunch under savage droughts; the eastern Great Plains, Midwest, and most of the South are being hit by a wildly unstable climate, with bone-dry dry years alternating with soggy wet ones; while the Appalachians and points eastward have been getting unsteady temperatures but reliable rainfall. Line up your subsistence strategy next to those climate shifts, and if you have the time and resources to relocate, you have some idea where to go.

All this presumes, of course, that what we're facing has much more in common with the crises faced by other civilizations on their way to history's compost heap than it does with the apocalyptic fantasies so often retailed these days as visions of the immediate future. There's no shortage of claims that it just ain't so, that everything I've just said is wasted breath because some vast and terrible whatsit will shortly descend on the whole world and squash us like bugs. There never has been a shortage of such claims. Meanwhile, all the dates by which the world was surely going to end have rolled past without incident, and the inevitable cataclysms have pulled one no-show after another, but the shrill insistence that something of the sort really will happen this time around has shown no sign of letting up. Nor will it, since the unacceptable alternative consists of taking responsibility for doing something about the future.

Now, of course, I've already pointed out that there's not much that can be done about the future on the largest scale. As the various factors traced out in this book head toward the red zone on the gauge, it's far too late in the day for much more than crisis management on a local and individual level. Even so, crisis management is a considerably more useful response than sitting on the sofa daydreaming about the grandiose project that's certain to save us or the grandiose cataclysm that's certain to annihilate us—though these latter options are admittedly much more comfortable in the short term.

What's more, there's no shortage of examples in relatively recent history to guide the sort of crisis management I have in mind. The tsunami of discontinuities that's rolling toward us out of the deep waters of the future may be larger than the waves that hit the Western world with the coming of the First World War in 1914, the Great Depression in 1929, or the Second World War in 1939, but from the perspective of the individual, the difference isn't as vast as it might seem. I'd encourage my readers to visit their local public libraries and pick up books about the lived experience of those earlier traumas. I'd also encourage those with elderly relatives who still remember the Second World War to sit down with them over a couple of cups of whatever beverage seems appropriate, and ask about what it was like on a day-to-day basis to watch their ordinary peacetime world unravel into chaos.

I've taken part in such conversations, and I've also done a great deal of reading about historical crises that have passed below the horizon of living memory. There are plenty of lessons to be gained from such sources, and one of the most important also used to be standard aboard sailing ships in the days before steam power. Sailors in those days had to go scrambling up the rigging at all hours and in all weathers to set, reef, or furl sails; it was not an easy job—imagine yourself up in the rigging of a tall ship in the middle of a howling storm at night, clinging to tarred ropes and slick wood and trying to get a mass of wet, heavy, wind-whipped canvas to behave, while below you the ship rolls from side to side and swings you out over a raging ocean and back again. If you slip and you're lucky, you land on deck, with a pretty good chance of breaking bones or worse; if you slip and you're not lucky, you plunge straight down into churning black water and are never seen again.

The rule that sailors learned and followed in those days was simple: "One hand for yourself, one hand for the ship." Every chore that had to be done up there in the rigging could be done by a gang of sailors who each lent one hand to the effort, so the other could cling for dear life to the nearest rope or ratline. Those tasks that couldn't be done that way, such as hauling on ropes, took place down on the deck—the rigging was designed with that in mind. There were emergencies where that rule didn't apply, and even with the rule in place, there were sailors who fell from the rigging to their deaths, but as a general principle, it worked tolerably well.

I'd like to propose that the same rule might be worth pursuing in the crisis of our age. In the years to come, many of us will face the same kind of scramble for survival that so many people faced in the catastrophes of the twentieth century's first half. Some of us won't make it, and some will have to face the ghastly choice between sheer survival and everything else they value in life. Not everyone, though, will land in one or the other of those categories, and many those who manage to stay out of them will have the chance to direct time and energy toward the broader picture.

Exactly what projects might fall into that latter category will differ from one person to another, for reasons that are irreducibly personal. I'm sure there are plenty of things that would motivate you to action in desperate times, dear reader, that would leave me cold, and of course, the reverse is also true. In times of crisis, of the kind we're discussing, it's personal factors of that sort that make the difference, not abstract considerations of the sort we might debate here. I'd also encourage readers to reflect on the question themselves: in the wreck of industrial civilization, what are you willing to make an effort to accomplish, to defend, or to preserve?

In thinking about that, I'd encourage my readers to consider the traumatic years of the early twentieth century as a model for what's approaching us. Those who were alive when the first great wave of dissolution hit in 1914 weren't facing forty years of continuous cataclysm but a sequence of crises of various kinds separated by intervals of relative calm in which some level of recovery is possible. More likely than not, the first round of trouble here in North America will be a major economic crisis; at some point not too far down the road, the yawning gap between our senile political class and the impoverished and disaffected masses promises the collapse of politics as usual and a descent into domestic insurgency, or one of the other standard ways by which former democracies destroy themselves. As already noted, there are plenty of other things bearing down on us—but after an interval, things will stabilize again.

Then it'll be time to sort through the wreckage, see what's been saved and what can be recovered, and go on from there. First, though, we have a troubled time to get through, and that can be a very challenging thing for those who have been taught to assume that history has some kind of obligation to give them the future they want. It's by stepping beyond that overdeveloped sense of entitlement that it becomes possible to plan for a future worth having.

Nothing will be easier, as the descent into the deindustrial dark age begins to pick up speed around us, than giving in to despair—and nothing will be more pointless. Those of us who are alive today are faced with the hugely demanding task of coping with the consequences of industrial civilization's decline and fall and saving as many as possible of the best achievements of the past few centuries so that they can cushion the descent and enrich the human societies of the far future. That won't be easy. So? The same challenge has been faced many times before, and quite often it's been faced with relative success.

The circumstances of the present case are in some ways more difficult than past equivalents, to be sure, but the tools and the knowledge base available to cope with them are almost incomparably greater. All in all, factoring in the greater challenges and the greater resources, it's probably fair to suggest that the challenge of our time is about on a par with other eras of decline and fall. The only question that still remains to be settled is how many of the people who are awake to the imminence of crisis will rise to the challenge and how many will fail to do so.

Some of the ones who will be taking that latter option are going out of their way to announce that fact to the world in advance. I'm thinking here of the very large number of people whose sole response to the approach of an unwelcome future is the hope that they'll die before it arrives. Some of them are quite forthright about it, which at least has the virtue of honesty. Rather more of them conceal the starkness of that choice behind a variety of convenient evasions, the insistence that we're all going to die soon anyway from some global catastrophe or other being the most popular of these just now.

I admit to a certain macabre curiosity about how that will play out in the years ahead. I've suspected for a while now, for example, that the baby boomers will manage one final mediagenic fad on the way out, and the generation that marked its childhood with coonskin caps and hula hoops and its puberty with love beads and Beatlemania will finish with a fad for suicide parties, in which attendees reminisce to the sound of the tunes they loved in high school, then wash down pills with vodka and help each other tie plastic bags over their heads. Still, I wonder how many people will have second thoughts once every other option has gone whistling down the wind, and will fling themselves into an assortment of futile attempts to have their cake when they've already eaten it right down to the bare plate. We may see some truly bizarre religious movements, and some truly destructive political ones, before those who go around today insisting that they don't want to live in a de-industrial world finally get their wish.

There are, of course, plenty of other options. One of the most promising is a strategy I've described wryly as "collapse first and avoid the rush": getting ahead of the curve of decline, in other words, and downshifting to a much less extravagant lifestyle while there's still time to pick up the skills and tools needed to do it competently. Despite the strident insistence from defenders of the status quo that anything less than business as usual amounts to heading straight back to the caves, it's entirely possible to have a decent and tolerably comfortable life on a tiny fraction of the energy and resource base that middle-class Americans think they can't possibly do without. Mind you, you have to know how to do it, and that's not the sort of knowledge you can pick up from a manual, which is why it's crucial to start now and get through the learning curve while you still have the income and the resources to cushion the impact of the inevitable mistakes.

The difficulty with this plan is that a growing number of North Americans are running out of time. I don't think it's escaped the notice of many people that despite all the cheerleading from government officials, despite all the reassurances from dignified and clueless economists, despite all those reams of doctored statistics gobbled down whole by the watchdogs-turned-lapdogs of the media and spewed forth undigested onto the evening news, the economy is not getting better. Outside a few privileged sectors, times are hard and getting harder; here in the US, more and more people are slipping into the bleak category of the long-term unemployed, and a great many of those who can still find employment work at part-time positions for sweatshop wages with no benefits at all.

Despite all the same cheerleading, reassurances, and doctored statistics, furthermore, the economy is not going to get better: not for more than brief intervals by any measure, and not at all if "better" means returning to some equivalent of North America's late-twentieth-century boom time. Those days are over, and they will not return. That harsh reality is having an immediate impact on some of my readers already, and that impact will only spread as time goes on. For those who have already been caught by the economic downdrafts, it's arguably too late to collapse first and avoid the rush; willy-nilly, they're already collapsing as fast as they can, and the rush is picking up speed around them as we speak.

For those who aren't yet in that situation, the need to make changes while there's still time to do so is paramount, and one of the most important changes involves the way people in today's industrial societies make a living. A great many people, to judge by the requests for advice I receive online, want to know what jobs might be likely to provide steady employment as the industrial economy comes apart. That's a point that needs careful assessment, since its implications intersect the whole tangled web in which our economy and society is snared just now. In particular, it assumes that the current way of bringing work together with workers, and turning the potentials of human mind and muscle toward the production of goods and services, is likely to remain in place for the time being, and it's becoming increasingly clear to me that this won't be the case.

It's important to be clear on exactly what's being discussed here. Human beings have always had to produce goods and services to stay alive and keep their families and communities going; that's not going to change. In nonindustrial societies, though, most work is performed by individuals who consume the product of their own labor, and most of the rest is sold or bartered directly by the people who produce it to the people who consume it. What sets the industrial world apart is that a third party, the employer, inserts himself into this process, hiring people to produce goods and services and then selling those goods and services to buyers.

That's employment, in the modern sense of the word. Most people think of getting hired by an employer, for a fixed salary or wage, to produce goods and services that the employer then sells to someone else, as the normal and natural state of affairs. It's a state of affairs that is already beginning to break down around us, however, because the surpluses that make that kind of employment economically viable are going away.

What makes this even more challenging is that very few people in the modern industrial world actually produce goods and services for consumers, much less for themselves, by applying energy to raw materials. The vast majority of today's employees, and in particular all those who have the wealth and influence that come with high social status, don't do this. Executives, brokers, bankers, consultants, analysts, salespeople—well, I could go on for pages—the whole range of what used to be called white-collar jobs is supported by the production of goods and services by the working Joes and Janes managing all the energy-intensive machinery down there on the shop floor. So is the entire vast maze of the financial industry, and so are the legions of government bureaucrats—local, state, and federal—who manage, regulate, or oversee one or another aspect of economic activity.

As noted in an earlier chapter, all these intermediaries are understandably just as interested in keeping their jobs as the working Joes and Janes down there on the shop floor, and yet the energy surpluses that made it viable to perch such an immensely complex infrastructure on top of the production of goods and services for consumers are going away. The result is a frantic struggle on everyone's part to make sure that the other guy loses his job first. It's a struggle that all of them will ultimately lose—as the energy surplus needed to support so drastic a degree of intermediation dwindles away, so will the entire system that's perched on that high but precarious support—and so, as long as that system remains in place, getting hired by an employer, paid a regular wage or salary, and given work and a workplace to produce goods and services that the employer then sells to someone else is going to become increasingly rare and increasingly unrewarding.

That transformation is already well under way. Outside of a handful of industries, very few people who work for an employer in the sense I've just outlined are prospering in today's North American economies. Most employees are having their benefits slashed, their working conditions worsened, their hours cut, and their pay reduced by one maneuver or another, and the threat of being laid off is constantly hovering over their heads. None of this is accidental, and none of it is merely the result of greed on the part of the very rich, though admittedly the culture of executive kleptocracy at the upper end of the North American social pyramid is making things a good deal worse than they might otherwise be.

The people I know who are prospering right now are those who produce goods and services for their own use, and provide goods and services directly to other people, without having an employer to provide them with work, a workplace, and a regular wage or salary. Some of these people have to stay under the radar screen of the current legal and regulatory system, since the people who work in that system are trying to preserve their own jobs by making life difficult for those who try to do without their intermediation. Others can do things more openly. All of them have sidestepped as many as possible of the infrastructure services that are supposed to be part of an employee's working life—for example, most of them aren't getting trained at universities, since the academic industry in the United States these days is just another predatory business sector trying to keep itself afloat by running others into the ground, and they aren't going to banks for working capital for much the same reason. They're using their own labor, their own wits, and their own personal connections with potential customers, to find a niche in which they can earn the money (or barter for the goods) they need or want.

I'd like to suggest that this is the wave of the future—not least because this is how economic life normally operates in nonindustrial societies, where the vast majority of people in the workforce are directly engaged in the production of goods and services for themselves and their own customers. The surplus that supports all those people in management, finance, and so on is a luxury that nonindustrial societies don't have. In the most pragmatic of economic senses, collapsing now and avoiding the rush involves getting out of a dying model of economics before it drags you down, and finding your footing in the emerging informal economy while there's still time to get past the worst of the learning curve.

Playing by the rules of a dying economy is not a strategy with a high success rate or a long shelf life. Those of my readers who are still employed in the usual sense of the term may choose to hold onto that increasingly rare status, but it's not wise for them to assume that such arrangements will last indefinitely; using the available money and other resources to get training, tools, and skills for some other way of getting by would probably be a wise strategy. Those of my readers who have already fallen through the widening cracks of the employment economy will have a harder row to hoe in many cases; for them, the crucial requirement is getting access to food, shelter, and other necessities while figuring out what to do next and getting through any learning curve that might be required.

ॐ

Another crucial aspect of our predicament just now, though it's not often recognized as such, is that most of our modern technologies are very poorly adapted to the long term. Most of the technologies used by today's industrial societies depend directly or indirectly on nonrenewable resources that, in the broad scheme of things, simply won't be around all that much longer. Those technologies that can't be reworked to use entirely renewable inputs, or that stop being economical once the costs of renewables have to be factored in, will go away in the decades and centuries to come, with profound impacts on human life.

In that light, it's comforting to realize that our species has managed to come up with a certain number of extremely durable technologies. Agriculture, despite the assertions of its modern neo-primitivist critics, is capable of being one of those. The rice paddies of eastern Asia, the wheat fields of Syria, and the olive orchards and vineyards of Greece and Italy, to name only a few examples, have proven sustainable over many millennia, and will likely still be viable long after today's idiotically unsustainable petrochemical agriculture has become a footnote in history books written in languages that haven't evolved yet.

There are other examples. One in particular, though, plays an important role in my own hopes for the future, not least because I work with it every day: the technology of the book.

One volume on my bookshelf right now makes as good an example as any. It's an English translation of *The Tale of Genji*, one of the world's first and greatest novels. It was written by a Japanese noblewoman, Murasaki Shikibu, at the beginning of the eleventh century for a circle of friends, and it wove together her wry reflections on court life with a sense of the impermanence of all earthly things. Like so many novels of an earlier age, it demands more patience than most of today's readers like to give to fiction; it unfolds at a leisurely pace, following the path of its decidedly unheroic hero, Prince Genji, through the social milieu of his time. Think of it as *War and Peace* without the war: the political struggles that frame Genji's career, sending him from the capital into exile and then returning him to the upper reaches of power, all take place without a hint of violence.

This is all the more striking because the society in which Murasaki lived was well on its way to a violent decline and fall. Her lifetime marked the zenith of the age Japanese historians call the Heian period. Over the next century and a half, the Japanese economy came apart, public order disintegrated in a rising spiral of violence, and the government lost control of the provinces where the new samurai class was taking shape. The civil wars that began in 1156 shredded what was left of Heian society and plunged Japan into a dark age four and a half centuries long.

Countless cultural treasures vanished during those years, but *The Tale of Genji* was not among them. One of the advantages of books is that, properly made, they are extremely durable; another is that they have very little value as plunder, and so tend to get left behind when looters come through. Both these advantages worked in favor of Murasaki's novel, and so did the patient efforts of generations of Buddhist monks and nuns who did for their culture what their equivalents in Dark Age Europe did a few centuries earlier.

It's not the only volume on my bookshelves that came through the fall of a civilization intact. A good shelf and a half of Greek philosophy and mathematics hid out in Irish monasteries and Arab libraries while Rome crashed to ruin and nomads fought over the rubble, and so did literary works from Greece and Rome, including a couple—Homer comes to mind—that came out of the dark ages before Greece and Rome, and so get extra credit. The Chinese classics on another shelf went through more than that. Chinese civilization has immense staying power, but its political systems tend to be fragile, and such seasoned survivors as Lao Tsu's *Tao Te Ching* have shrugged off half a dozen cycles of decline and fall.

Still, the granddaddy of them all is next to the Greek classics. The *Epic of Gilgamesh* was first composed well over five thousand years ago by some forgotten poet of Sumer, the oldest literate society anybody has yet been able to find. It's not something most people read in school, which is ironic, because the epic of Gilgamesh is the kind of story we most need to read these days: a story about limits. When he first strides into the story, Gilgamesh is about as far from Prince Genji as a fictional character can get.

Superhumanly strong, with an ego to match, he makes Conan the Barbarian look like Caspar Milquetoast, but his ego sends him on a long journey through love, loss, and a shattering confrontation with the human condition that leaves little of his arrogance intact. It's a story well worth reading even, or especially, today.

The astonishing thing, at least to me, is that I can take that book from its place on the shelf today and take in a story that had readers enthralled five thousand years ago. Precious little else from Sumer survives at all. Five thousand years is a long time, especially in a corner of the world where more civilizations have risen and fallen than just about anywhere else. That's what I mean about the durability of books as a technology of information storage and transfer. Even though individual books break down over time, it costs little to manufacture them and little except time to copy them, and they weather copying mistakes remarkably well. Unlike today's data storage methods, where a very small number of mistakes can render data hopelessly corrupt, a book can still pass on its meaning even when the copy is riddled with scribal errors.

All this bears directly on the shape of the deindustrial dark age ahead of us. Our age will certainly leave its share of legacies to the far future, but as already noted, most of those are the opposite of helpful. Of our positive achievements, on the other hand, the ones most likely to reach our descendants five thousand years from now are the ones written in books.

Thus I'd like to suggest that books, and the technologies that produce and preserve them, might well deserve a place well up on the list of useful things that need to be preserved through the long decline ahead of us. I wish it made sense to count on public libraries, but those venerable institutions have gotten the short end of the stick now for decades, and the dire fiscal straits faced by most state and local governments in the US now do not bode well for their survival. Like so many other things of value, book technology may have to be saved by individuals and local voluntary groups, using their own time and limited resources.

It might come down to copying books with pen and ink onto handmade paper, but there may well be another viable option. Letterpress technology is simple enough to make and maintain—the presses that sparked a communications revolution in Europe in the fourteenth century were built entirely with hand tools—and brings with it the power to produce a thousand copies of a book in the time a good scribe would need to produce one. With printing presses, something like the book culture of colonial America, complete with local bookstores, libraries open to anyone willing to pay a modest subscription, and private book collections, comes within reach, at least in regions that maintain some level of stability and public order. This may not seem like much in an age of internet downloads, but it beats the stuffing out of Dark Age Europe, when most people could count on living out their lives without turning the pages of a book.

This principle isn't limited to books, of course. The sort of local, decentralized approach to the survival of book technology suggested here is a template for the kind of strategy that could work for many other things as well. Five points that might help guide such projects come to mind.

First, it's crucial to remember that our predicament is anything but unique. The fantasy that today's industrial societies are destiny's darlings, and therefore exempt from the common fate of civilizations, needs to be set aside. So does the equally misleading fantasy that today's industrial societies are the worst of all possible worlds and are getting the cataclysmic fate they deserve. The societies of the industrial world are human cultures, no better or worse than most. For a variety of reasons, they happened to stumble onto the reserves of stored carbon hidden in the Earth and used most of them in three centuries of reckless exploitation; now, having overshot their resource base, like so many other societies, they're following the familiar trajectory of decline and fall. Letting go of the delusion of our own uniqueness enables us to learn from the past and also makes it easier to set aside some of the unproductive cultural narratives that hamstring so many attempts to respond to our predicament.

Second, one of the lessons the past offers is that the fall of civilizations is a slow, uneven process. None of us are going to wake up one morning a few weeks, or months, or years from now and find ourselves living in the Dark Ages, much less the Stone Age. Thus trying to leap in a single bound to some imagined future is unlikely to work very well. Rather, the most effective strategies will be aimed at muddling through, trying to deal with each stage of the descent as it comes into sight, and being prepared to make plenty of midcourse corrections. Flexibility will be more useful than ideology, and making do will be an essential survival skill.

Third, another of the lessons offered by the past is that the long road down is not going to be easy. Like every human society in every age, the future ahead of us will have opportunities for happiness and achievement, of course, and there will doubtless be significant gains to set in the balance against the inevitable losses, especially for those who long for simpler lives at a slower pace. Still, the losses will be terrible; it's crucial not to sugarcoat them, despite the very real temptation to do so, or to ignore the immense human tragedy that is an inevitable part of the slow death of any civilization.

Fourth, the harsh dimensions of the future can be mitigated, and the positive aspects fostered, by preparations and actions that are well within the reach of individuals, families, and communities. Not all declines and falls are created equal; in many failed civilizations of the past, a relatively small number of people willing to commit themselves to constructive action have made a huge difference in the outcome, and not only in the short term. The same option is wide open today; the one question is whether there will be those willing to take up the challenge.

Fifth, while this book has attempted to sketch out the most likely overall shape of the deindustrial dark age ahead, we can only guess at many of the details. Drawing up detailed plans and predictions may be a source of comfort in the face of a relentlessly unpredictable future, but that same unpredictability makes any plan, no matter how clever or popular, a dubious source of guidance at best. Nor is consensus a useful guide; one further lesson of history is that, in every age, the consensus view of the future is consistently wrong. Instead, the deliberate cultivation of diverse and even conflicting approaches by groups and individuals maximizes the likelihood that the broadest possible toolkit will reach the waiting hands of the future.

All this implies that we are much less helpless in the face of the future than it's become fashionable to assume. While it's inevitable that much will be lost in the descent into the coming deindustrial dark age, the evidence of the past shows that the efforts that are needed to preserve scientific, intellectual, and cultural legacies through a dark age and out the other side are well within the reach of individuals—and to judge from history, the selection of legacies from the past that reach the far side of the dark age will play a crucial role in determining the shape of the renaissance that follows.

And there will be a renaissance. That's the final secret history has to teach us about dark ages: like civilizations, they are temporary phenomena. Like civilizations, they transform their environments until the conditions that allowed them to come into being no longer permit them to continue. The fall of Rome thus eventually led to the rise of Renaissance Europe, the fall of Mycenean Greece led to the rise of Classical Greece, the fall of Heian Japan led to the rise of Tokugawa Japan, and so on through history's long litany of civilizational rise and fall.

In exactly the same way, the fall of modern industrial society— in North America and elsewhere—will eventually lead to the rise of the successor societies of the far future, the cultures and civilizations that will build on our ruins. What the people in those successor societies will bring with them on the road to a renaissance, the lessons they will have learned and the technologies and cultural creations that will be ready to hand—that will be determined, at least in part, by the choices we make now.

Endnotes

Chapter 1: The Wake of Industrial Civilization

1. The literature on this subject is immense. See Meadows et al. 1973 and Catton 1980 for good overviews.
2. Greer 2011.
3. Catton 1980, pp. 126–142.
4. Censorinus 1900, p. 30.
5. Toynbee 1939c., pp. 321–326.
6. Crossley-Holland 1984, pp. 59–60 gives a complete translation.

Chapter 2: The Ecological Aftermath

1. Than 2015.
2. Friedman 2007.
3. Anderson (undated).
4. See Pielou 1991 for a useful summary.
5. Mullins 1985, p. 20.
6. See Gamble and Soffer 1990 for a global survey.
7. I have used Pielou 1991 and Straus et al. 1996 for the following summary.
8. Alley 2000.
9. See, among many others, Holthaus 2015 and Oskin 2014.
10. Weaver 2003.
11. Moore 2007, p. 99.
12. Fuchs et al. 2004.
13. Dean 2006.
14. Jarlett 2013.
15. Mahaffey 2014.

Chapter 3: The Demographic Consequences

1. Lengnick 2015.
2. I insist on the prefix, because what passes for political thought these days has nothing to do with either liberalism or conservatism as these were understood as little as a few decades ago.
3. Fengler 2014.
4. Chamie and Mirkin 2014.
5. Grant 1990.
6. Webster 2002.
7. Blumberg 1980.
8. Thompson 1999.
9. Morris 1973, p. 98.
10. Morris 1973, pp. 126–132.
11. Morris 1973, pp. 103–104.
12. Morris 1973, pp. 91–92.

Chapter 4: The Political Unraveling

1. Greer 2008, pp. 225–240.
2. Souyri 2003.
3. See Blumberg 1980 for a detailed discussion.
4. See, for example, Icke 2004.
5. Toynbee 1939a, pp. 133–244.
6. Grant 1990.
7. Toynbee 1939b, pp. 35–193.
8. I have discussed this at length in Greer 2014.
9. Toynbee 1939b, pp. 141–337.
10. Toynbee 1954, pp. 12–44.
11. Morris 1973, pp. 56–62.
12. Friday 2004.

Chapter 5: The Economic Collapse

1. Ruskin 1967.
2. Roberts 2015.
3. Scheyder 2015.
4. Turner and Alexander 2014.
5. Rines 2015.
6. Greer 2009, pp. 19–36.
7. Schumacher 1973, pp. 171–190.
8. Weatherhead 1979.

9. Kunstler 2007.
10. Elgin 1981 was the most popular book on the subject.
11. France 1894, p. 118.
12. Marx 1952, pp. 85–111.
13. Fukuyama 1989.
14. Jones 1959.
15. Morris 1973, pp. 429–430.
16. de Roover 1958.
17. Dante 1954, pp. 107–108.
18. Abraham 1972.
19. Hatto 1964 and Finch 1965, respectively, are good English translations.
20. Tolkien 2014, pp. 100–103.
21. A complete translation of this poem is in Crossley-Holland 1984, pp. 53–56.

Chapter 6: The Suicide of Science

1. Jahnke 2015.
2. Oreskes 1999 is a good history of attitudes toward the continental drift theory.
3. See, for instance, Woolgar and Latour 1979.
4. Chuvin 1990 is a well-written account.
5. Mangan 2013.
6. Snow 1959.
7. Gornall 2015.
8. See, among many other studies, Fanelli 2009.
9. O'Hehir 2015.

Chapter 7: The Twilight of Technology

1. Ward-Perkins 2005.
2. Wiener-Bronner 2014.
3. Dale 2015.
4. Heinberg 2015.
5. Matthews 2014.
6. Dizard 2013; see also Heinberg 2013.

Chapter 8: The Dissolution of Culture

1. See especially Debord 1970.
2. Barfield 1965 explores this phenomenon at length.

3. Thomson 2000.
4. Tolkien 1965, p. 188.
5. Edwards 1997.
6. "Quote Investigator" 2012.
7. Toynbee 1939a, pp. 119–132.
8. Domhoff 2013.
9. Toynbee 1939b, pp. 459–480.

Chapter 9: The Road to a Renaissance

1. Hirsch et al. 2005.
2. Sider 2015.

Bibliography

Abraham, Arthur, "Nyagua, the British, and the Hut Tax War," *International Journal of African Historical Studies*, vol. 5 (1972), pp. 94–98.

Alley, Richard B., *The Two-Mile Time Machine: Ice Cores, Abrupt Climate Change, and Our Future* (Princeton, NJ: Princeton University Press, 2000).

Andersen, Poul, *The Winter of the World* (New York: New American Library, 1976).

Anderson, Kevin, "Hypocrites in the air: Should climate change academics lead by example?" Kevinanderson.info, kevinanderson.info/blog /hypocrites-in-the-air-should-climate-change-academics-lead-by -example/, undated, accessed 23 December 2015.

Barfield, Owen, *Saving the Appearances: A Study in Idolatry* (New York: Harcourt Brace Jovanovich, 1965).

Blumberg, Paul, *Inequality in an Age of Decline* (New York: Oxford University Press, 1980).

Calder, Nigel, *The Weather Machine* (New York, Viking Press, 1974).

Catton, William R., Jr., *Overshoot: The Ecological Basis of Revolutionary Change* (Urbana, IL: University of Illinois Books, 1980).

Censorinus, *The Natal Day*, trans. William Maude (New York: Cambridge Encyclopedia Company, 1900).

Chamie, Joseph, and Barry Mirkin, "Russian Demographics: The Perfect Storm," *YaleGlobal*, 11 December 2014, yaleglobal.yale.edu/content /russian-demographics-perfect-storm, accessed 23 December 2015.

Chew, Sing C., *World Ecological Degradation* (Walnut Creek, CA: Altamira Press, 2001).

Chorlton, Windsor, *Ice Ages* (New York: Time Life Books, 1983).

Chuvin, Pierre, *A Chronicle of the Last Pagans* (Cambridge, MA: Harvard University Press, 1990).

Crossley-Holland, Kevin, ed., *The Anglo-Saxon World: An Anthology* (Oxford: Oxford University Press, 1984).

Dale, Daniel, "Baltimore, Detroit threaten thousands with water shut-off," *The Star*, thestar.com/news/world/2015/04/22/baltimore-detroit-threaten-thousands-with-water-shut-off.html, accessed 5 December 2015.

Dante Alighieri, *The Inferno*, trans. John Ciardi (New York: Mentor Books, 1954).

Dean, Cornelia, "Study Sees 'Global Collapse' of Fish Species," *New York Times*, 3 November 2006, nytimes.com/2006/11/03/science/03fish.html, accessed 23 December 2015.

Debord, Guy, *The Society of the Spectacle* (London: Black & Red, 1970).

de Roover, Raymond, "The Concept of the Just Price," *The Journal of Economic History*, vol. 18 no. 4 (December 1958), pp 418–434.

Dizard, John, "US Shale Is a Surprisingly Unprofitable Miracle," *Financial Times*, 11 October 2013, ft.com/cms/s/0/3e56228a-2ce4-11e3-8281-00144feab7de.html, accessed 25 December 2015.

Domhoff, G. William, "Wealth, Income, and Power," Who Rules America? February 2013, www2.ucsc.edu/whorulesamerica/power/wealth.html, accessed 25 December 2015.

Doyle, William, *The Origins of the French Revolution* (New York: Oxford University Press, 1999).

Edwards, Lynda, "Myths over Miami," *Miami New Times*, 5 June 1997, miaminewtimes.com/1997-06-05/news/myths-over-miami/, accessed 23 December 2015.

Elgin, Duane, *Voluntary Simplicity* (New York: Harper, 1981).

Fanelli, Daniele, "How Many Scientists Fabricate and Falsify Research? A Systematic Review and Meta-Analysis of Survey Data," *PLoS ONE*, vol. 4 no.5, 2009.

Fengler, Wolfgang, "The Rapid Slowdown of Population Growth," *Future Development*, 9 September 2014, blogs.worldbank.org/futuredevelopment/rapid-slowdown-population-growth, accessed 23 December 2015.

Finch, R. G. (trans.), *The Saga of the Volsungs* (London: Nelson, 1965).

France, Anatole, *Le Lys Rouge* (Paris: Calman-Levy, 1894).

Friday, Karl, *Samurai, Warfare and the State in Early Medieval Japan* (London: Routledge, 2004).

Friedman, Thomas, *Hot, Flat, and Crowded* (New York: Farrar, Strauss, & Giroux, 2008).

———, "The People We Have Been Waiting For," *New York Times*, 2 December 2007, nytimes.com/2007/12/02/opinion/02friedman .html?_r=0, accessed 23 December 2015.

Fuchs, M., A. Lang, and G. A. Wagner, "The history of Holocene soil erosion in the Phlious Basin, NE Peloponnese, Greece, based on optical dating," *The Holocene*, vol. 14 no. 3 (2004), pp. 334–345.

Fukuyama, Francis, "The End of History?" *The National Interest*, Summer 1989.

Galbraith, John Kenneth, *The Culture of Contentment* (Boston: Houghton Mifflin Co., 1992).

Gamble, C., and O. Soffer, eds., *The World at 18,000 BP: High Latitudes* (London: Unwin Hyman, 1990).

Gornall, Jonathan, "Sugar: Spinning a web of influence," *British Medical Journal*, 11 February 2015, sciencedaily.com/releases/2015/02 /150211204055.htm, accessed 25 December 2015.

Grant, Michael, *The Fall of the Roman Empire: A Reappraisal* (New York: Colliers, 1990).

Greer, John Michael, *Apocalypse Not* (San Francisco, CA: Cleis Press, 2011).

———, *Decline and Fall: The End of Empire and the Future of Democracy in 21st Century America* (Gabriola Island, BC: New Society, 2014).

———, *The Long Descent: A User's Guide to the End of Industrial Civilization* (Gabriola Island, BC: New Society, 2008).

———, *The Ecotechnic Future: Envisioning a Post-Peak World* (Gabriola Island, BC: New Society, 2009).

Hatto, A. T., (trans.), *The Nibelungenlied* (London: Penguin, 1964).

Heinberg, Richard, *Snake Oil: How Fracking's False Promise of Plenty Imperils Our Future* (Santa Rosa, CA: Post Carbon Institute, 2013).

Hirsch, Robert L., Roger Bezdek, and Robert Wendling, *Peaking of World Oil Production: Impacts, Mitigation, and Risk Management* (Washington, DC: US Department of Energy, 2005).

Holthaus, Eric, "The Point of No Return: Climate Change Nightmares Are Already Here," *Rolling Stone*, 5 August 2015, rollingstone.com /politics/news/the-point-of-no-return-climate-change-nightmares -are-already-here-20150805, accessed 25 December 2015.

Icke, David, *And the Truth Shall Set You Free* (Ryde, UK: Bridge of Light, 2004).

Illich, Ivan, *Energy and Equity* (New York: Harper & Row, 1974).

Jahnke, Art, "Who Picks Up the Tab for Science?" *BU Today*, 2015, bu.edu/research/articles/funding-for-scientific-research/, accessed 25 December 2015.

Jarlett, Harriet, "Coccolithophores thrive despite ocean acidification," Planet Earth Online, 21 May 2013, planetearth.nerc.ac.uk/news /story.aspx?id=1465, accessed 23 December 2015.

Johnson, Warren, *Muddling Toward Frugality* (Boulder, CO: Shambhala, 1978).

Jones, A. H. M., "Over-taxation and the Decline of the Roman Empire," *Antiquity* 33 (1959), pp. 39–49.

Kafka, Franz, *The Castle* (New York: Alfred A. Knopf, 1968).

Korten, David, *The Great Turning* (San Francisco: Berrett-Koehler, 2006).

Kunstler, James Howard, "Making Other Arrangements," *Orion*, January 2007, https://orionmagazine.org/article/making-other-arrangements/, accessed 25 December 2015.

Kurzweil, Ray, *The Singularity is Near* (New York: Viking, 2005).

Lengnick, Laura, *Resilient Agriculture: Cultivating Food Systems for a Changing Climate* (Gabriola Island, BC: New Society, 2015).

Mahaffey, James, *Atomic Accidents: A History of Nuclear Meltdowns and Disasters: From the Ozark Mountains to Fukushima* (New York: Pegasus Books, 2014).

Mangan, Dan, "Medical Bills Are the Biggest Cause of US Bankruptcies: Study," CNBC, 25 June 2013, cnbc.com/id/100840148, accessed 25 December 2015.

Mann, Thomas, *Royal Highness*, trans. A. Cecil Curtis (New York: Vintage Books, 1983).

Marx, Karl, *Capital*, trans. Samuel Moore and Edward Aveling (Chicago: William Benton, 1952).

Matthews, Chris, "Wealth inequality in America: It's worse than you think," *Fortune*, 31 October 2014, fortune.com/2014/10/31/inequality -wealth-income-us/, accessed 25 December 2015.

Meadows, Donnella, Dennis Meadows, Jorgen Randers, and William W. Behrens III, *The Limits to Growth* (New York: Universe, 1972).

Moore, Gary S., *Living with the Earth, Third Edition: Concepts in Environmental Health* Science (New York: CRC Press, 2007).

Morris, John, *The Age of Arthur: A History of the British Isles from 350 to 650* (New York: Charles Scribner's Sons, 1973).

Mullins, Rita Thieron (as "The Editors of Time Life Books"), *Grasslands and Tundra* (New York: Time Life Books, 1985).

O'Hehir, Andrew, "Anti-vaxxers are not the enemy: Science, politics and the crisis of authority," *Salon*, salon.com/2015/02/07/anti_vaxxers _climate_deniers_and_the_crisis_of_authority/, accessed 5 December 2015.

Oreskes, Naomi, *The Rejection of Continental Drift* (Oxford: Oxford University Press, 1999).

Oskin, Becky, "Catastrophic Collapse of West Antarctic Ice Sheet Begins," *LiveScience*, 12 May 2014, livescience.com/45534-west -antarctica-collapse-starts.html, accessed 25 December 2015.

Pielou, E. C., *After the Ice Age: The Return of Life to Glaciated North America* (Chicago: University of Chicago Press, 1991).

Ponting, Clive, *A Green History of the World* (New York: St. Martin's Press, 1992).

Quote Investigator, "The Future Has Arrived," quoteinvestigator.com /2012/01/24/future-has-arrived/, 24 January 2012, accessed 25 December 2015.

Rines, Samuel, "Secular Stagnation: The Dismal Fate of the Global Economy?" *The National Interest*, 11 September 2015, national interest.org/feature/secular-stagnation-the-dismal-fate-the-global -economy-13819, accessed 23 December 2015.

Roberts, David, "None of the world's top industries would be profitable if they paid for the natural capital they use," *Grist*, grist.org/business -technology/none-of-the-worlds-top-industries-would-be-profitable -if-they-paid-for-the-natural-capital-they-use/, accessed 5 December 2015.

Ruskin, John, *Unto This Last* (Lincoln, NB: University of Nebraska Press, 1967).

Scheyder, Ernest, "North Dakota: Oil producers aim to cut radioactive waste bills," Reuters, reuters.com/article/2015/01/28/us-usa-north -dakota-waste-idUSKBN0L11Z420150128, accessed 5 December 2015.

Schumacher, E. F., *Small Is Beautiful: Economics As If People Mattered* (New York: Perennial Library, 1973).

Science Daily, "Investigation reveals network of links between public health scientists and sugar industry," sciencedaily.com/releases/2015 /02/150211204055.htm, accessed 5 December 2015.

Sider, Alison, "Fracking Firms That Drove Oil Boom Struggle to Survive," *The Wall Street Journal*, 23 September 2015, wsj.com/articles /fracking-firms-that-drove-oil-boom-struggle-to-survive-144305 3791, accessed 25 December 2015.

Silverberg, Robert, *The Time of the Great Freeze* (New York: Holt, Rinehart & Winston, 1964).

Snow, C. P., *The Two Cultures and the Scientific Revolution* (New York: Cambridge University Press, 1959).

Souyri, P. F., *The World Turned Upside Down: Medieval Japanese Society* (New York: Columbia University Press, 2003).

Straus, Lawrence G., B. V. Eriksen, Jon M. Erlandsen, and David R. Yesner, *Humans at the End of the Ice Age: The Archaeology of the Pleistocene-Holocene Transition* (New York: Plenum Press, 1996).

Tainter, Joseph, *The Collapse of Complex Societies* (Cambridge; Cambridge University Press, 1988).

Than, Ker, "Arctic Meltdown Opens Fabled Northwest Passage," *Livescience*, livescience.com/1884-arctic-meltdown-opens-fabled-northwest-passage.html, accessed 23 December 2015.

Thompson, E. A., *The Huns* (Oxford: Blackwell, 1999).

Thomson, Belinda, *Impressionism: Origins, Practice, Reception* (London: Thames & Hudson, 2000).

Tolkien, J. R. R., *Beowulf: A Translation and Commentary* (Boston: Houghton Mifflin Harcourt, 2014).

———, *The Fellowship of the Ring* (New York: Ballantine Books, 1965).

Toynbee, Arnold, *A Study of History, Vol. 4: The Breakdowns of Civilizations* (London: Oxford University Press, 1939); cited as Toynbee 1939a.

———, *A Study of History, Vol. 5: The Disintegrations of Civilizations* (London: Oxford University Press, 1939); cited as Toynbee 1939b.

———, *A Study of History, Vol. 6: The Disintegrations of Civilizations, Continued* (London: Oxford University Press, 1939); cited as Toynbee 1939c.

———, *A Study of History, Vol. 8: Heroic Ages, and Contacts Between Civilizations in Space* (London: Oxford University Press, 1954).

Turner, Graham, and Kathy Alexander, "Limits to Growth was right. New research shows we're nearing collapse," *The Guardian*, theguardian.com/commentisfree/2014/sep/02/limits-to-growth-was-right-new-research-shows-were-nearing-collapse, accessed 5 December 2015.

Ward-Perkins, Bryan, *The Fall of Rome and the End of Civilization* (Oxford: Oxford University Press, 2005).

Weatherhead, Peter, "Do Sparrows Commit the 'Concorde Fallacy'?" *Behavioral Psychology and Sociobiology*, 5 (4), pp. 373–381.

Weaver, Andrew J., et al., "Meltwater Pulse 1A from Antarctica as a Trigger of the Alleröd-Bölling Warm Interval," *Science*, vol. 299 no. 5613 (14 March 2003), pp. 1709–13.

Webster, David, *The Fall of the Ancient Maya* (London: Thames and Hudson, 2002).

Wiener-Bronner, Danielle, "Report Shows Cyber Crime is on the Rise," *The Wire*, 22 April 2014, thewire.com/technology/2014/04/report -shows-cyber-espionage-is-on-the-rise/361024/, accessed 25 December 2015.

Woolgar, Steve, and Bruno Latour, *Laboratory Life: the Construction of Scientific Facts* (Princeton, New Jersey: Princeton University Press, 1979).

Index

abstract concepts, 183–187, 189
abstract value, 118–119, 121
After the Ice Age, 128–129
agriculture, 11, 12, 30–31, 39–40, 43, 89, 220. *See also* homesteading; topsoil.
Alleröd, 24–25
American Revolution, 77–78
Anderson, Kevin, 19
anthropogenic climate change, 7, 16–18, 23, 128
anti-vaxxers, 143, 144, 145
appropriate technology, 99
arts and literature, 123–124. *See also by name.*
A Study of History, 5
atheist movement, 130, 131, 145
Attila, 52, 55–56
Augustine, 123

Baltimore, 168, 169, 171, 172, 176
banking and finance industry, 209–210
barter economy, 114, 115, 116
Beowulf, 120, 121
bioremediation, 37
birth rates, 43–47. *See also* population.

Boeing, 159–160
Bölling, 24
books, as technology, 220–223
Boreal phase, 25
bottleneck technologies, 155, 156, 157, 158
Britain, 46, 53, 78, 117
Britannia, 52, 54, 87
British colonialism, 77–78, 117
bubble activity, in United States, 169, 170, 201–202
bureaucratic systems, 74–76, 80, 81
Bush, George W., 149
business models, in the United States, 171–172

Calder, Nigel, 128, 129
California, 27
cancer, 37–38
capital, maintenance costs, 59–60, 62, 76, 83. *See also* social capital.
carbon dioxide (CO_2), 25–26, 33
castes, 51, 61–62, 84–85. *See also* feudalism.
catabolic collapse, 60–63, 79
Central Asia, 52, 54
charismatic leaders, 8, 10, 12, 52, 55–56, 80, 87, 194–195

charts, and technology categories, 152–156

cheap energy, 97, 104, 156–157, 193. *See also* charts.

Childeric, 53

Chorlton, Windsor, 129

Christianity, 135–137, 138–139, 145, 195–196

City of God, The, 123

classes, in society, 60–61, 63. *See also* castes; elite classes; social hierarchies.

climate, in North America, 18, 20–23, 210. *See also* droughts.

collapse, 10, 12, 17, 32, 36, 55, 59, 78, 80, 81, 209, 213, 215–216. *See also* catabolic collapse; Tainter, Joseph.

Collapse of Complex Societies, The, 91, 97

collective knowledge, 191–192

colonialization, 99–100, 133, 208. *See also* British colonialism.

concentrated energy, 98–99, 100

Concorde, 159, 160

Concorde fallacy, 100

conflicts, 55, 72, 86. *See also* ethnic conflict.

Constantine, 136

cost per worker, in workplaces, 99

creative minority, 83

crises, in economic system, 103

crisis management, 211–213

cultural productions, 123–124

cultural resources, 10–11

culture, in society, 177, 178

Culture of Contentment, The, 76, 173

culture of poverty, 171

Dade County. *See* homeless children.

dark ages, characteristics, 4–5, 12–13

death rate, 12, 43, 44–46

decline and fall
basis of, 59–60
and elite classes, 67–82
patterns of, 4–6, 8–10, 12, 28, 44, 49–52, 84, 124, 223–224

deindustrial dark ages, 34, 37, 40, 48, 57, 104–105, 147, 168, 214–215

demand destruction, 20

demographic transition, 42

depopulation, 44

Detroit, 168, 169, 171, 172, 176

diminishing returns, 91, 92, 94, 95, 104, 124

disintermediation, 101, 103–105

dominant minority, 82–83, 84, 87. *See also* elite classes.

droughts, 54, 56, 210

ecological damage, 30. *See also* climate.

ecological succession, 96

economic contraction, 9, 11, 50, 55, 63, 101–102, 103, 108, 125–126

economic growth, 9, 92, 93, 101

economic stagnation, 102–103, 112. *See also* secular stagnation.

ecosystems, 4, 21, 22–23, 33–34, 37, 96, 97–98

Ecotechnic Future, The, 31

electrical grid, 168, 169

elite classes, 60–61, 63–65, 67–82. *See also* patrician elite; senile elite.

in mature civilizations, 68, 71, 72, 74–80, 85, 190–191

selection process, 68–72, 78–79, 88

senility of, 73, 85, 88, 173–174, 176

in United States, 65–66, 73, 81–82, 173–174

employment, 100–101, 106, 216–219. *See also* business models; unemployment.

Energy and Equity, 180

energy per capita, 1, 42–43, 96, 97, 103–104, 156, 174

energy sources, 97, 206. *See also* nonrenewable resources; renewable resources.

energy technologies, 202, 206. *See also* energy sources; *and by name.*

environmental damage, 92–93

Epic of Gilgamesh, 195, 221–222

ethnic conflict, 49–51, 57

ethnic consolidation, 51

ethnic dissolution, 84

ethnic divisions, 51, 52, 82, 84

ethnogenesis, 41, 48

Euripides, 123

externalities, 92–93, 94, 180

externalization, of the mind, 183, 187–188, 189

external proletariat, 86, 194

feudalism, 62, 110–113, 122

fisheries, 33–34

Flavius Aetius, 81

Florida, 27, 56. *See also* homeless children.

foreign policy, United States, 75, 149

fossil fuels, 19–20, 22, 31, 97, 174–175, 199, 202, 207

fracking, 92–93, 94, 170, 175, 209–210

France, Anatole, 105–106

French Revolution, 64, 72, 76–77, 78, 173

Friedman, Thomas, 18

Fujiwara family, 87–88

Fukuyama, Francis, 107

Galbraith, John Kenneth, 76, 173

gift economy, 115, 116

global meltwater pulses, 26

global weirding, 18, 20, 26

gold, 119, 120, 121, 122

goods and services, exchanges of, 9, 62, 93–94, 97, 99, 100, 106, 121, 216–18. *See also* disintermediation; employment; market economy; money, absence of.

greenhouse gases, 19, 20–21, 25

Greenland, 24, 25, 26, 28, 56

Gulf Coast, 22, 27, 29, 47

health care system, US, 95, 96, 101, 102, 131, 137

alternative, 101, 102, 131, 142

Hegel, Georg, 107

Heian Japan, 55, 87–88, 220–221, 225

Hengist, 87, 88

Higg, story of, 110–112

Hirsch, Robert, 207

history

ages of, 4–5

lessons from, 223–225

hoarding, of personal wealth, 120–122

Holocene Climatic Optimum. *See* Hypsithermal.
homeless children, secret stories, 189–190
homesteading, 208–209
Hudson's Bay, 56
human ecology, 11–12
Huns, 52, 54
Hypatia, 136–137
Hypsithermal, 21, 22

Ice Age, 129
ice ages, 23–24, 129
ice sheets, 23, 24–25, 26
Illich, Ivan, 180
illth, 92
illusion of invincibility, 72–73
imagination, 2, 113, 159, 183, 187–188, 189
imitation. *See* mimesis.
immediate experience, 186–187
immigration policy, 41, 43
Impressionists, 184, 185
industries, 163, 165. *See also by name.*
inflation, 104, 162, 172
information technologies, 165, 166. *See also* internet.
infrastructure, 27–230
institutional frameworks, 73–79
intellectual projects, 123–124
interest rates, 94, 162
interface technologies, 154–155
interglacials, 23–24
intermediate technology, 99
intermediation. *See also* marketing.
  in the market, 106–107, 108–109, 113–119, 217

and social complexity, 95–97, 101–102
internal proletariat, 82, 83, 84, 85, 87, 176, 191, 194, 195–196
internet, 160–168, 170, 181
internet service providers (ISPs), 162
involuntary simplicity, 104
iron industry, 98

Japan, 62. *See also* Heian Japan; *Tale of Genji, The*

kerogen shale, 19
Kunstler, James Howard, 100

laboring class, 61, 85, 100–101, 104, 106
LESS (Less Energy, Stuff, and Stimulation), 203–205
Liebig's law of the minimum, 97–98
lifestyles, 199, 201, 202–206, 215
Limits to Growth, The, 43, 93
literature, 4, 12–13, 185–186, 187
local food, 101
localized economies, 9, 101, 103, 115–116, 166, 167
Long Descent, The, 60

marine transgression, 27. *See also* sea levels.
maritime trade, 29–30
market, the, 105–110
market economy, 104–106
marketing, 79–181, 104, 141, 187
Marx, Karl, 107
mass media, 187–188
mass migrations, 41, 55, 56, 89

materialistism, 182
Maya, 46–47, 55, 86
media fast, 181
medical industry, 127–128
medieval society, 62, 113, 120
methane, 25, 26
Midwest, 22, 40, 48, 210
Milankovich cycle, 23–24
mimesis, 190–193, 194–195, 196
Minamoto clan, 88
minorities, 50, 63. *See also* dominant minority; elite classes; overseer class.
Miocene epoch, 23
Mississippi River area, 30, 39, 56
money economy, 113–119
Muslims, 149
Mycenean civilization, 32, 225

negative returns, 92, 103, 104
Neoplatonism, 134–135, 139
net energy, 19–20, 97
New Orleans, 27, 30
Nibelungenlied, 120–121, 122
nonindustrial societies, 218–219
nonrenewable resources, 60, 97. *See also* fossil fuels.
nuclear accidents, 35–37
nuclear power, 34–37, 201

oceanic food chains, 33
oceans, 33–34. *See also* Gulf Coast; sea levels.
Odoacer, 53–54, 80, 82
oil prices, 94, 175, 206
Older Dryas, 24
one percent, the, 8, 63
online crime, 163–164
oral traditions, 4, 120

overpopulation, 40–43
overseer class, 63–64, 85, 87

Pagan religion, 136
patrician elite, of Roman Empire, 136
peasant economy, 61
philosophy, classical, 133–135, 138–139. *See also* religion; Situationists.
Pielou, E.C., 128–129
Planet Earth, 129
Pleistocene epoch, 23
political fragmentation, 8–10
pollutants, 37. *See also* greenhouse gases; toxic effluents.
poor people. *See also* labouring class.
    in Roman Empire, 66–67, 135–136, 195–196
    and science, 137–138
    in social order, 83–84, 137–138
    in United States, 169, 171, 172
population, 11–12, 40–49
post-Roman Europe, 41, 54, 55, 88, 109–110, 120
power
    and force, 48–49
    in mature civilizations, 73–80
    and social hierarchies, 82–83
precious metals, 119, 120
prosthetics, and technology, 178–183, 187–188

racism, 82
rainfall, 22–23
Reagan era, 66
religion, 132, 195, 196. *See also* atheist movement; Christianity; Pagan religion.

renaissance, 225
renewable resources, 60, 201–202
replicators, 188–189
repression, by elites, 64, 66
reproduction campaigns, 41–42
retail sector, 210
Roman Empire, 66–67, 79, 80–81,
    86, 120, 133–134. *See also* patri-
    cian elite.
    and agriculture, 32
    ceramic industry, 157–158
    energy per capita, 174
    internal proletariat, 195–196
    market economy, 109–110
Romulus Augustulus, 53–54
Ruskin, John, 92
Russian Revolution, 72, 78

Sacramento, 47
Salon, 143
Saxons, 53, 54
Schumacher, E. F., 99–100
science
    and business interests, 140–141
    as one entity, 150
    and the public, 129–130, 139–140,
        145–146, 192
    social role of, 132–133
scientific ethics, 140–142
scientific research, and resources,
    124–127, 131–132, 193
"Seafarer, The," 122
sea levels, 24–25, 26–30
secular stagnation, 93–94
senile elite, 73, 83, 85
Situationists, 181–182
Snow, C. P., 139
social capital, 62–63
social complexity , 94–97, 99

social hierarchies, 62–65, 82–85,
    99, 106
Socrates, 135
solar power, 202
Southwest, 21, 56, 210
Soviet Union, 35, 43
subsystems, 18
sunk costs, 100
supersonic transport (SST), 159–
    160
supply and demand, 112, 114, 115
support technologies, 154–156
systems approach, 15–18

taconite, 98, 156
Tainter, Joseph, 91, 94, 96, 97, 99,
    104
Tale of Genji, The, 220–221
taxes, 9, 66–67, 117, 163, 169
technic societies, 31
technological fragmentation, 157–
    158
technological suites, 154–156, 157–
    158
technology
    and externalities, 180
    as one entity, 150–151
    and resources, 125–126, 152–156,
        219–220
    social role of, 132–133
"The Ruin," 13
Third World nations, 99
3-D printers, 188–189
thresholds, in systems, 17
tools, and technology, 178
topsoil, 31–32
toxic effluents, 33–34
Toynbee, Arnold, 5, 82–83, 86, 190,
    193–194

transition, 104, 194, 200–201, 205, 207, 214, 215
Two Cultures, The, 139
Tyson, Neil DeGrasse, 192, 193–194

unemployment, 108, 170, 209–210, 216
universities, in United States, 69–71, 218

vaccinations. *See* anti-vaxxers.
values, and facts, 118–119
Varro, Marcus Terentius, 4
village economies, 115
violence, and power, 8
voluntary simplicity, 104
Vortigern, 87

warbands, 55–56, 86–89
warlords, 54, 56, 66–67, 80, 88–89, 194–195. *See also* Flavius Aetius.
water systems, 168, 169, 171, 172, 174
water temperatures, 34
wealth, distribution of, 11–12, 49, 55, 60–61, 66, 86, 138, 172–173, 193. *See also* elite classes; social hierarchies
Weather Machine, The, 128
West Antarctica, 24, 25, 26, 27, 28
White's law, 96, 97, 174

Younger Dryas, 25

zero marginal return, 91, 92, 95

About the Author

John Michael Greer, historian of ideas and one of the most influential authors exploring the future of industrial society, writes the widely cited weekly blog "The Archdruid Report" and has published more than thirty books on ecology, history, and nature spirituality. His involvement in sustainability issues dates back to the early 1980s, when he was active in the Appropriate Technology movement and be-  came certified as a Master Conserver. He is the author of numerous titles, including *The Long Descent, The Ecotechnic Future, The Wealth of Nature,* and *After Progress.* He lives in Cumberland, MD, an old mill town in the Appalachians, with his wife Sara.

A Note About the Publisher

NEW SOCIETY PUBLISHERS (www.newsociety.com), is an activist, solutions-oriented publisher focused on publishing books for a world of change. Our books offer tips, tools, and insights from leading experts in sustainable building, homesteading, climate change, environment, conscientious commerce, renewable energy, and more — positive solutions for troubled times.

The interior pages of our bound books are printed on Forest Stewardship Council®-registered acid-free paper that is 100% post-consumer recycled (100% old growth forest-free), processed chlorine-free, and printed with vegetable-based, low-VOC inks, with covers produced using FSC®-registered stock. New Society also works to reduce its carbon footprint, and purchases carbon offsets based on an annual audit to ensure a carbon neutral footprint. For further information, or to browse our full list of books and purchase securely, visit our website at: **www.newsociety.com**

New Society Publishers
ENVIRONMENTAL BENEFITS STATEMENT

For every 5,000 books printed, New Society saves the following resources:[1]

26	Trees
2,327	Pounds of Solid Waste
2,560	Gallons of Water
3,339	Kilowatt Hours of Electricity
4,230	Pounds of Greenhouse Gases
18	Pounds of HAPs, VOCs, and AOX Combined
6	Cubic Yards of Landfill Space

[1]Environmental benefits are calculated based on research done by the Environmental Defense Fund and other members of the Paper Task Force who study the environmental impacts of the paper industry.

MIX
Paper from responsible sources
FSC® C016245